D1508269

Religion and Technology in India

Religion tends to flourish when technological developments create new possibilities for communication and representation, and simultaneously change as a consequence of these developments.

This book explores intersections between religion and technology in India, at the present and in the colonial past, and how various forms of techno-religious intersections transform and open up for new religious practices, discourses, communities, and institutions. With focus on Indian contexts and religions, it discusses various empirical and theoretical aspects of how technological innovations create, alter, and negotiate religious spaces, practices and authorities. The book provides rich and multifaceted empirical examples of different ways in which technological practices relate to meanings, ideas, and practices of religions. The techno-religious intersections generate several questions about authority and power, the politics and poetics of identity, community and place, and how religious agency, information, and experience are mediated, commodified, and adjusted to new demands of societies. The chapters explore the Hindu, Jain, and Sikh traditions in relation to new technological developments and media, such as photography, new means of visualization, TV serials, mobile phones, and online communication.

The book will be of interest to academics studying modern and contemporary India and South Asia, and especially the role of religion and technology.

Knut A. Jacobsen is Professor in the study of religions at the University of Bergen, Norway. His research focuses on Yoga, Sāṃkhya, and Hindu conceptions and rituals of space and time. He is the editor in chief of the six volumes *Brill's Encyclopedia of Hinduism* (2009–2015). His most recent book published by Routledge is *Yoga in Modern Hinduism: Hariharānanda Āraṇya and Sāṃkhyayoga* (2018).

Kristina Myrvold is Associate Professor of the study of religions at Linnaeus University, Sweden. Her research interests focus on Sikh practices, migration, scriptures, and print history in Punjab. She has published numerous articles and edited several books on India and the Sikhs and currently works on project on religious miniature scriptures.

Routledge South Asian Religion Series

For more information about this series, please visit: https://www.routledge.com/asianstudies/series/RSARS

Rethinking Religion in India
The Colonial Construction of Hinduism
Edited by Esther Bloch, Marianne Keppens and Rajaram Hegde

Health and Religious Rituals in South Asia
Disease, Possession and Healing
Edited by Fabrizio M. Ferrari

Time, History and the Religious Imaginary in South Asia
Edited by Anne Murphy

Cross-disciplinary Perspectives on a Contested Buddhist Site
Bodhgaya Jataka
Edited by David Geary, Matthew R. Sayers and Abhishek Singh Amar

Yoga in Modern Hinduism
Hariharānanda Āraṇya and Sāṃkhyayoga
Knut A. Jacobsen

Women, Religion and the Body in South Asia
Living with Bengali Bauls
Kristin Hanssen

Religion, Space and Conflict in Sri Lanka
Colonial and Postcolonial Contexts
Elizabeth J. Harris

Religion and Technology in India
Spaces, Practices and Authorities
Edited by Knut A. Jacobsen and Kristina Myrvold

Religion and Technology in India

Spaces, Practices and Authorities

Edited by
Knut A. Jacobsen and Kristina Myrvold

Routledge
Taylor & Francis Group

LONDON AND NEW YORK

First published 2018
by Routledge
2 Park Square, Milton Park, Abingdon, Oxon OX14 4RN

and by Routledge
711 Third Avenue, New York, NY 10017

Routledge is an imprint of the Taylor & Francis Group, an informa business

British Library Cataloguing in Publication Data
A catalogue record for this book is available from the British Library

Library of Congress Cataloging in Publication Data
Names: Jacobsen, Knut A., 1956- editor.
Title: Religion and technology in India : spaces, practices, and authorities
/ edited by Knut A. Jacobsen and Kristina Myrvold.
Description: New York : Routledge, 2018. | Series: Routledge South Asian
religion series ; 11 | Includes bibliographical references and index.
Identifiers: LCCN 2017061109| ISBN 9780815384168 (hardback) |
 ISBN 9781351204798 (ebook)
Subjects: LCSH: Technology–Religious aspects. | India–Religion. |
Technology–India.
Classification: LCC BL265.T4 R39 2018 | DDC 201/.660954–dc23
LC record available at https://lccn.loc.gov/2017061109

ISBN: 978-0-8153-8416-8 (hbk)
ISBN: 978-1-351-20479-8 (ebk)

Typeset in Times New Roman
by Taylor & Francis Books

Contents

Illustrations

Figures

Tables

Contributors

Anna Bochkovskaya is an Associate Professor at the Department of South Asian History, Institute of Asian and African Studies, Lomonosov Moscow State University. Her research interests include contemporary history of India, Punjab studies, and religious studies. She is the author of chapters on Sikhism and Current Trends in Hinduism in Russian-language university textbooks *Introduction to Religious Studies* (2008, 5th edition), *The History of Religions* (2014, 4th edition), and *Religious Studies: BA Level* (2016, 2nd edition); chapters and translations in *Death in Maharashtra: Imagination, Perception and Expression* (2012). She is a member of the interdisciplinary research project "Under the Skies of South Asia" launched in 2011 jointly with colleagues from the Institute of Oriental Studies, Russia's Academy of Sciences. She vastly contributed to the volumes published under this project: *Portrait and Sculpture* (2014) and *Mobility and Space* (2015), and edited Volume 3 (*Under the Skies of South Asia: Territory and Belonging*, 2016). Her most recent publications focus on religion and caste controversies in the Indian Punjab.

Kenneth M. George is Professor of Anthropology at the Australian National University, having served previously at Harvard University, and as Editor of the *Journal of Asian Studies* (2005–2008). His ethnographic research has been supported by the Social Science Research Council, the Aga Khan Trust for Culture, the John Simon Guggenheim Foundation, and the Institute for Advanced Study, Princeton. His books include showing *Signs of Violence: The Cultural Politics of a Twentieth Century Headhunting Ritual* (1996); *Spirited Politics: Religion and Public Life in Contemporary Southeast Asia* (2005, co-editor); and *Picturing Islam: Art and Ethics in a Muslim Lifeworld* (2010). His current research (with Kirin Narayan) explores the intermingling of religion, technology, and infrastructure in South and Southeast Asia.

Robert M. Geraci earned his Ph.D. at the University of California, Santa Barbara, and is currently Professor of Religious Studies at Manhattan College. He is the author of *Apocalyptic AI: Visions of Heaven in Robotics, Artificial Intelligence, and Virtual Reality* (Oxford, 2010) and *Virtually*

Sacred: Myth and Meaning in World of Warcraft and Second Life (Oxford, 2014). His research has been supported by the U.S. National Science Foundation, the American Academy of Religion, and a Fulbright-Nehru Senior Research Award. Thanks to the last of these, he is in the finishing stages of a book on religion, science, and technology in contemporary India (forthcoming from Lexington).

Knut A. Jacobsen is Professor in the study of religions at the University of Bergen, Norway and author and editor of many books and numerous articles in journals and edited volumes on various aspects on religions of South Asia and in the South Asian diasporas. His research focuses on Sāṃkhya and Yoga, pilgrimage and religion in public space, and religious pluralism. He is the author of *Prakṛti in Sāṃkhya-Yoga: Material Principle: Religious Experience, Ethical Implications* (Peter Lang, 1999), *Kapila: Founder of Sāṃkhya and Avatāra of Viṣṇu* (Munshiram Manoharlal, 2008), *Pilgrimage in the Hindu Tradition: Salvific Space* (Routledge, 2013) and *Yoga in Modern Hinduism: Hariharānanda Āraṇya and Sāṃkhyayoga* (Routledge 2018). Other recent publications include the edited volumes *Yoga Powers: Extraordinary Capacities Attained through Meditation and Concentration* (Brill, 2012) and *Routledge Handbook of Contemporary India* (Routledge, 2016). Jacobsen is the founding Editor-in-Chief of the six volumes *Brill's Encyclopedia of Hinduism* (Brill, 2009–2015) and the *Brill's Encyclopedia of Hinduism Online*.

Brigitte Luchesi is a trained sociologist, social anthropologist, and historian of religion. She obtained her Ph.D. at the Free University of Berlin. She has taught at the Institute for Ethnology and the Institute for Jewish Studies in Berlin and from 1989 to 2008 at the Department of Comparative Religion at the University of Bremen, Germany. After her retirement she moved back to Berlin where she continues to work in the fields she always has been most interested in: forms of local religion in North India and the religious practices of Hindu and Christian immigrants from South Asia in Germany.

Kristina Myrvold is Associate Professor of Religious Studies at Linnaeus University, Sweden. Her research focuses on Sikh religious uses of texts, ritual practices, historiographies, and Sikh and Indian migration, integration processes and identity formations in Europe. Myrvold has published numerous journal articles and book chapters on Sikh practices in Sweden and in India, and contributed chapters on the Sikhs in Sweden and Europe to different handbooks on religions. She is the author of *Inside the Guru's Gate: Ritual Uses of Texts among the Sikhs in Varanasi* (Lund, 2007) and editor of the publications *The Death of Sacred Texts* (Ashgate, 2010), *Sikhs in Europe* (with K. A. Jacobsen, Ashgate, 2011), *Sikhs across Borders* (with K. A. Jacobsen, Bloomsbury, 2012), *Objects of Worship in South Asian Religions* (with K. A. Jacobsen and M. Aktor, Routledge, 2014,),

Young Sikhs in a Global World (with K. A. Jacobsen, Ashgate 2015), and *India: Research on Cultural Encounters and Representations at Linnaeus University* (with S. Billore, Makadam, 2017). Her recent research focuses on intersections of religion and technology in Punjab, print history of religious Sikh texts, and the production and use of miniature books in Sikh and Islamic traditions. Myrvold is one of the editors of the *Brill's Encyclopedia of Sikhism* (2017–2019) in two volumes.

Kirin Narayan is Professor of Anthropology and South Asian Studies at the Australian National University. She is author of *Storytellers, Saints and Scoundrels: Folk Narrative as Hindu Religious Teaching* (1989) that won the Victor Turner Prize for Ethnographic Writing; *Love, Stars and All That* (1994), a comic novel about academia; *Mondays on the Dark Night of the Moon: Himalayan Foothill Folktales* (1997), a collaboration with Urmila Devi Sood who shared and discussed her folktale repertoire; *My Family and Other Saints* (2007), a family memoir of spiritual quests; *Alive in the Writing: Crafting Ethnography in the Company of Chekhov* (2012), a manual for writing; and *Everyday Creativity: Singing Goddesses of the Himalayan Foothills* (2016), an ethnography of women's engagement with mythological songs in Kangra. Her current research (with Ken George) explores Vishwakarma traditions in relation to competing cultural conceptions of creativity and technology in contemporary India.

Moumita Sen is post-doctoral fellow at the University of Oslo looking at Adivasi politics and Hindu Nationalism in India. Her doctoral dissertation "Clay-modelling in West Bengal: Between art, religion and politics" was a study of visual culture in West Bengal. She is interested in caste, visual arts, and the relationship between religion and politics in South Asia.

Hindol Sengupta is the author of eight books including *Recasting India: How Entrepreneurship is Revolutionizing the World's Largest Democracy* (Palgrave Macmillan, 2014), which is the only Indian book ever to be shortlisted for the Hayek Prize given by the Manhattan Institute for original writing in economics in memory of the Nobel laureate F. A. Hayek. He is the winner of the PSF award for public service which has among its earlier winner the late Indian scientist and President A. P. J. Abdul Kalam. He is a World Economic Forum Young Global Leader and a Knight Bagehot Fellow at Columbia University. He is Editor-at-Large for the Indian edition of the *Fortune* magazine and an Aspen Italy columnist.

Iris Vandevelde is a teaching assistant and post-doctoral researcher at the Department of Languages and Cultures of Ghent University in Belgium. She earned her Ph.D. in Film Studies and Visual Culture from the University of Antwerp in 2012, based on her research into Indian cinema in the South Asian diaspora. Her main research interests are media and visual cultures in India, Indian cinema, transnationalism and diaspora, Hindu nationalism and reconversion, Hindi, and Jewish film culture. She is currently involved with the FWO-funded project "Online religion in a transnational context: representing and practicing Jainism in diasporic communities."

Tine Vekemans is a research assistant at the Department of Languages and Cultures of Ghent University in Belgium. Her research interests include contemporary Jainism, the Jain diaspora, and the interactions of religion, migration, and digital media. She is currently involved with the FWO-funded project "Online religion in a transnational context: representing and practicing Jainism in diasporic communities."

Xenia Zeiler is Associate Professor of South Asian Studies at the University of Helsinki, Finland. Her research is situated at the intersection of digital media, religion and culture, in India and the worldwide Indian community. Her research foci are digital Hinduism, global Hinduism, Ethno-Indology and Tantric traditions. She is the author of a monograph on current trans-formations of Tantric traditions in India and of numerous articles and book chapters on mediatized and digital Hinduism, including the first-ever article on video games and Hinduism, on popular religion in contemporary India, and on global Hinduism. Her current projects include Mediatized Religion in Asia, Video Gaming and Cultural Heritage in Asia, a Digital Humanities Initiative India-Finland, and Methods for researching Video Games and Religion. Together with Kerstin Radde-Antweiler, she is co-founder and co-editor-in-chief of *Gamevironments: Games, Religion, and Stuff* (http://www.gamevironments.org/), the first academic journal with a specific focus on video gaming, religion and culture.

Introduction

Knut A. Jacobsen and Kristina Myrvold

This book explores intersections between religion and technology in India, at the present and in the colonial past, and how various forms of techno-religious intersections transform and open up for new religious practices, discourses, communities, and institutions. Starting from a broad definition of technology, technological developments at different times in history include new machines and technologies in a broader sense, such as the invention of writing, printing technology, and new means of transportation and communication, and more lately the Internet which have facilitated new spaces of religion. The techno-religious intersections generate several questions about authority and power, community and place, and how religious agency, information, and experience are mediated, commodified, and adjusted to new demands of societies. With focus on the Indian contexts and religions, this book discusses various empirical and theoretical aspects of how technological innovations create, alter, and negotiate religious spaces, practices, and authorities. The book provides empirical examples of different ways in which technological imaginaries and practices in relation to religion become rich and multifaceted, by linking the concrete techniques, tools, and knowledge with meanings, ideas and practices of religions (Ornella, 2015; Stolow, 2013). Technological developments facilitate new "techno-religious spaces" in which different forms of poetics and politics of identity and community can be played out and alter religious practices and power relations. From this perspective are new technologies being "socialized" and may cause both democratization and struggles for domination and control based on the access and use of technologies (Kong, 2001; Crang et al., 2012).

Since the mid-1990s, researchers have increasingly examined the relation between new media and religion from the perspective of religious change (e.g. Dawson and Cowan, 2004; Campbell, 2012; Stout and Buddenbaum, 2008). The acclaimed 1995 publication on *Media and the Transformation of Religion in South Asia* edited by Lawrence A. Babb and Susan S. Wadley included essays on three types of media: printed images, audio recordings, and films and videos (Babb and Wadley, 1995). At that time, around twenty years ago, these represented the leading media technology in India and, as the title stated, these media were thought to have transformed religion in South Asia and had created new ways both to express religion, to spread religion, and to access it. A comparison between the changes in media and communication technology in the twenty-first century with those discussed in *Media and the Transformation of Religion in South Asia*, reveals some striking new developments. Printed images, audio recordings, and films and videos were in the book identified as the examples of the "second wave" of the modern change in the media, which communicate and transmit religion in South Asia (Babb and Wadley, 1995: 5). Babb and Wadley refers to the first wave as the printing press, which had an enormous influence on religion since the nineteenth-century colonial India, while printed images, audio recordings, and films and videos were the second wave, which according to them were thought to have influenced in particular mobility, simplifications and standardizations (Babb and Wadley, 1995: 4–5). By waves Babb and Wadley seem to refer to the point of time when new media become available to a large number of people because of cheap production, transport, and dissemination. The changes in the communication technology that is taking place in the twenty-first century with the new technologies of the Internet, mobile phones and smartphones have been so important that it can perhaps be called a "third wave" of change in the media, which communicate religion in India. *Media and the Transformation of Religion in South Asia* was published just before these new technologies of the "third wave" started to impact religious life in India. For the past twenty years the digital technologies have revolutionized communication and have not the least influenced the speed of communication, the availability of information, and the ways of communication with the ability to reach people almost everywhere in an instant. The digital revolution of Internet and mobile phones created a new reality as physical distance no longer was a hindrance of communication, and communication could happen in an instant. Instant dissemination characterizes mobile phones and Internet communication and printed pictures, audio cassettes and videos that depended on cheap production, transport and dissemination now belonged to a previous stage of communication technology.[1]

Religious actors in India have learned how to use the new media to their advantage. Ability to reach people in an instant, wherever they are located, characterizes the new media. Religion flourishes when technologies create new possibilities for communication. However, while new technologies give new opportunities for communication, they may also, as a consequence, lead to changes in religion. Building upon the theoretical academic discussions on *online religion* and *religion online* (see. e.g. Dawson and Cowan, 2004; Helland, 2000), several contributions in this book illustrate how the digital media is used by religious communities and individuals to communicate information about religious groups, traditions, ideologies, rituals, and so on, and is also employed for creating practices that involve a more interactive religious and ritual participation in communities through the media, whether it concerns participation in rituals online, spiritual counseling, cooperation and communication with co-devotees, or the organization of religious events.

Overview of the content of the chapters

The first two chapters of the book explore the issue of technology related to the Hindu pantheon. Hinduism has its own god of technology, Vishwakarma, a god who is both *of* the machine and *in* the machine. The first chapter of Kirin Narayan and Ken George analyzes the Hindu god of technology, whose worship goes back as far as to the *Rigveda*. In the Epics and the Puranas he is celebrated for his technological and infrastructural inventions for the gods, such as celestial machines, weapons, and palaces, and cities. Kirin Narayan and Ken George discuss Vishwakarma as the divine craftsman, architect, and engineer and his association with artisans as well as with modern technology and industry. They argue that Vishwarkarma's presence has grown with the spread of machinery, industry, and technology, confirming the view that there is a religiosity of technology and a technologization of religion. As modern technology expands, so does the worship of the god associated with it and the current rapidly growing infrastructural networks are providing new arenas for his worship.

Another example of the close relationship between technology and religion from contemporary India is the promotion by Hindu nationalism of the idea that modern technology was present in Vedic religion. In Chapter 2, Robert M. Geraci analyzes this idea and its role in Indian politics and shows how it has a long history in shifting political environments. The idea that modern technology was present in Vedic religion flourished already as an ingredient of the resistance to British colonial rule. The influential founder of Arya Samaj, Dayananda Sarasvati (1824–1883), argued famously for the presence of flying machines, steamships, and advanced exploding weapons in ancient India. This discourse continued beyond the end of colonialism into expressions of anti-Western sentiments. Geraci shows that this mixture of myth, technology, and history represents a glorification of the past, which follows from the Hindu view of the *yuga*s which claims that the past was better than the present but that the current Hindu improvements of science and technology also support the view that we now have entered an ascending *yuga*. The chapter illustrates that in contemporary India the glorification of the technological achievements of an imagined Indian mythological past is not limited only to the uneducated, but the views, surprisingly, are shared also by many persons educated in and working in the technological sciences.

Chapters 3 and 4 discuss new technologies of visualization. In Chapter 3 Kristina Myrvold, based on research of surviving photographic material and colonial records on Punjab, analyzes the impact of photography on the Sikhs, especially the visual images of them in colonial photographic representations. She illustrates how these representations were underpinned by orientalism and racial ideologies but also how technological developments created new opportunities and visual imaginaries that challenged the colonial power. Myrvold shows that the new technology of photography became an agent of change that had consequences not only for the visual representations of the

Sikhs but also for developments in the society at large. Myrvold concludes that the nineteenth-century images portraying the Sikhs as ideal warriors have in the twenty-first century assumed new religious meanings in contemporary Sikh identity and commemoration projects.

In Chapter 4, Moumita Sen describes the changes in clay-modeling in Bengal in the middle of the twentieth century which led to the appearance of the "Artistic Durga" in contrast to the traditional "Sabeki" Durga statue. With the influence of naturalism, the visual image of goddess Durga was transformed from a traditional image into a Western image making the goddess into a picture of a real, living woman. This remarkable change in visual image was due to new institutions of education in the arts in which traditional craftsmen were trained in a naturalist style of art that started to affect the making of god images in the whole of Bengal. Sen describes this change as an influence from perspectivalism and naturalism, combined with European Enlightenment values of science and reason, and argues that *techne*, or the knowledge of making and doing things, can best describe the "hybridaized," vernacularized knowledge systems of contemporary clay-modelers of Bengal.

Chapter 5 by Xenia Zeiler analyzes religion and popular TV serials and particularly how the serials portray the position of Hindu widows in society. Zeiler points out that the widow has very negative associations in Hinduism; she was thought to be inauspicious and polluting and even potentially dangerous. This was probably related to the outsider position of widows in the society and the attempts to exclude them. The author first describes the textual history of these views on widows and widowhood and then analyzes three Hindi TV serials which portray new and partly reformed views on widows. Zeiler demonstrates how mass media narratives have become powerful vehicles of change in society and these serials contribute to new representations of widowhood in contemporary India. The TV serials manage to bring out the contrast between the expectations of widows described in religious texts and the contemporary more liberal approaches to widowhood. Especially the TV serial set in the pilgrimage city of Benares, which promotes the widow's right to take own decisions about her life, can contribute to legitimate new choices and values about widows in contemporary India.

The following chapter by Brigitte Luchesi analyzes various changes in religious life in the state of Himachal Pradesh, and especially in the district of Kangra, that have been caused by new technological developments. In spring 2015 when Luchesi observed a religious ritual and asked a participant about some details a young boy, who witnessed Luchesi, advised her to find the information on the Internet, indicating how the Internet has increasingly become a legitimate place for finding religious knowledge in rural areas, even replacing other forms of authority that were previously communicated through oral traditions. As Luchesi's chapter illustrates, technology and religion have intersected to the extent that some rituals have expanded as ritual commodities and become more frequent, such as in the technological modernization in the presentation of *jhanki*s, in which living persons expected to remain motionless and silent represent Hindu gods and goddesses. But Luchesi also notes that the story-telling that previously was linked with the ritual has diminished and has been replaced by television, leading to the vanishing of faith in the traditional stories. The "switching on" of the television whenever people had free time, as well as the downloading on computers and mobiles, has also led to the disappearance of traditional songs.

The remaining four chapters deal with different aspects of the new technology of mobile phones and online communication. In Chapter 7, Knut A. Jacobsen analyzes recent changes in the *shraddha* ritual at Kapilashram in the town of Siddhpur in Gujarat. An important function for the *shraddha* ritual at Kapi-lashram is to give opportunity to appease the souls (*preta*s) of dead mothers or grandmothers. This is especially urgent when they are understood to be a source of problems for the surviving families. Kapilashram is the main place in India for these *shraddha* rituals for the dead mothers and grandmothers and is unique by being the only Hindu pilgrimage site that is exclusively promoted and functions as a place for the performance of *shraddha* to deceased mothers. Jacobsen's chapter shows how the new communication technology is being used to propagate the pilgrimage places, to attract pilgrims, and to organize travels for pilgrims, and how this has transformed the ritual practices at the pilgrimage place.

In Chapter 8, Hindol Sengupta explores a new Hindu spiritual movement called the Hindutva Abhiyan that is headquartered in central India. The chapter analyzes the work and methodology of the Hindutva Abhiyan in using social media and technology to pitch the ideology of Hindutva, especially their ideas about caste. The Hindu nationalist V. D. Savarkar, who coined the term *hindutva*, was against caste discrimination because caste hindered unity among the Hindus. Sengupta looks at Hindutva Abhiyan's interpretation of V. D. Savarkar's visions of a caste-free Hindu society and analyzes the attempts by the contemporary association to present a definition that puts casteless-ness or a caste-free Hindu society at the heart of the message and the role of social media in promoting it. Hindutva Abhiyan is entrepreneurial in nature and uses social media as a tool to disseminate everyday messages. The chapter analyzes how the use of social media by Abhiyan is cast in metaphors of eating together from the same utensils and seen as a tool to push for a caste discrimination-free Hindu unity.

In Chapter 9, Anna Bochkovskaya looks at *dera*s in Punjab, the majority of the devotees of which are made up of Dalits. Bochkovskaya argues that the lower-castes are trying to get their share of societal resources and assert themselves in Punjab's politics. To attain this they resort to new forms of religion and distance themselves from traditional Sikh authorities due to the overwhelming dominance of upper Sikh castes (mostly Jats) in the ritual sphere and in religious institutions. Both Sikh places of worship (gurdwaras) and the Sikh scripture (Guru Grant Sahib), according to Bochkovskaya, are nowadays regarded by many Punjabi Dalits as manifestations of high-caste power. Her chapter focuses on the Internet performance of one of the largest and most controversial *dera*s, Dera Sacha Sauda, founded in 1948. In the early twenty-first century, the *dera*s have been using online marketing options for promoting their ideologies and attracting new followers. One component of Sacha Sauda's success is its propaganda activity carried out by its media center that is continuously expanding. There have been several attempts by the *dera* leaders in the past to adopt their own holy books and, as Bochkovskaya illustrates, an online text was intended to create a general image of Dera Sacha Sauda as an independent religious entity promoting its own "spiritual" book, but which also might be considered as a version of counter-scripture in relation to mainstream Sikhism. Bochkovskaya argues that the *dera* online is presented as a business project, but also represent a fusion of religious and social components. Its success is due to "a well-calculated social strategy, flexible propaganda policy, and pragmatism involving the use of cutting edge media technologies" (p. 177).

The last chapter of the book, Chapter 10, treats Jain online ritual tools and resources in the context of an Indian diaspora. Tine Vekemans and Iris Vandevelde note that over the past decades Jainism has developed an increasing presence online, which consists mainly of informational websites, discussion groups, mobile applications, and social media accounts, but also ritual tools and resources. The authors argue that the diaspora plays an important role in the developments of Jainism and the new media, by being an important target audience and by representing more active online communities with about half of the Jain websites being hosted outside of India. The chapter analyzes three different types of online ritual tools and resources: religious downloads, live *darshan*, and online *puja*, and explains how they fit into Jain ritual offline practices. As their study based on fieldwork among Jains in the USA and Belgium illustrate, online *darshan* is preferable before online *puja*, and most devotees would turn to home shrines rather than using online alternatives. As Vekemans and Vandevelde question, if computer mediated ritual is acceptable in theory, then why is it so little used in practice? Online practices are certainly not denounced, but they are also not accepted as alternative to offline ritual practices. The authors show that the absence of social and sensory elements and the questions related to appropriate mind-set and commodification are the main reasons. Many of their respondents doubted that it was possible to establish the right mind-set while surfing the Internet, but supported that online practices can be useful for contemplation and education. Since Jain monks and nuns do not travel abroad, Internet becomes particularly important for the diaspora in keeping with religious authorities in the "homeland" and for gathering information.

Inspired by the theoretical directions derived from interdisciplinary research on religion, media, and technology, which has illustrated how religion and technology implicate each other in various and changing ways, this book thus provides empirical examples of how different technological developments in Indian contexts intersect with specific religious traditions and communities and alter religious spaces, practices, and power relations.

Note

1 In the Introduction of the *Media and the Transformation of Religion in South Asia* the authors noted that "from a pure technological standpoint, technological advance in communications tends to be seen primarily as a means of overcoming physical distance" and that words and pictures, audio recordings, videos and tapes could be transported cheaply over large distances and if cheaply produced disseminated to large number of people (Babb and Wadley, 1995: 3).

References

Babb, Lawrence and Susan Wadley (eds.) (1995) *Media and the Transformation of Religion in South Asia*. Philadelphia, PA: University of Pennsylvania Press.

Campbell, Heidi (ed.) (2012) *Digital Religion: Understanding Religious Practice in New Media Worlds*. Abingdon and New York: Routledge.

Crang, Mike, Phil Crang and Jon May (1999) *Virtual Geographies: Bodies, Space and Relations* (Sussex Studies in Culture and Communication). London: Routledge.

Dawson, Lorne L. and Douglas E. Cowan (eds.) (2004) *Religion Online: Finding Faith on the Internet*. New York: Routledge.

Helland, C. (2000) "Online Religion/Religion Online and Virtual Communitas," in J.K. Hadden and D.E. Cowan (eds.), *Religion on the Internet: Research Prospects and Promises*, New York: JAI Press, pp. 205–224.

Kong, Lily (2001) "Religion and Technology: Refiguring Place, Space, Identity and Community." *Area* 33(4), pp. 404–413.

Ornella, Alexander (2015) "Towards a 'Circuit of Technological Imaginaries': A Theoretical Approach," in Daria Pezzoli-Olgiati (ed.), *Religion in Cultural Imaginary: Explorations in Visual and Material Practices*. Baden-Baden: Nomos, pp. 303–332.

Stout, Daniel A. and Judith M. Buddenbaum (2008) "Approaches to the Study of Media and Religion: Notes from the Editors of the Journal of Media and Religion with Recommendations for Future Research." *Religion* 38(3): 226–232.

Stolow, Jeremy (ed.) (2013) *Deus in Machina: Religion, Technology, and the Things in Between*. New York: Fordham University Press.

1 Vishwakarma

God of technology

Kirin Narayan and Kenneth M. George

Returning in 2015 to a Kangra village that she has been visiting on and off since 1975, Kirin Narayan was once again disoriented by extensive changes to the landscape and ways of life. Like many other places across India, this western Himalayan foothill region has since the 1990s become a giant construction site. All along Kangra valley, at the base of the towering Dhauladhar range, networks of new roads are now flanked by brightly painted new shops and houses; stacks of red brick, sacks of cement, and hillocks of stone and sand disclose plans for yet more buildings. Sounds of construction reverberate across the landscape: a pervasive chip-chip-chip of chisels breaking river stones; the whirr and whine, the buzz and the bleats of large machines. Side by side with these physical transformations of the landscape, images of the Hindu deity Vishwakarma – the divine craftsman, architect and engineer – have been proliferating. Driving past the open shop fronts of timber mills, furniture workshops, welding units, garages, and computer repair shops, one glimpses Vishwakarma calendar art on the walls. Entering workspaces, one discerns Vishwakarma nestled in alcoves beside tailors bent over their sewing machines, near the kiln in potteries, or presiding over electricity circuits for tea-processing machinery. In the town of Palampur, a new pink Vishwakarma temple rises beside the road leading toward the developing Nagri Industrial Area. Why has Vishwakarma's presence grown with the spread of machinery, industry, technology, and infrastructural systems? In the stimulating introduction to his edited volume *Deus in Machina: Religion, Technology and the Things in Between*, Jeremy Stolow argues that though religion and technology may seem categorically distinct, there is much to be gained by looking at "the technologization of religion and the religiosity of technology" (2012: 4).[1]

Cautioning that we need to acknowledge how Christian associations linger amid these conceptual categories and are reinforced by Western technological hegemony, Stolow welcomes the "many hybrids that lie beneath this semantic divide, each awaiting its own opportunity to be made visible as a god *in* the machine" (2012: 19). In India, it appears that Vishwakarma is the god *in* the machine and *of* the machine. His historical association with the simple technology of hand tools has extended towards the complex technology of machines and building projects more generally, as well as the expansion of infrastructures. Vishwakarma, then, offers a valuable prism to view a spectrum of approaches in the interface between technology and religion in India.

We begin by offering an overview of Vishwakarma's role in Hindu and Buddhist myths and legends, and also his presence in vernacular Islam. Next, we examine how he is associated with artisans working by hand with tools. We then trace the association of Vishwakarma with machines and industry, and their politicization. Finally, we discuss how rapidly expanding infrastructural networks – the technofunctional systems enabling the movement of things, people, and information (Larkin, 2013) – appear to be offering new arenas for Vishwakarma worship. As we are at the beginning of a larger research project, our remarks have yet to rest on the dense authority of extended fieldwork. Nonetheless, we use this opportunity to propose some provisional thoughts about what Vishwakarma worship may tell us about religion, society and technology.

Vishwakarma as all-maker

Vishwakarma's association with creating and making has deep Indic roots. In the Vedas he is known as Vishwakarman "'the Maker of Everything' (or literally 'who has the making of everything')" (Jamison and Brereton, 2014: 1513) and also as Tvastar (or Tvashtri "the "Fashioner," who "adorned all creatures with their forms" (*ibid.*: 51). A hymn to Vishwakarman in the Rig Veda (X, 81: 3) in particular carries a verse (beginning "*vishvastash cakshuruta vishvatomukho*") that to this day is widely anthologized in devotional texts.[2] Many who today recite these praises might perceive them as saluting a generalized creator, and not necessarily just Vishwakarma:

> Whose eyes and face are turned in every direction, whose arms and feet move in every direction, producing heaven and earth, he forges them together with his arms, with his fan(-bellows) – he the god alone. (Jamison and Brereton, 2014: 1514)

A different translation of this same verse emphasizes how as Vishwakarma "creates the Earth and Heavens/ he welds them together with whirring of arms and wings" (Pannikar, 1977: 808). This protean, welding and whirring activity of creation can be located in the imagery of the pumping of a blacksmith's feathered bellows (Kali, 2011: 206). Reading with an eye for the work of craftsmen, our attention was drawn also to the next verse that extends the forging of metal to carpentry, to ask, "What was the wood? What was the tree? – out of which they fashioned heaven and earth?" (Rig Veda X: 81.4, in Jamison and Brereton, 2015: 1514). The end of the same hymn requests Vishwakarma for help as "he who is luck for everyone, whose work succeeds" (Rig Veda X: 81, 7, in Jamison and Brereton, 2015: 1515) – an appeal that resonates with contemporary invocations to Vishwakarma for the successful completion of work projects.

For reasons we have yet to discover, Vishwakarma's role shifts in the epics and the Puranas. Brahma becomes the Creator, while Vishwakarma becomes the *deva-shilpi*, the divine craftsman and architect, acting either in person or through his sons to serve other gods. He is celebrated for making ingenious creations for the gods: for example powerful weapons, self-moving celestial vehicles, magnificent palaces and expansive, magical cities like Dvaraka (Wilkins, 1980 [1882]: 77; Mani, 1975: 869–72; Vishwakarma, 2002). The multiplicity of Vishwakarma's talents is celebrated in the epigraph introducing the marvelous images of art brought together by the art historian Ananda K. Coomaraswamy in 1914. Introducing Indian art to Western audiences in *Vishwakarma,: Examples of Indian Architecture, Sculpture, Painting, Handicrafts*, Coomaraswamy draws on this verse from the *Mahabharata*:[3]

> Vishwakarma, Lord of the arts, master of a thousand handicrafts, carpenter of the gods and builder of their palaces divine, fashioner of every jewel, first of craftsmen, by whose art men live, and whom, a great and deathless god, they continually worship. (Coomaraswamy, 1914: 2)

In Buddhist literature too, Vishwakarma is a capable maker. In Jataka tales, particularly in the last ten births of the Buddha Siddhartha, he appears at Sakka or Indra's command whenever these earlier Hindu incarnations of the Buddha need a dwelling. With the movement of both Hindu and Buddhist faiths and narratives, Vishwakarma has traveled beyond the confines of India and can be found under similar names in Sri Lanka, Bangladesh, Nepal, Thailand, Cambodia, and even as far as Kyoto – that, however, would be the subject of a different paper. Vishwakarma's presence at the conjunction of Hindu and Buddhist beliefs is materialized also in his association with the Ellora caves: for some artisans this is a sacred space where his presence remains after he has left his body, and for others, he is manifest in the statue of the Buddha in Cave 10, to which we will shortly return (see e.g. Mukherjee, 1994: 40).

We have also found Vishwakarma's presence in vernacular Islam in Bengal. Patua painters, who move between Muslim and Hindu identities, see themselves as having descended from Vishwakama (Korom, 2006: 32; Mukherjee, 1994: 52–53). The artist Meera Mukherjee retells several tales of Vishwakarma's association with Gaji Pir and with the flying of kites (Mukherjee, 1994: 43–44, 67, 70).

Vishwakarma appears to have been historically worshipped in the form of tools, with anthropomorphic iconographies only developing later. For example, in his ethnographic novel *Govinda Samanta*, later reissued as *Bengal Peasant Life*, that is, described as "an authentic history," the Reverend Lal Behari Day emphasizes the importance of tools in the worship of Vishwakarma:[4]

> Visvakarma, the engineer of the celestials, is represented by the figure of a man painted white, having three eyes, wearing on his head a crown, a

necklace of gold, and bangles on his wrists, and holding a club in his right hand. But the image is seldom made, its place being supplied by the implements and tools in the various departments of mechanical labour. Every peasant, every artizan [*sic*], worships the tools of his trade in his own house. (Day, 1913: 351)

Day continues with a description of the festivities that he locates in the month of *Chaitra* (March/April), indicating the sorts of tools that characters engaged in different caste occupations set up in worship.

On that day Govinda set up in a corner of his house the plough, the hoe, the sickle, and other implements of husbandry; Nanda, his hammer, his anvil and his bellows; Kapila, his axe, his wedge, his inclined plane; Chatura, his razors, his basin, and the sharp instruments for paring off the nails; Bokaram, his loom and shuttle, the fisherman, his nets, his rods, and lines; the oilman, his oil-mill; the potter, his wheel; the mason, his trowel and plumb-line; the shoemaker, his awl; the washerman, his beetle, his mallet, and his ironing instrument – they all washed and cleaned these implements, and set them apart for the day from ordinary use. (Day, 1913: 352)

While such tool worship continues today, marked by both the lunar and solar calendar in different regions, today we also find iconographies of Vishwakarma so diverse that they are almost unrecognizable across regions. Vishwakarma is invariably represented as holding tools, with more tools arranged in a nimbus behind him. He is found especially in the following forms:

1 Vishwakarma as a white-bearded and crowned grandfather with four arms, usually surrounded by five sons. A white swan or goose beside him suggests an association with Brahma. This white-bearded form is found particularly in India's western and northwestern regions. It also appears to be gaining broader currency across the country. More recently, this form is sometimes depicted seated on the ground, balancing a globe on his lap, and chiseling away at the continents (see Figure 1.1).
2 Vishwakarma as a muscular young man with a black moustache and four arms, with an elephant vehicle, suggesting an association with Indra or Brihaspati. His sons are not represented. This form is prevalent in eastern India and used when making clay icons of Vishwakarma for annual worship and ritual submergence each September 17 (see Figure 1.2).
3 Vishwakarma as a clean-shaven, five-faced and ten-armed companion to the goddess Gayatri sitting side by side in lotuses. Sometimes, figures of the five sons surround them; other times not at all. Before them, a cow and tiger are drinking from the same source with the tiger cub suckling the cow and the calf suckling the tiger, suggesting the harmonious mixing of opposites. This form predominates in South India. This same five-headed

and ten-armed form – sometimes accompanied by two goddesses touching his feet – is known as "Virat [Immense] Vishwakarma" in iconographies from India's western region.

Two further forms deserve mention though they are less often encountered:

1   Vishwakarma as a clean-shaven young man modeled after the seated Buddha from the celebrated Cave 10 in the ancient rock cut cave complex at Ellora. This cave, known as "the Carpenter's Hut" (Sutar ki jhopri), has arched, wood-like beams. Vishwakarma's hands, arranged in the teaching pose, carry no tools and two elephants flank him; in one poster we located he is titled "Guru Vishwakarma" (the Teacher Vishwakarma).
2   Vishwakarma as a clean-shaven, two-armed standing young man carrying a ruler in his right hand and a palm leaf manuscript in his left. No sons are present. As Samuel Parker, who reproduces this image in an article about temple architects in Tamil Nadu comments, "Images of Vishvakarma or of sculptors or architects are extremely rare in Indian tradition, hence the word 'Vishvakarma' is inscribed in Tamil beneath the bare feet, removing any possible ambiguity in the iconography" (Parker, 2003: 132). We note that this two-armed, ruler-bearing form also appears to be worshipped at technical colleges and vocational schools in Thailand.[5]

While a ruler (*gaj*) is often present, emphasizing the importance of measuring and ratios, the other tools around Vishwakarma can display tremendous variation. As a four-handed grandfather (Form 1; see Figure 1.1), Vishwakarma's ruler is in his upper left hand, and in his right, he holds what is clearly a plumb bob in older iconographies but that has now, in some modern representations, given way to a measuring tape, which duplicates the ruler's function. His lower left hand holds a water pot, once again showing a kinship with Brahma (though possibly not for sprinkling holy water so much as for cooling heated metal).[6] His lower right hand holds a treatise on building. By contrast, the Indra-like Vishwakarma (Form 2) is more varied. In posters, he carries a bow and arrow in his upper left hand, what appears to be a socket wrench in the upper right; while the lower left hand holds a scale and the lower right an axe; in images, this young form may have a hammer in his upper right hand, and a kite and spool for thread in the upper left, with a lower right palm raised in blessing, or he may be surrounded by kites marking the kite-flying on the day of his celebration (see Figure 1.2). The South Indian ten-armed Vishwakarma, however, holds an array of more traditional weapons rather than tools, and also a lute-like musical instrument known as the *veena* (*vina*).

The metal tools organized in a wide halo-like arc around the deity's head display tremendous artistic invention and close observation of craftsmen's key tools. The grandfather Vishwakarma (Form 1) may display such tools as an axe, saw, T-square, hammer, mallet, spanner, plier, scale and more. The young Vishwakarma (Form 2) might have a wide array of tools for building as well

Figure 1.1 Vishwakarma as a grandfather surrounded by his five sons in a poster
source: https://en.wikipedia.org/wiki/Vishvakarman#/media/File:Vishwakarmaji.png,
accessed 12.13.2017.

as a sickle, scissors, knife, water pump, cooking dish, lock, sewing machine
and other metal tools and implements we have yet to identify. The other three
forms do not carry extra tools.

Along with the regional variation in forms, tremendous variation can be found
around the dates associated with Vishwakarma's worship. September 17 is

Figure 1.2 Vishwakarma image from annual *puja* in Bengal
Photo courtesy of Moumita Sen.

celebrated as Vishwakarma Jayanti in Eastern India with images of Vishwakarma worshipped, taken out in massive processions and ceremonially sub-
merged (Kumar, 1988: 204–208). This date is linked to *Kanya Sankranti* or the
last day of the Bengali month Bhadra and so would shift slightly from year to
year; however, it has become standardized to September 17 (Mukherjee, 1994:
24–29). To India's west, though, the key period of Vishwakarma worship is from
the fifth to the thirteenth day after the Magh new moon (January/February),
while to the north he is mostly worshipped the day after the festival Divali
(October Worship of Vishwakarma often involves ceremonially assembling,
washing, and anointing tools (Narayan and George, 2017).

The association with making and with tools, then, forms the most obvious
and powerful link between Vishwakarma and technology. People in Kangra
explain that Vishwakarma *must* be worshipped wherever metal tools or
machines are in use; his presence, they say, brings blessings to the undertaking
while protecting the user from harm. As a young hereditary carpenter from
Kangra told Narayan, during periods of worship, the tools were being given a
rest. An engineer likened the cessation of all machine work in his workshop
on Vishwakarma Day to a "tools-down strike."[7]

Vishwakarma in the work of artisans

Vishwakarma does not only work alone. He is assisted by his sons, who in many accounts are five, each son specializing in the transformation of a particular form of matter. These sons thus represent different forms of craft technology. Most often, these are viewed as the ancestors of blacksmiths, carpenters, brass workers, sculptors and goldsmiths, respectively. It is in this claim of a hereditary connection directly to Vishwakarma that different artisan castes, embodying his presence, can be known as "Vishwakarma," "the sons of Vishwakarma," or even on account of the number five, the "Panchalas" (from *panch* or five). In some cases, the social structure of the Vishwakarma-related communities is visible in the deity's iconographic form, with the five heads representing five emanations/sons who were the ancestors of five caste groups, or alternately these same caste groups being represented through the form of five sons standing at his side.

Perhaps because of the centrality of iron to tools used by other artisans, blacksmiths are often listed as first among these five key groups, as Jan Brouwer has shown in *The Makers of the World: Caste, Craft and Mind of South Indian Artisans* (Brouwer, 1985: 55). The emergence of a wider identity beyond particular *jati* groups, to be seen as a single family of Vishwakarma, appears to be partly consolidated around historical circumstances in which a shared corporate identity emerges. So, for example, the historian Vijaya Ramaswamy observes that "[i]t is in the context of temple building where these five craft groups worked in such close coordination that the concept of 'Vishwakarma kula" [Vishwakarma's family] seems to have predominated over that of separate caste identities" (Ramaswamy, 2004: 553; cf. Ramaswamy, 1985).

Beyond the paradigmatic five sons, there appears to be certain flexibility in numbers. So for example, in his treatise on Hindu temple building, Alain Danielou describes the key artisan players who are directed by a Brahman site foreman as "divided into four categories: architect (*sthapati*), mason (*sutra-grahin*), sculptor (*takshaka*) and painter-decorator (*vardhakin*)" (Danielou, 2001: 30). From these temple-centered four, Danielou expands the list to nine more sons that includes smiths of more standard groupings:

> According to legend, Vishwakarman, the architect of the universe, beside his building workmen, had nine sons born of a woman belonging to the worker caste. These were the garland maker (*malakara*), the smith (*kar-makara*), the polisher of mother-of-pearl (*shankakara*), the weaver (*kuvindaka*), the potter (*khumbhakara*), the painter (*chitrakara*), and the goldsmith (*svarnakara*) (Danielou, 2001:30).

Working among artisans in Karnataka in the 1980s Jan Brouwer emphasized how Vishwakarma communities connect their work back to the god's primordial Vedic identity, emphatically staking out their own view as different from epic and Puranic depictions of Vishwakarma as merely a craftsman for other gods. As he writes, "[t]he Visvakarma view of Lord Visvakarman should not be confused with the Brahmans' view of Visvakarman as celestial architect, i.e. Visvakarman reduced to a servant of the deities" (Brouwer, 1995: 41). Working in the 1960s on the ethnography of caste in Tamil Nadu, Brenda Beck similarly observed the gap between the Vedas and epics in a footnote, pointing out that the self-identifying term for artisans as Visvakarma Brahmins "refers both to the god Visvakarman or "world creator" of the Rig Veda and to the demigod Visvakarman or "craftsman – creator" of the Ramayana ... group members see their status as craftsmen in this world as a counterpart to that of divine creator in another" (Beck, 1970: 789, cited in Brouwer, 1995: 41).

Artisans who do *not* honor Vishwakarma mark the edges of a more Hindu or Hinduized identity. For example, in an older detailed study of the cosmology and material practices of Agaria tribal iron smelters and blacksmiths of central India, Verrier Elwin noted how Agaria distinguished themselves from Hindu blacksmiths, the Lohar, partly through their mythological affiliation:

> The Agaria have an elaborate mythology of which the heroes are Logundi Raja, Jwala Mukhi and Kariya Kuar, but they are ignorant of the Hindu Vulcan, Twashtri or Vishwakarma, the artisan of the gods, who made the fiery weapon Agneyastra and revealed the Sthapatya-veda, the science of mechanics and architecture. The Lohar, on the other hand, who are ignorant of the tribal heroes, derive their caste and its profession from Twashtri or Vishwakarma (Elwin, 1942: 2).

More recently, working in industrial settings in now transformed tribal regions, Jonathan Parry notes that at the Bhilai steel plant and in private sector factories, Vishwakarma puja is observed on September 17 each year, sponsored by management. Since this is fixed by the Western solar calendar rather than the lunar Hindu one, a group of workers speculated to Parry that Vishwakarma had perhaps arrived from abroad along with the industrial machines (Parry, personal e-mail communication, February 11, 2015).

Vishwakarma and industrial technology

The historian Smritikumar Sarkar has documented how with industrialization in colonized India, artisans sometimes innovatively adopted new technologies for their work (Sarkar, 2013). Across regions, Vishwakarma may have moved with artisans who left hereditary workplaces, seeking employment instead in urban and industrial spaces, as Hein Streefkerk has described for Gujarat (Streefkerk, 2006). Vishwakarma's connection to the material aspects of technology appear to have made for a logical extension from hand tools to complex machines, and then his being honored by fellow workers from different caste backgrounds. In Kangra, for example, Kirin Narayan has been told that since "Technical Work A-Z" involves Vishwakarma, all factories including grain mills and printing presses come to a halt on the regional Vishwakarma Day (after Diwali). Simultaneously, on regular workdays, workers engaged with machines might ask the god for the safety (*salamat*) of their hands and feet, along with skill and success.

The association of both artisans and factory workers with Vishwakarma is well-documented in Nita Kumar's book *Artisans of Benares*. Kumar notes how Vishwakarma Puja as a public celebration on September 17 each year "started out as Vishwakarma *puja*, a domestic workshop of the tools and the God of the trade" (Kumar, 1988: 204). Kumar found that those who observe this Puja are both artisans and people from a range of castes who work in factories, with products that "range from diesel locomotives to nuts and bolts, from consumer goods like fans and aluminum trays. They may also be engaged in motor and machine repairs, be employees in electricity or water supply offices, or be unskilled workers in a press" (*ibid.*: 204). Further, Kumar observed trade union support of this observance and an interest in declaring this a national holiday or Labour Day with a strong Hindutva inflection (*ibid.*: 205).

Vishwakarma's worship by industrial workers has been widely noted in Bengal. Most prominent mention of this worship is by historian Dipesh Chakrabarty, who draws on a description from the 1930s of Vishwakarma's worship at jute mills featuring an altar filled with tools, and the sacrifice of a goat, to raise the larger question of how historians might "handle this problem of the presence of the divine or the supernatural in the history of labor as we render this enchanted world into our disenchanted prose" (Chakrabarty, 2007 [2000]: 77). Rather than reducing such gods and spirits into secular historical accounts, he argues for ways of writing that also point to how this religious mode of thinking is itself contingent and finite. In relation to the theme of this essay, Chakrabarty's plea could be read as an argument to look for the spaces and forces that conjoin, rather than separate, religion and technology.

The sociologist Leela Fernandes, who studied Bengal's jute mills in the 1990s, points to how Vishwakarma is mobilized by workers and trade unions, in counterpoint to the power of employers, producing an "oppositional class relationship" (Fernandes, 1997: 105). She describes how the occasion of preparing these shrines and worshiping at them can become "a space of autonomous worker activity on the factory floor that temporarily challenges the authority of management" (*ibid.*: 104). Simultaneously, as different trade unions competed with different shrines, representations of Vishwakarma became "transformed into symbols of power of the mill trade unions" (*ibid.*: 103); that is, a religious frame was given to the system of social and political relations around technology as a system of production. Fernandes also found that the Hindu nature of these observances was underlined by the Bharatiya Mazdoor Sangh trade union affiliated with the BJP, who lobbied for this date to become a National Labor Day, with "the implicit assumption that the Indian worker is synonymous with the 'Hindu' worker" (*ibid.*: 37).

In her account of Bengali shipyard workers who undertake Vishwakarma puja, Laura Bear (2015) poignantly describes the men's pride in their sense of workmanship. As "Vishwakarma putra" (sons of Vishwakarma) they identify themselves as "men of steel" and as such they are offering their very *shakti*, power, through their labor. They enact reciprocal kinship relations with each other and with Vishwakarma on the occasion of Vishwakarma puja that connects also to the worship of goddess Monosha and a domestic *ranna puja*. While acknowledging that Muslim workers do not participate in these *puja*s, Bear uses the example of Vishwakarma worship to elaborate her view that the austerity capitalism of the present brings into focus a *homo deus*, who "overcomes uncertainty by associating their powers with the permanence and eternal return of the life forces of nature and the divine" (Bear, 2015: 173), and that laborer's assertion of an ethos of mutual trust and care reminds us to think beyond economic measures of public good towards ethical and political accountability.

A web search reveals many "Vishwakarma Industries" as well as "Vishwakarma Industrial Zones." The name and image of Vishwakarma can also be used to brand tools, machines and products used in carpentry and construction. For example, carpenter relatives in small village in Kathiawar shared with Narayan an illustrated storybook about Vishwakarma distributed by the Pidilite Industries, which manufactures Fevicol wood glue. George Varghese K. (2003) suggests that free calendars distributed by the same corporation have been a source of standardization for iconography, bringing the white-bearded grandfather of the north to Kerala (Varghese K., 2003: 4800).

Though Vishwakarma worship is no longer confined to artisan castes, its expansion into the industrial labor force and worksites may still involve caste politics. Because of Vishwakarma's historical association to artisan castes, his name can signal an association with the "Other Backward Castes" (OBCs) for whom government affirmative action programs have been a contested political realm since 1990.[8] To pay respects to the god can be a way of winning votes from caste organizations and workers' organizations alike.

Vishwakarma's association with industry has come to be marked by *Vishwakarma Rashtriya Puraskar* (VRP) or the Vishwakarma National Awards that are awarded on Vishwakarma Day, or September 17 each year in New Delhi by the Government of India's Ministry of Labour and Employment. A website notes that this award was first known as "Shram Vir" (Labor Hero) when established in 1965, though does not detail when the new name was adopted. The rationale for the award explains the need for workers to be recognized along with other national award winners: "With the growing tempo of industrialization, it was considered desirable to provide for public recognition of outstanding achievement on the part of the workers, at the national level, so that, the workers could feel that they were accorded a place similar to that of other recipient of Rashtriya Puraskars for outstanding achievements in the other walks of life"(Ministry of Labour & Employment, n.d.).

Clearly, political maneuvering and often Hindutva agendas lead different state governments to observe Vishwakarma Day (Vishwakarma Jayanti) – standardized to the industrialized eastern date of September 17. For example the impetus for the national recognition of this date that Kumar had already noted in 1982 was officially declared in 2016, with an announcement from the Labour and Employment Minister in the National Democratic Alliance government that Vishwakarma Day would henceforth also be considered National Labour Day. Indeed, looking beyond the nation, the Minister proposed that "Vishwakarma Day needs to be celebrated by the whole world as a tribute to the working class"; before outlining various government schemes for workers, he described Vishwakarma as the inventor of "equipment for the livelihood of thousands of workers" and "the first engineer in the country" (webIndia123, 2016).

Vishwakarma and the growth of infrastructure

Returning again to Nita Kumar's valuable historical ethnography, we learn that the celebrations of Vishwakarma Puja in Benares were linked to infrastructural institutions, such as the Benares Waterworks and Electricity and Power Offices (Kumar, 1988: 207–208); fascinatingly Kumar remarks, "Some informants considered Vishwakarma Puja to have begun in the 1950s with the opening of the Diesel Locomotive Works!" (*ibid*.: 208).

While the Diesel Locomotive Works manufactures engines and spare parts for the Indian Railways, Vishwakarma may also be viewed as overseeing this entire infrastructural grid. For example, in 2004 when the colorful Laloo Prasad Yadav was serving as the Railway Minister under the United Progressive Alliance government, he absolved himself of responsibility for safety in India's railway network. Instead, he pointed to Vishwakarma as "God of machines." As the newspaper *Times of India* reported from Patna:

> Railway passengers, caution. Gone are the days when railway ministers used to resign, owning responsibility for train mishaps. With Bihar supremo Laloo Prasad Yadav at the helm, Lord Vishwakarma, God of machines, and not the railway minister is to blame for, God forbid, such mishaps. 'Indian Railways is the responsibility of Lord Vishwakarma. So is the safety of passengers ... It is His duty, not mine. I have been forced to don His mantle,' Laloo said before a section of media persons at the CM house here late on Thursday evening. The minister said he is merely a medium of the God ... He has put a picture of Lord Vishwakarma in his office. 'I keep telling Him whatever accident or incident takes place on the tracks is His responsibility,' the rail minister said. (Prakash, 2004)

Vishwakarma in this statement has moved from artisanal workshops to industries to an infrastructural domain. One cannot know for sure how seriously or cynically this statement was made, or for what political ends his image was installed in the Minister's office. Nonetheless, Yadav's shrugging off his responsibility affirms Vishwakarma's association not just with machines, but with the complex infrastructural network of railways, too.

Vishwakarma communities themselves may also celebrate the growth of infrastructure as evidence of Vishwakarma's power. So for example, a website of the Vishwakarma Samaj of Karnataka states,

> Everything in this world we see like huge dams, the repositories, spans, high rises, planes and all mechanics and builds [*sic*] around which our life spins are the result of Hammer and Chisel which speak to Shree Vishwakarma. (Vishwakarma Samaja, 2013)

Even as India's infrastructure grows, in an unexpected conjuncture, Vishwakarma Day, celebrated annually on 17 September, turns out to coincide with Narendra Modi's birthday. A week after Vishwakarma Day in 2014, when PM Modi launched his "Make in India" campaign to increase industrial production and foreign investment, a popular mythological website immediately rebranded Vishwakarma as "The 'Make-in- India' God" (Talking Myths Project, 2014). The Prime Minister has subsequently used Vishwakarma Day to promote his decidedly pro-development agenda. A series of tweets sent in 2015 to his enormous Twitter following (estimated in February 2016 to be at 17.5 million) exhorts, "Vishwakarma is known for innovations, we must dedicate this day for new researches," and ends by advocating, "Success of initiatives like 'Skill India' and 'Make in India' would be a fitting tribute to Vishwakarma" (Narendra Modi, 2015).

This juxtaposition of Vishwakarma with the "Make in India" agenda is evident in a press release from November 9, 2015, describing the renaming of the Shipwright School at the port of Visakhapatnam:

> VISAKHAPATNAM: Navy Chief Admiral R K Dhowan today commissioned the erstwhile Shipwright School (SWC) and premier training establishment of the Indian Navy as INS Vishwakarma at the Eastern Naval Command (ENC) here. 'Transforming the Indian Navy to a designer's and builder's Navy in keeping with the 'Make in India' vision,' Dhowan said. (PTI, 2015)

While the Admiral refers to the training of designers and the builders, Vishwakarma appears in other educational settings linked to developing job skills within expanding India's infrastructure. Institutes of Technology and of Information Technology frequently carry his name. Further, celebrations of Vishwakarma Day may occur in educational settings. So, for example, Uttaranchal University's Mechanical Department describes the celebration of Vishwakarma Puja on the university's website as "a resolution time for students and faculty to dedicate themselves to the cause of advancement of technology and gain divine inspiration for creating novel products" (News Desk, 2014). Further, we learn that:

> Vice Chancellor Prof (Dr) SC Joshi, in his speech stated that the students should make a promise to update themselves in latest innovations and technologies. Prof. N K Joshi, Director, Uttaranchal Institute of Technology stated that Lord Vishwakarma is believed to be the creator of the universe and the lord of labour and hard work. Worshipping Lord Vishwakarma is a way of showing respect to hard work. (News Desk, 2015)

Accompanying photographs on the site depict male and female students in uniform, with ties, saluting the grandfatherly form of Vishwakarma or anointing machines with ceremonial red markings. These future engineers and designers – members of the white-collar "creative class" – are in such settings exposed to Vishwakarma as a patron deity of their undertaking. Just as Vishwakarma is said to have once built the palaces and cities of deities, then, he is now invoked in the vast building projects associated with hypermodernity.

Conclusions

Walking between villages in Kangra, Kirin Narayan recognized the carpenter's son who was now a grown man with a wife and son beside him. In the intervening years, he had become a carpenter, but unlike his father who made wooden farm implements, he worked on constructing buildings. Learning of our interest in researching Vishwakarma traditions, the young man and his articulate wife lit up. "Wherever you have machines," the young man said, beaming, "there you have Vishwakarma. All this technology; it's all given by god."

In this chapter, we have traced how Vishwakarma has been associated historically with artisans, their tools, and their craft. With the rise of industrial technology, Vishwakarma has continued to be honored in new spaces like factories and workshops. He can be invoked in the building of infrastructure – roads, bridges, waterways and even information technology systems. When associated with a religious nationalist ideology, the deity's multifaceted association with other religious traditions and many regional variations may be eclipsed.

Homo faber – humans as makers – is basic to human evolution, and to the enchantment opened out through the processes of making facilitated by technology (cf. Gell, 2006). Urging scholars to move beyond Christian and Western associations around the terms religion and technology, Stolow suggests that we think of how "different religious regimes impose distinct constraints on the range of possible engagements with the pragmata of tools, devices and machines, while at the same time such appropriations enable quite different modes of embodied perception, action, and imagination" (Stolow, 2012:19). When a creator god is celebrated as a craftsman with tools, as Vishwakarma is, might technology become more likely viewed as an extension of religious creativity, rather than at odds with religion? Here, comparative work on Hephaestus, the Greek god of metalworking and sculptor; Vulcan, the Roman blacksmith god; and even Lu Ban or Lo Pan the Chinese carpenter deity and patron saint of builders, would be useful to explore, along with moments in Western history – for example in Free-masonry – when a divine force has been associated with craftsmanship and machines.

Before leaving Kangra in 2015, Narayan made a point of visiting the new "Baba Vishwakarma" temple in the town of Palampur that she had driven by several times. The pink temple contained an image of Vishwakarma holding tools, his vehicle of a swan beside him, and a few other small images. Continuing into the compound beyond, she discovered that this was the Mechanical Engineering Subdivision of the Himachal Pradesh Public Works Department (HP PWD). An engineer sat at an office desk, a spangled Vishwakarma print on the wall to his right. Learning of our proposed research, he warmly invited us to attend the communal worship and feast held annually at the temple on the day after Divali. A younger co-worker recollected episodes of Vishwakarma miraculously building the city of Dwaraka in the Shree Krishna television serial. In a further conjunction of religion and technology, he advised that we could learn about Vishwakarma's key projects by simply studying the mythological retellings on Youtube.

Notes

1 Compare Alfred Gell juxtaposing enchantment and technology (Gell, 2006 [1999]).
2 This mantra is also integrated in many later texts, especially the *Vajasaneyisamhita*, 17:19 TS 4.6.2.4, *Atharvaveda* 13.2.26 and *Shvetashvatarapanishad* (see Kali, 2011: 206–208, 442).
3 *Mahabharata* I: 2592. This verse was also reused as an epigraph in Renaldo Maduro's 1996 book on the Nathadwara painters who seek daily inspiration through meditation on Vishwakarma.
4 Though not acknowledged this passage is cited almost verbatim in Wilkins' entry on Vishwakarma in his influential *Hindu Mythology* (Wilkins, 1980 [1882]: 77).
5 We are grateful to Anthony Lovenheim Irwin for sharing his insights and images of this worship with us (personal communication, January 4, 2016).
6 We are grateful to Frank Korom for this insight.
7 See Narayan (2014: 117–118) for more details on different days for the worship of Vishwakarma.
8 Even though, ironically, many of these artisan communities fought landmark law cases to be recognized as "Vishwakarma Brahmans" or "Vishwabrahmins" in the nineteenth and earlier twentieth centuries (Kshirsagar, 1921).

References

Bear, Laura (2015) *Navigating Austerity: Currents of Debt along a South Asian River.* Palo Alto, CAL: Stanford University Press.

Beck, Brenda (1970) "The Right-Left Division of South Indian Society." *Journal of Asian Studies* 29(4): 779–799.

Brouwer, Jan (1995) *The Makers of the World: Caste, Craft and Mind of South Indian Artisans.* Delhi: Oxford University Press.

Chakrabarty, Dipesh (1989) *Rethinking Working Class History: Bengal 1890–1940.* Princeton, NJ: Princeton University Press.

Chakrabarty, Dipesh (2007 [2000]) *Provincializing Europe: Postcolonial Thought and Historical Difference.* Princeton, NJ: Princeton University Press.

Coomaraswamy, Ananda K. (1909) *The Indian Craftsman.* London: Probsthain and Co.

Coomaraswamy, Ananda K. (1914) *Vishvakarma: Examples of Indian Architecture, Sculpture, Painting, Handicrafts.* London: Otto Harrasowitz.

Danielou, Alain (2001) *The Hindu Temple: Deification of Eroticism.* Trans. by Ken Hurry. Rochester, VT: Inner Traditions.

Day, Lal Behari (1913) *Bengal Peasant Life.* London: Macmillan and Company.

Elwin, Verrier (1942) *The Agaria.* London: Oxford University Press.

Fernandes, Leela (1997) *Producing Workers: The Politics of Gender Class and Culture in the Calcutta Jute Mills.* Philadelphia, PA: University of Pennsylvania Press.

Gell, Alfred (2006[1999]) "The Technology of Enchantment and the Enchantment of Technology." In E. Hirsch, (ed.), *The Art of Anthropology: Essays and Diagrams.* New York: Berg, pp. 159–186.

Hingorani, Alka (2013) *Making Faces: Self and Image Creation in a Himalayan Village.* Honolulu: University of Hawaii Press.

Jamison, Stephanie and Joel Brereton (translation) (2014) *The Rigveda: The Earliest Religious Poetry of India.* Vol. III. New York: Oxford University Press.

Kali, Devadatta (translation and commentary) (2011) *Shvetashvatarapanishad: The Knowledge that Liberates.* Lake Worth, FL: Nicolas Hays.

Korom, Frank J. (2006) *Village of Painters: Narrative Scrolls from West Bengal.* Santa Fe, NM: Museum of New Mexico Press.

Kshirsagar, Narayan Ravaji Shastri (1921) *Vishvabrahmakulotsaha or History of Vishvabrahmins.* Poona: Kalika Prasad Press.

Kumar, Nita (1988) *The Artisans of Banaras: Popular Culture and Identity, 1880–1986.* Princeton, NJ: Princeton University Press.

Larkin, Brian (2013) "The Politics and Poetics of Infrastructure." *Annual Review of Anthropology* 42: 327–343.

Maduro, Renaldo (1976) *Artistic Creativity in a Brahman Painter Community.* Berkeley, CA: Center for South and Southeast Asian Studies.

Mani, Vettam (1975) *The Puranic Encyclopedia.* Delhi: Motilal Banarsidas.

Ministry of Labour and Employement (n.d.) Available at: http://labour.nic.in/content/award/vishwakarma-awards.php (accessed February 16, 2016).

Modi, Narendra (2015) "PM Greets the People on Vishwakarma Jayanti." Available at: www.narendramodi.in/pm-greets-the-people-on-vishwakarma-jayanti-293941 (accessed December 16, 2015).

Mukherjee, Meera (1994) *In Search of Viswakarma.* Calcutta: Printco.

Narayan, Kirin (2014) "Narrating Creative Process." *Narrative Culture* 1(1):109–124.

Narayan, Kirin and Kenneth M. George (2017) "Tools and World-Making in the Worship of Vishwakarma." *South Asian History and Culture* 8(4): 478-492.

News Desk (2014) "Vishwakarma Puja Celebration in Mechanical Department." UIT News, September 18. Available at: http://uttaranchaluniversity.ac.in/vishwakarma-puja-celebration-mechanical-department/ (accessed January 2, 2016).

News Desk (2015) "Vishwakarma Puja was celebrated on 17 September 2015 in UIT, Uttaranchal University." UIT News, September 17. Available at: https://uttarancha luniversity.ac.in/vishwakarma-puja-was-celebrated-on-17-september-2015-in-uit-utta ranchal-university/ (accessed January 3, 2016).

Pannikar, Raimundo (1977) *The Vedic Experience Mantramanjari.* Berkeley, CA: University of California Press.

Parker, Samuel (2003) "Making Temples/Making Selves: Essentialism and Construction in the Identity of the Traditional South Indian Artist." *South Asian Studies* 19(1):125–140.

Prakash, Manisha (2004) "Boarding a Train? Pray to God." *The Times of India,* July 2. Available at: http://timesofindia.indiatimes.com/city/patna/Boarding-a-train-Pray-to-God/articleshow/761797.cms (accessed May 9, 2016).

PTI (2015) "Navy Chief Admiral RK Dhowan Commissions INS Vishwakarma." *The Economic Times,* November 14. Available at: http://economictimes.indiatimes.com/news/defence/navy-chief-admiral-r-k-dhowan-commissions-ins-vishwakarma/article show/49784044.cms (accessed December 16, 2016).

Ramaswamy, Vijaya (1985) "Artisans in Vijayanagar Society." *Indian Economic and Social History Review* 22(4): 417–444.

Ramaswamy, Vijaya (2004) "Vishwakarma Craftsmen in Early Medieval Peninsular India." *Journal of the Economic and Social History of the Orient* 47(4): 548–582.

Sarkar, Smritikumar (2013) *Technology and Rural Change in Eastern India 1830–1980.* Delhi: Oxford University Press.

Stolow, Jeremy (2012) "Introduction: Religion, Technology and the Things in Between." In J. Stolow, (ed.), *Deus in Machina: Religion, Technology and the Things in Between.* Bronx, NY: Fordham University Press, pp. 1–22.

Streefkerk, Hein (2006) *Tools and Ideas: The Beginnings of Local Industrialization in South Gujarat, 1970–2000.* New Delhi: Manohar.

Talking Myths Project (2014) "The 'Make-in-India' God." September 25, 2014. Available at www.talkingmyths.com/the-make-in-india-god/ (accessed January 3, 2016).

Varghese, K. George (2003) "Globalisation Traumas and New Social Imaginary: Visvakarma Community of Kerala." *Economic and Political Weekly* 38(45): 4794–4802.

Vishwakarma, Dr. Ishvar Sharan (2002) *Bharatiya Sahitya tatha Shilp mein Visvakarma* [Visvakarma in Indian Literature and Art]. Delhi: Prathibha Prakashan.

Vishwakarma Samaja (2013) "Welcome to Vishwakarma Samaja." Available at: www. vishwakarmasamaja.com/index.html (accessed December 15, 2016).

webIndia123 (2016). "Vishwakarma Day needs to be celebrated by all: Dattatreya." September 18. Available at: http://news.webindia123.com/news/Articles/India/20160918/2945989.html (accessed December 1, 2016).

Wilkins, W.J. (1980 [1882]) *Hindu Mythology: Vedic and Puranic.* 2d ed. Bombay and Delhi: Rupa and Co.

2 Saffron glasses

Indian nationalism and the enchantment of technology

Robert M. Geraci

In 2014, Prime Minister Narendra Modi made headlines by claiming that Indians had mastered genetic engineering and plastic surgery during Vedic times. This claim, made at the opening of a new research hospital in Mumbai, is in keeping with similar claims about the invention of rockets and powered flight, as "described" in the *Mahabharata* and *Ramayana*. But the controversy that erupted around Modi's public revelation does not reveal anything new about Indian discourses around religion and science, though such ideas have been largely ignored in academic research. Despite the general silence until Modi's remarks, the underlying idea – that Vedic technology prefigured many twentieth-century advancements – has considerable cachet in Indian conversations about science and technology, and is credible in the minds of many Indian scientists and educated members of the public. Modi's remarks are a departure, however, from previous political speech. They show that the politics of religion and technology are inextricably bound to the politics of nation-building and contemporary reflections upon Hindu religious traditions. The nationalist use of religion and technology is at least as old as the resistance to British imperialism. The same strategy was taken in the anti-colonial movements of the nineteenth and early twentieth century, where *kali yuga* (and its end) was tied to British rule and where the *swadeshi* (self-sufficiency) movement grounded nationalist thinking in the economy and technological lives of Indians (Banerjee-Dube, 2015: 103, 229, 401). In this vein, Gandhi's *charkha* (the spinning wheel) was simultaneously a symbol of indigenous and *swaraj* [1] technology, and one element in a religious package of ascetic practices (*ibid.*: 293, 334). Gandhi was, for example, visualized in divine form (as Shiva) with the *charkha* in hand, and *swadeshi* was crucial to the religious practices of his Satyagraha Ashram (Trivedi, 2007: 7–8, 48). [2] Along these more mundane examples, Indian nationalists also cited ancient epics as evidence that modern technology and science are indigenous to India, and not merely the imports of British conquerors.

Ascriptions of Vedic technology, which are quite common now, had their political origin in the nineteenth century. Swami Dayananda Saraswati (1824–1883), among the first modern Indians to claim Vedic priority for modern technology, did so in the nineteenth century as a form of counter-colonialism: he argued that ancient Indian references to flying vehicles, explosive devices, and more demonstrate that advanced technologies were actually present at the time of the texts' authorship.[3] This includes steamships (Saraswati, 1908: 282), modern weaponry (*ibid.*, 292) and flying machines (*ibid.*, 312). Indeed, he goes so far as to assert that "it is a fact, that all the sciences and arts and religions, that are now found in the whole world, took their original start from Aryavarta [north India]" (*ibid.*, 293). Drawing on the examples of a flying machine and a fan that never ceased operating, both allegedly detailed in the *Bhoja Prabandha* (11th CE), Saraswati wrote that "had these two inventions come down to these days, the Europeans would not have been so puffed up with pride, as they are now-a-days" (*ibid.*: 312). The anti-British sentiment in Swami Dayananda's historical revisionism is now often replaced with anti-Western motivations, as visible in the online comments to Modi's remarks, which will be discussed below.

It is likely that continued allegiance to Swami Dayananda's position remains, at heart, what Karl Marx calls "the sigh of the oppressed" (see Marx, [1844] 2002: 171). While India is fast catching up with (or even superseding) Western countries in technological development, the nation remains mired in poverty and continues to have significant needs in political and economic development. Resistance to Western domination often emerges, in the Indian context, out of a self-understanding in which the past was better than the present.

Just as Indian astrology indicates that we are always "falling backward into the past" (Larson, 2012: 122; Larson, 2016), the larger cosmological cycles of *yuga*s indicate that the merits of the contemporary world can never be anything other than restorations of past accomplishments. On account of this historical understanding of progressive decline, "in the Hindu conception, the past must have been more developed than the present ... a significant number of Indian élites defined 'progress' as a movement towards achieving the heights of the glorious past" (Deshpande, 1979: 11). Within that context, Modi's government draws strength from a combination of modernization and anti-western nationalism; just so, the persistence of Vedic science and technology in political debate makes almost as much sense as it did during the British colonial era.

The idea that modern technology actually existed in Vedic times has had little academic traction, with most Indian historians wrestling with the question of pre-British scientific ecologies and/or the Nehruvian drive toward modernization. Such authors had other historical trajectories to question, ones they felt were closer to the heart of authentic historical scholarship. This preference is despite the fact that, as Gyan Prakash points out, belief in the Indic origins of modern science "won widespread support among the Western-educated elite and became a key nationalist idea" in the nineteenth century (Prakash, 1999: 86). Though surely well meant, this absence of sustained inquiry into the social relevance of Vedic technology means that few intellectual tools were available when Modi remarked on genetic engineering and plastic surgery.

In fact, the only meaningful investigation into Vedic technology was undertaken by engineers, not historians (Mukunda, Desphande, Negendra, Prabhu, and Govindaraju, 1974). That study, published in a journal virtually unknown outside of India and now, seemingly, defunct, is still the definitive statement on whether or not ancient Indians had flying machines (the authors conclude that there were not any such devices or the scientific ecology to support them).

Despite the effort of those engineers and recent news media criticism by historians, many Indians share Modi's view of history. For example, readers of the Indian newspaper *The Hindu* believe that Modi's comments were, at the least, acceptable, and in many cases admirable. Reactionary criticism to Modi's remarks misses the way in which faith in the scientific testimony of the *Ramayana* and *Mahabharata* is ingrained in contemporary discourses about science and technology, including within scientific communities and among the educated public.

Modi's position is couched in nationalist rhetoric that is mixed with actual political processes, such as a presentation on Vedic-era flight at the 2015 Indian Science Congress (ISC). But while these ideas are definitely a part of the political conflicts between Modi's Bharatiya Janata Party (BJP) and their left-leaning opponents, neither Modi nor the speakers at the ISC have articulated a new claim. The claims are controversial, surely, but not new. The novel part of this process is the public revelation of deep-seated and widely shared beliefs, occasionally as definite support for, but more often as a refusal to dismiss the possibility of advanced technology in the Vedic era. Bringing this to light offers insight into the nature of politics in the analysis of religion, science, and technology, and from there on the landscape of Indian religious life.

The envisioning of technology through "saffron glasses" – through a nationalist vision in which modern technologies circulate through Indian media, politics, science, and religion – reveals the dynamic imagination that surrounds technology. No technology exists in an intellectual or emotional vacuum; rather, participation in the intellectual and emotional worlds of human beings is a vital element in technological development, and such participation is distributed through the social world of people, ideas, and other technologies. "Technological imaginaries are thick, rich, and multimodal practices because they link material, concrete, and tangible objects and practices with meaning and the immaterial" (Ornella, 2015: 310). The technological imaginary includes material objects, a search for the sublime, a focus on narratives and aesthetics, and more (*ibid.*: 322). There are, of course, precursors to the saffron imaginary of early twenty-first-century India.

Just as other cultures have possessed or presently integrate technology into their worldviews,[4] Indians have long had their own ways of thinking about and using technology. Geographical expansion under the Gupta dynasty, for example, led to changing economic policies, these in turn creating a host of religious innovations that impacted Indian ways of living (Nath, 2001). More recently, science and technology were key in the struggle to identify the essence of India as a nation (Khilnani, [1997] 1999: 61–106). In the case of Vedic technology, the circulation of technology – its use in political, scientific, and religious discourse – means that the "on the ground" experience of technology in contemporary India unites religious and scientific visions in a nationalism that cannot be wholly explained without recourse to this unification of religion, science, and technology.

Politics, technology, and mass media participation

When Modi expressed the popular sentiment that there was plastic surgery and genetic engineering in Vedic times – taking the epic tale, the *Mahabharata*, as evidence – he revealed a current of Indian life that had been largely ignored in historical circles. That claim was rapidly embraced by a sizeable minority of Indians, who saw Modi criticized online and subsequently responded with support for him and for claims of Vedic priority in science and technology. While the majority may not agree that scriptural testimony amounts to historical proof, online commentary on *The Hindu* and Twitter indicate that many Indians appreciate how Vedic appropriation of modern technology advances their national cause.

Specifically, Modi declared that "it is said in the *Mahabharata* that Karna was not born from his mother's womb. This means in the times in which the epic was written genetic science was very much present. We all worship Lord Ganesha; for sure there must have been some plastic surgeon at that time, to fit an elephant's head on a body of a human being" (quoted in K. Thapar, 2014). The claim was remarkable specifically, as Karan Thapar points out in *The Hindu*, for its utterance by the Prime Minister and the scientific location at which it was given. Further, the claim was perhaps predictable given the nationalist rhetoric that swirls around Modi.

Thapar criticized Modi in *The Hindu*, and a polarized debate ensued in the online comments. On the popular level, an analysis of news item comment fields reveals that many readers see Modi's comments in a favorable light. Such impressions are visible in written comments but also through the like/dislike features implemented online. Such analysis has obvious limitations, as one cannot reliably extract data about the entire community from a limited set of information that comes from English-readers willing and able to respond through Internet comment fields.

That said, the data clearly demonstrate that many readers of *The Hindu* believe that Modi's comments were, at the least, acceptable and perhaps even admirable. Therefore, it is important that we not fall into the trap of seeing this nationalist mixture of myth, science, and history as merely a rhetorical trap for the uneducated. English language comments and responses indicate an educated readership, more than capable of finding alternative viewpoints and considering different options. In fact, it is possible, though unlikely, that the nationalist faith in Vedic technology is limited exclusively to educated audiences.

Responding to Thapar's indictment, *The Hindu*'s readership rushed to comment online. As of November 12, 2014, 86 online comments opposed the likelihood of Vedic technology, while 43 were either apparently or vigorously in support of Modi's comments and Vedic technology. Another 77 made comments too vague to identify their positions, though many of these reflect negatively upon the truth claims of other religions (e.g. Christianity) and thus might be considered to lean in the direction of accepting Vedic technology (see K. Thapar, 2014). The comments rejecting Modi's position averaged 160 "likes" and 60 "dislikes" from the article's readers (rounding to the nearest whole number); meanwhile, the comments supporting Modi and Vedic technology averaged 128 "likes" and 217 "dislikes." A similar piece by Vikram Soni and Romila Thapar, arguing that mythology must be held distinct from history, was halted at 50 comments. Of these, 11 seemed to or definitely do support Vedic technology, while 13 rejected it (see Soni and Thapar, 2014). The following examples offer representative positions from the two essays:

> Let India's modern, clear thinking, rational and brilliant scientists (and I'm sure there are many) come forward and write a joint letter to the Hindu Newspaper stating their view that myth is myth and science is science. India desperately needs to move from mythological unreality to sound science, and accurate and unbiased history. At the moment it seems to be going in the opposite direction (220 likes, 56 dislikes). (Thapar, 2014)
>
> I completely agree. Myths are myths, they can't be treated like history or history of science. People always like fantasy and that' why they created all this kind of story like today's super hero. Just don't mix it with science (77 likes, 1 dislike). (Soni and Thapar, 2014)
>
> Karan is a known Modi hater … That fact apart, Why cannot we think that this would have been possible 4000 years back? The human brain (Homo Sapiens) has not evolved or changed in the past 10,000 or so years. The 'Raw' materials required to produce the ideas of Plastic Surgery or Gene Technology were there then and is there now … Again, The Brain is the same, The opportunity to use the 'Brain' was lot more possible I guess in the 'olden days' than now where everything equates to money (114 likes, 251 dislikes). (Thapar, 2014)
>
> We had everything in the past, that other cultures still can't even dream of, but it was lost because of our culture of segregation. Only few castes were allowed to read Sanskrit and read the Vedas, even among them there were multiple divisions with practices of not eating together and not marrying with each other. So, we can assume that we had all these inventions but only a few people were allowed to use them, making their presence limited, and making them susceptible to being lost. Instead of giving grants for scientific research, government should redirect the money to the discovery of these inventions. They were much bigger than anything science can offer even now (human-animal hybrid, human-flight, floating

cities) and we had a tradition of writing so putting effort and money in finding them makes more sense than spending money on stupid research) (0 likes, 37 dislikes). (Soni and Thapar, 2014)

Clearly, the readers of *The Hindu* more often favored Thapar's position than Modi's; but just as clearly Modi has a considerable audience in the educated, English-reading community, and there is a willingness to believe that ancient Indians possessed advanced technology to match the claims of India's great epics. Many of these readers probably belong to the "Internet Hindus" group described by Juli Gittinger. "Internet Hindus" often paint themselves as uneducated and oppressed despite the discontinuity between this image and the reality of their Internet and social media presence, and have rallied around Modi and the BJP government (Gittinger, 2015: 11–13).

The relationship among science, technology, and India's role in the global economy is empirically visible in Hindu nationalism online. Comparing Hindu, Kashmiri, and Sikh nationalism in the twentieth century, Rohit Chopra notes that "globality" is the most frequently used theme in Hindu nationalist websites, and the second most common is science and technology (Chopra, 2008: 217). In fact, Hindu nationalist references to science and technology account for 76.49 percent of all such references among the three nationalist communities online, showing that, in India, science and technology are uniquely important to the Hindu nationalist movement (*ibid.*: 221).

The authority claimed for Vedic technology traces to a more generalized approach to Indian scripture, which integrates material that – today – we might differentiate as being either scientific or religious, but not both. Jonathan Parry recognizes the nationalist concerns in claims about Vedic technology, but he also notes that traditional scriptures show "no conceptual divide between 'religious' and 'scientific' knowledge. Without any sense of the incongruity the texts known as Puranas contain terrifying accounts of the fate of the souls of sinners, sandwiched between sections on – say – mineralogy and medicine" (Parry, 1985: 207).

In his ethnographic work with the Brahmin community in Benares, Parry also identifies a local approach to authority, which may bear relevance on the public perception of Vedic technology. He describes a distinction between what is scriptural (*shastrik*) and what is popular (*laukik*), and reports that while there are misunderstandings between the two (e.g., ritual sacrifice is believed by many to be popular practice when in fact it has a long textual history), "that which is *believed* to be textual is – at least in principle – beyond debate, while that which belongs to the oral tradition is not. At the risk of belabouring the point, the *textual* tradition is here accorded an ideological immunity to sceptical scrutiny [*sic*]" (Parry, 1985: 205, emphasis original). If it is the case that practices erroneously conceived as scriptural must be authoritative, how much more so must those which are, indeed, documented in a wide variety of texts when they are properly identified as such? While the *Mahabharata* and *Ramayana* are not among the *shruti* literature, they remain authoritative scripture, and are deeply influential upon contemporary Indian life.

There is no doubt that ancient Indian scriptures reference flying vehicles, explosive magical attacks, and unusual births. If Parry is correct in understanding textual reports (even if they are only erroneously reported as scriptural) as being immune to skepticism or refutation, then the identification of those references with modern technologies becomes a natural hermeneutic move. After all, the ancient epics are literally inscribed across the Indian landscape, present everywhere through performances and images (Singer, 1972: 76); their ongoing presence in Indian cultural life can provide the impetus for reimagining modern technology. Given this, the popular support for Modi's position makes sense. While many Indians reject interpretations that read contemporary technology into ancient stories – which certainly do not provide clear depictions that match the present world – others find scriptural references sufficient cause to see ancient precedence in contemporary technological innovation. If that is the case, then identifying the ancient references with contemporary technology is no great leap.

Modi's own approach to these technologies is couched in nationalist rhetoric that is mixed with actual political processes, such as the presentation on Vedic-era flight at the 2015 Indian Science Congress (ISC) and his selection of members for the Indian Council for Historical Research. But while these ideas are definitely a part of the political conflicts between Modi's allies and their left-leaning opponents, neither Modi nor the speakers at the ISC have articulated a new claim, which is apparent in their wide acceptance among *The Hindu's* readership. In the 1980s, for example, Parry noted that

> in Benares I have often been told – and I have heard variants of the same story elsewhere – that Max Müller stole chunks of the *Sama-veda* from India, and it was by studying these that German scientists were able to develop the atom bomb. The *rishis*, or ancient sages, not only knew all about nuclear fission, but as (what we would call) mythology testifies, they also had supersonic aeroplanes and guided missiles. (Parry, 1985: 206)

As noted above, such claims trace back to the nationalist thinkers of the nineteenth and early twentieth century (e.g. see Prakash, 1999: 106). The claim to technological priority is one part of Modi's nationalist strategy, one that mirrors the approach to the Internet in which he walks a tightrope of returning "India to her prior glory while at the same time ushering a new epoch of technology so that India can take her place on the global stage" (Gittinger, 2015: 15).

The public is thus open to suggestion that lost technological knowledge is consistent with worldly decline as seen in the *yuga* cycle, but nationalists subsequently reverse this and acknowledge technological progress as a sign of national progress. According to the *yuga* theory, "whatever good there is in the world today is the inheritance from the past ages" (Deshpande, 1979: 6;

see also Prakash, 1999: 98); so if technological mastery represents a human good, then it must similarly represent an historical reality. Centuries ago, the *yuga* cycle served as a way of addressing "the challenges posed by changing social order" (Nath, 2001: 39). Today, the cycle of *yugas* provides a mythical reference point from which to situate modern technology and the changes it has wrought. Indeed, the *yuga* cycle domesticates technology, and makes it part of an historical process already well-integrated into contemporary Indian practice and provides a point of departure for nationalist propaganda.

Politically, Modi has already drawn on advocates who intertwine technology, progress, and the *yuga* cycle. Those who see technology as a sign of worldly progress principally rely upon *The Holy Science*, composed by Sri Yukteswar Giri in the late nineteenth century. For Sri Yukteswar Giri, not only did we enter an ascending *yuga* at the beginning of the eighteenth century, but improvements in science and technology prove this (Giri, [1894] 1972: xvii–xxi; see Geraci, 2016). The loudest spokesperson for this position is David Frawley, founder of the American Vedic Institute (see Frawley, 1990: 69–60; Frawley, 2012). Though Frawley is American, he is held in high esteem in Indian nationalist political groups and was awarded the *Padma Bhushan*, India's third highest civilian honor by the Modi government. He received the award in 2015 – the same year that Bill and Melinda Gates received the *Padma Bhushan* for their humanitarian work. So while Frawley might be an unreliable witness to historical realities and a surprising choice for the interpretation of Indian religion and the role of technology in it, his interpretations cannot be discounted. Frawley is a clear expositor of the belief that technological mastery indicates religious and historical progress, and thus has been embraced by the nationalist engine of the Modi era.

Naturally, it makes sense for a nationalist movement of revivalism to prefer the ascending *yuga* cycle model. Rather than wallowing in the misery of a *kali yuga* whose end is centuries off, Modi's regime can paint its work as a key indicator of progress; but such progress can be had only if the *yuga*s are ascending. As such, the government's approbation of Frawley should be seen as part of a larger nationalist project. It is not just a religious statement about the nature of cosmic history, but a political statement about the nature of Modi's government.

This politico-religious move justifies a certain vision of technology, but it is also often the case that scientific or pseudoscientific explanations are also used to communicate and justify religious traditions. In 2014, Indian historians went on a (justified, but ultimately futile) crusade when Modi appointed Y. Sudershan Rao as the head of the Indian Council of Historical Research (e.g., R. Thapar, 2014; Firstpost staff, 2014; and Ghosh, 2015). Among India's historians, Rao is infamous for his claims that one can understand ancient Indian life by reading the *Mahabharata* and the *Ramayana*, and for the now familiar claim that modern technologies are but rediscoveries of technology possessed in Vedic times. Just as airplanes hearken to *pushpaka vimana* (the flying vehicle that Rama takes after defeating Ravana and by which he returns home to Ayodhya) and mobile phones to a variety of long-distance telepathic communications, scientific theories and religious myths can be taken as interdependent support for one another. This strategy, employed professionally by Rao, also plays a role (albeit more modest) in public life and in scientific and engineering communities. One IT professional, for example, told me that "the Darwinian idea and fact of evolution is captured" in the concept of Vishnu's ten avatars because the god takes on different forms over the course of time (starting with a fish and ending in advanced humanity). And so Darwinian selection is "reasonable" on account of the fact that Vishnu was incarnated in different, perhaps increasingly complex, forms. The politicized version of this that Rao exemplifies and Modi uses places the integration of religion and technology at the beating heart of nationalism.

Modi's use of social media reveals the significance of science and technology in his public outreach, and continues the Hindu nationalist approach. In 2015, Modi used Twitter to make regular reference to science and technology and give pride of place to technological initiatives. For example, his five most frequently used "mentions" were @narendramodi, @pmoindia, @un, @david_cameron, and @MakeInIndia. Leaving aside the first two, which are self-referential, the nationalistic economic and manufacturing initiative *Make In India* was the third most used mention on his Twitter account.[5] During that year, Modi used variations on the word science (e.g. science, scientist, scientific, etc.) 47 times and variations on the word technology 54 times (which was thus the 115th most common word in his Twitter account, out of 7,217 English words used)[6]. These are in addition, of course, to other technological words, such as digital, which appears 32 times (inclusive of the related hashtags and mentions).

At the same time, Modi uses Twitter for nationalist advocacy; his most frequently used hashtag – by a large margin – was #IncredibleIndia. That hashtag appears almost twice as frequently as the runner up, #YogaDay (171 uses to 96). Overall, his hashtags and mentions indicate both assertive support for India and frequent references to science and technology. Since #IncredibleIndia is a tourist marketing campaign, it does not cross paths with science and technology references on the Prime Minister's Twitter account. That is, the hashtag's frequency shows the importance of advertising India, but it is not used in braggadocio to accompany other claims, such as those related to scientific accomplishments. Modi thus uses Twitter to advertise India, while also using it to advertise India's accomplishments. This combination of scientific and technological outreach and national propaganda illustrates Modi's strength in the digital arena, and reflects the larger narrative of Indian nation-building that has characterized public discourse about technology in India's modern era. Others seem to follow Modi's approach in this: in 2015, #hindurise was the most popular hashtag, aside from #vedicscience, that Twitter users paired with the term "vedicscience[7]."

Nationalism is strongest when grounded in a mythical narrative that provides inspiration and motivation. Indian nationalist groups, Thomas Blom Hansen has noted, typically tell stories of how their communities have formed and use those stories (which cannot generally be authenticated) as rhetorical tools of conversion and internal reinforcement. Hansen notes that such myths serve two basic purposes: first, to show the vitality of the community, and second to produce a new interpretation of history (Hansen, 1999: 90–91). Claims of Vedic priority do both of these things, and thus provide powerful narratives for modern Indian nationalism. As such, stories capitalize on many Indians' commitment to the veracity of ancient scripture; they provide a nearly unassailable tool for building local pride and rejecting foreign domination.

Rebuilding the present

In scientific circles, the belief that modern technology existed in ancient times often operates as an intellectual hypothesis, a strategy of communication, or as a source of inspiration; but it also stands in tension with the political aspirations of scientists who advocate in favor of public appreciation for science and greater government support of modern research. There is very little disdain for belief in Vedic technology, even among those scientists and engineers who consider it a fantasy; and many scientists and engineers consider Vedic technology appropriate to conversations about contemporary work. Nevertheless, the political processes that surround Vedic technology threaten to disenfranchise modern scientific work and they may even undermine the democratic ideals articulated in India's constitution.

Scientists at elite research centers in Bangalore, India recognize the need for a greater public awareness of modern science and scientific work. One molecular biologist explained to me that "no scientist can go and talk to a common man on the street and explain him what he is doing. So that this, there is a big separation, distance between the common man and the scientist. The common people don't know what is a, who is a scientist, what they do" and one of his graduate students separately argued that "the need is that the, the gap between the scientists and the common people has to be bridged, which is not very clear right now" and the media "are not very accurate...there is a huge gap."[8] Similarly, an electrical engineer argued that closing the distance between scientists and the public is both part of his work and part of India's political heritage. He lauded Gandhi's "attempts to democratize knowledge" through *khadi* (India's handspun cotton) and hoped to overcome the incomprehensibility of science for most people. While there are groups dedicated to bridging this gap, and bringing science to the public, at present these groups have had little success in changing public policy or forcing India's state and national government to give science the level of prestige they desire in public education and discourse (see Quack, 2012).

Difficulties in bridging the gap between scientists and the public extend to politics. It is the belief of many scientists with whom I spoke while in residence at the Indian Institute of Science in Bangalore in 2012 and 2013 that politicians do not always offer appropriate support to India's researchers. "The politicians think the scientists are not anywhere, not world class," reported a researcher in machine learning; "government will listen to me, but it's out of politeness." He did not expect that he could change a politician's mind about matters of science policy. At the same time, scientists recognized that government has an important role to play in funding and directing research in socially valuable directions. A researcher in information processing technologies explained that "scientists, they should be free" but that "the work of the scientist should be toward mankind...politicians are ... empowered to, given the right policies, to enable scientists perform ... to promote the right set of reforms, to essentially make scientists function."

Naturally, if science policies are set at the governmental level, and if the public is presently divorced from scientific research practices, then the Modi government's descriptions of Vedic technology are profoundly important. Conflating modern technology and ancient myths could further the divide between scientists and the public, and could promote unreasonable public policies. For an example of the latter, consider the online news comment above, the author of which desires that the Indian government focus its funding on uncovering details about ancient technologies rather than supporting contemporary research.

Frustratingly for India's "rationalist" communities, many scientists permit the ongoing comparisons and conflations between Vedic technology and modern technoscience (see Quack, 2012: 213–214; Tyagi, 2014). For many of my interviewees in Bangalore, such comparisons provide easy modes of comparison to illustrate what a new technology might do. For example, an information technology entrepreneur described the ancient epics as "an inspiration for innovation ... and some of these things, we just discuss it when we do a product, brainstorming. To just take away that inhibition of something which is unknown." Others, however, went one step further, alleging that one should not dismiss the possibility that the ancient epics' testimony is accurate. "Much of this knowledge could have ... existed, existing before," one nanotechnology engineer explained to me. Similarly, an AI systems researcher told me that:

> [t]here could be some great technology, which we are not able to really foresee, which really existed. So it's quite possible. If somebody asks for a proof. The proof is that okay we believe the scripture that exists. That is the proof ... Many of us personally believe ... the scriptures, whatever they have stated is true. Just because we have no, we cannot do ... it does not mean, they are also not done. It is not just a story that somebody has floated. So, we have a long way to go.

These latter researchers held similar positions to Parry's interviewees in Benares, who firmly believed that the ancient *rishis* possessed advanced scientific knowledge (Parry, 1985: 206). The difference is that these individuals are, themselves, scientists and engineers. The credibility they grant to Vedic technology may not directly affect their research priorities, but it does affect how they think about technology and about historical progress. And, further, it affects public discourse: when elite scientists and engineers permit the conflation of myth and modernity, the public has little reason to do otherwise.

For some contemporary scientists, the challenge of having religious and scientific concepts converge produces ambivalent responses. During my stay at the Indian Institute of Science in Bangalore, a presentation on *pushpaka vimana* took place on campus (Tiwari, 2013), though one professor with authority over the event vociferously described it to me as simply an opportunity for students to hear a lecture in Hindi. V.V. Raman, well-known in American conversations about religion and science, takes a gentler, but even more ambiguous approach. On the one hand, he writes of parallels in ancient Indian texts that "it is important not to take such parallels too far" (Raman, 2011: 154) and that claims of electronics, flying vehicles, and rocketry in the epics are "more embarrassing than pleasant for scientifically enlightened Hindus" (*ibid.*: 49). But when referencing biological anomalies in the *Mahabharata* he remarks that "it is difficult to know what to make of such passages" and that:

> such references make one wonder whether the known history of civilizations is really complete, whether perhaps there might have been phases of human history of which we may have completely lost track … it is not persuasive to say that everything we read in ancient epics is purely creative writing. The reading of mythology as records of a world that has somehow disappeared altogether, except as vague remembrances enshrined in legends of ages past, could turn out to be closer to the truth than now seems the case. (*ibid.*: 197)

Raman, like some others, maintains a tenuous balance between the credulous and the skeptical even as he attempts to avoid what he calls the error of "nostalgia" (*ibid.*: 198–199, 225). Precisely where he stands on the matter remains, however, unclear, especially given that in other respects, he counsels that modern scientists look to Indian traditions, as when he claims that modern cosmology might rely upon the *yuga* cycle for new insights (*ibid.*: 85–86).

Other scientists, however, reject Vedic technology out of hand, preferring to believe that by adherence to contemporary understandings of history and of modernity, India will strengthen scientifically and culturally. The well-known Indian cosmologist Jayant Narlikar, for example, cautions his readers, "let us not be carried away by myths, howsoever exciting and absorbing they might be" (Narlikar, 2003: 1). More impassioned in his approach, Mayank Vahia, an astrophysicist at the Tata Institute for Fundamental Research, published a 2015 essay calling for a total rejection of Vedic technology. In his article, Vahia rightly notes that ancient India lacked an appropriate knowledge ecosystem to support the described technologies and calls for scientists to join a public battle for the "soul of India" (Vahia, 2015: 2148). His concern, obviously, is political as well as scientific. Should scientists cede the interpretation of science and technology to political nationalism and mythic revivalism, the nation will suffer.

Narlikar and Vahia are, as of the early twenty-first century, minority voices. Most scientists and engineers tolerate the conflation of myth and technology, though not always for the same reasons. And while scientists largely tolerate (without espousing) faith in Vedic technology, politicians and their public seem increasingly vocal in their claims of technological priority. Irfan Habib, one of India's foremost historians, notes that after Modi's announcement similar remarks about Vedic technology have multiplied (see Mahaprashasta, 2015) Whether because politicians espouse them or because scientists do not always dismiss them, precisely such beliefs circulate in Indian conversations about technology, and can be leveraged for nationalist political rhetoric.

Conclusion

The focus upon and open acknowledgement of ancient tradition marks an important exercise in political and popular understandings of history. In India, many advocates embrace tradition, appropriating science and technology in their affirmation of the past. Meera Nanda has offered a powerful critique of this position in her discussion of scientific reasoning and postmodernity in science (Nanda, 2003). Among the wider community, Indian rationalist groups also decry any effort to unite traditional religion and modern science (Quack, 2012). Despite such opposition, many accept modern innovation as a return to past technologies and as a sign of our progress toward *satya yuga*. As such, the triumphs of the present are but imitations of the past and harbingers of a future that is, itself, a return to the past.

On the level of politics and wider Indian culture, the public tolerance of claims to Vedic priority has very serious outcomes. Just as U.S. school districts often press for the teaching of Creationism or Intelligent Design in science classrooms, Modi's apparent allies have sometimes successfully advocated for the inclusion of Vedic science and technology in Indian schools. Modi, himself, wrote the foreword to textbooks that were integrated into public education and which speak favorably of Vedic technology. Dinanath Batra, the textbooks' author, was an outspoken leader in the effort to ban the scholarly work of Wendy Doniger and is an executive of the Vidya Bharati (the educational wing of the conservative Rashtriya Swayamsevak Sangh social movement). His book, *Tejomay Bharat*, became part of compulsory education in the state of Gujarat in 2014; in that book and others he argues in favor of Indian priority in technical innovations including stem cell research, modern media, and more (see Sharma, 2014). Modi's involvement in Batra's textbooks no doubt proved helpful in getting them approved for the curriculum despite the conflict they present with India's national science standards, these latter mandated by the National Council of Educational Research and Training.

Government control over textbooks makes regime changes crucial to how history is understood. Romila Thapar argues that history must be removed from government control and put in the hands of professional historians and educators (see Perera, 2015: 47–9). But for the time being, the history of technology is caught up in cultural and political battles over India's ancient traditions. History, in this case the history of technology, is held hostage by nationalist religious fervor. From Dayananda Saraswati in the nineteenth century to Prime Minister Modi in the twenty-first, Vedic technology becomes a tool for national glorification, but it is one that comes with dangers to the very progress that it alleges to master.

Despite such dangers, Indian nationalism seems poised to continue its grip over science and technology, just as it now pervades much of Indian religious life. From before independence, Indian politics have been deeply religious, with neo-Hindu faith undergirding nationalism in both its Gandhian and, perhaps surprisingly, Nehruvian forms (Larson, 1995: 185–211). Daniel Gold notes that "great big broadly conceived Hindu processions seem to be part of the new religious wave" of the late twentieth and early twenty-first centuries (Gold, 2015: 158), and public discourse increasingly identifies Rama as a warrior defending his home rather than as a paragon of virtue (*ibid.*: 254). As an example, John Harriss cites a business leader from Chennai who follows the contemporary Swami Dayananda (1930–2015), citing that individual's approbation of religious strength, nationalism, and political support for the Rashtriya Swayamsewak Sangh (Harriss, 2003: 359). In both practice and belief, then, nationalism has found a home in Indian religious activity. Nationalism has thus been the unifying factor that draws religion, science, and technology together; it provides the rationale and the means for making technology religious even as religion provides the lens through which technology appears *swadeshi*, and hence nationalist.

Meera Nanda refers to the intersection of religion and science in India as a "counter-Enlightenment" that threatens to disrupt scientific and cultural progress in India. Nanda recognizes that "Hindu science" (the adoption of modern science into a Vedic worldview that transcends it) was a useful tool against colonial oppression and Orientalist stereotypes (Nanda, 2006: 495). But as I noted above, she sees the convergence as a fundamental failure of secularization and as conducive to continued social inequalities. Instead of a rational march toward egalitarian society, Nanda fears a regressive political stance of intolerant and aggressive nationalism (Nanda, 2007). Similarly, Romila Thapar argues that the Indian definition of secularism is "incomplete." She believes that Indian secularism has not yet progressed to the point where religious communities cease controlling social interactions, nor have marginalized religions attained social equality (see Shankar, 2015).

This examination of the revelation of Vedic technology points toward the importance of politics in the engagement of religion and science, and of the study of religion and science to Indian politics. Technology can be imbued with many different political valences and cultural values; so its history becomes a political process. People might be ignorant of the histories provided by professionals, but they are not ignorant in the sense of knowing nothing (though what they know may be factually incorrect). The professional practice of academic research is, of course, political. But more important is noting the practical implications of political versions of history. Reflections on religion, science, and technology, then, must also often be a study of politics – and be relentlessly aware of what contemporary people think. Only by gathering into itself such considerations can we appreciate the religious and nationalist impulses that provide an historical lens for the public technological imaginary.

Acknowledgments

The author is profoundly grateful to the U.S. – India Educational Foundation and the Council for International Exchange of Scholars, which provided him with a Fulbright-Nehru Senior Research Award in 2012–13 and to Manhattan College for providing sabbatical support during that time. During the Fulbright-Nehru research, the author was a member of the Centre for Contemporary Studies at the Indian Institute of Science. He thanks his colleagues there, especially Maheswari Satheesh and Dr. Raghavendra Gadagkar, for their friendship and support. In addition, the author recognizes that little of this work would have been possible or as relevant to contemporary India without the Indian scientists and engineers who sat down for interviews, both those who were included in this paper and those who were not. Finally, the author is indebted to Dr. Musa Jafar, whose expertise in data analytics and whose RStudio extension made it possible to evaluate Prime Minister Modi's use of Twitter.

Notes

1 *Swaraj* means "self-rule" or "home rule," and refers to both an individual's control over his or her own life and the people of India's control over the nation.
2 Indian nationalists hailed science and technology in non-religious ways also. Drawing upon Tanika Sarkar, Ishita Banerjee-Dube points out that Jagadishchandra Bose's *Plant Response* was "hailed by the journal *Prabasi* as the greatest swadeshi event of 1906, and the experiments of Prafullachandra Ray in chemistry, gave the Bengali intelligentsia the happy consciousness that a combination of science and patriotism were helping to put Bengal and India on the map of world culture" (Banerjee-Dube, 2015: 232). We might compare this to more recent efforts at championing India's place in global politics and culture through its IT industry and space program.
3 Similarly, there were late nineteenth and early twentieth century debates over whether ancient Indians had discovered vaccination prior to the advent of nineteenth century bacteriology (see Chakrabarti, 2012: 41–42).

4 David Nye (2003) offers, perhaps, the most articulate descriptions of this in his exploration of how technology was part of American visions of the frontier, Manifest Destiny, and the nation's Christian heritage.
5 To appreciate the nationalistic approach to technology at the heart of *Make in India*, consider the description of Make In India Week—2016: "A week that will spark a renewed sense of pride in Indian industry by showcasing the potential of design, innovation and sustainability across India's manufacturing sectors in the coming decade" (Make In India, 2016).
6 This number does not include those words sifted from the analysis, including definite and indefinite articles, tinyURLs, and image captions. It does include words used as mentions or hashtags.
7 Such pairings include mentions of individuals who include vedicscience in their Twitter IDs (e.g. @vedicscience or @vedicscience108), who use the #vedicscience, or who simply compress the words Vedic and science into one word. Among these, #Hindurise occurred alongside vedicscience 39 times in 2015. Other high frequency connections include #vedic (20 occurrences), #hinduism (18 occurences), #india (17 occurrences), #hindu (16 occurrences), and #indiansciencecongress (13 occurrences), #ancientindia (12 occurrences), #bharat (10 occurrences), and #vedanta (10 occurrences). The connections to the Indian Science Congress, which all occurred during the days of the Congress in January, reveal the immediate and automatic connection that Twitter users make between the political support of science, nationalist revival, and support for Vedic science and technology.
8 Interview data were collected by the author from December, 2012 to May 2013, during which time he was Fulbright-Nehru Senior Researcher and Visiting Professor at the Centre for Contemporary Studies, Indian Institute of Science (Bangalore). Interviews were conducted at the Indian Institute of Science and elsewhere in Bangalore's academic and industrial communities.

References

Banerjee-Dube, Ishita (2015) *A History of Modern India.* Delhi: University of Cambridge Press.

Chakrabarti, Pratik (2012) *Bacteriology in British India: Laboratory Medicine and the Tropics.* Rochester, NY: University of Rochester Press.

Chopra, Rohit (2008) *Technology and Nationalism in India: Cultural Negotiations from Colonialism to Cyberspace.* Amherst, NY: Cambria.

Deshpande, Madhav (1979) "History, Change and Permanence: A Classical Indian Perspective." In Gopal Krishna (ed.), *Contributions to South Asian Studies 1.* Delhi: Oxford University Press, pp. 1–28.

Firstpost staff (2014) "Historians Raise Questions about ICHR's New Boss Prof Y. Sudershan Rao." *Firstpost* (July 14). Available at: www.firstpost.com/living/historians-raise-questions-about-ichrs-new-boss-prof-y-sudershan-rao-1617971.html (accessed July 12, 2015).

Frawley, David (1990) *The Astrology of the Seers: A Guide to Vedic (Hindu) Theology.* Salt Lake City, UT: Passage Press.

Frawley, David (2012) "Secrets of the Yugas or World-Ages." American Institute of Vedic Studies webpage. Available at: http://vedanet.com/2012/06/13/secrets-of-the-yugas-or-world-ages/ (accessed June 2, 2015).

Geraci, Robert M. (2016) "A Tale of Two Futures: Techno-Eschatology in the U.S. and India." *Social Compass* 63(3): 319–334.

Ghosh, Arunabh (2015) "Killing Humanities in India." *The Times of India* (August 13). Available at: http://blogs.timesofindia.indiatimes.com/toi-edit-page/killing-huma nities-in-india-2/ (accessed August 13, 2015).

Giri, Sri Yukteswar ([1894] 1972) *The Holy Science*. Los Angeles, CA: Self-Realization Fellowship.

Gittinger, Juli L. (2015) "Modi-Era Nationalism and the Rise of Cyber-Activism." *Exemplar: The Journal of South Asian Studies* 3(1): 9–17.

Gold, Daniel (2015) *Provincial Hinduism: Religion and Community in Gwalior City*. New York: Oxford University Press.

Hansen, Thomas Blom (1999) *The Saffron Wave: Democracy and Hindu Nationalism in Modern India*. Princeton, NJ: Princeton University Press.

Harriss, John (2003) "The Great Tradition Globalises: Reflections on Two Studies of 'The Industrial Leaders' of Madras." *Modern Asian Studies* 37(2): 327–362.

Khilnani, Sunil ([1997] 1999) *The Idea of India*. New York: Farrar, Straus and Giroux.

Larson, Gerald James (1995) *India's Agony over Religion*. Albany, NY: SUNY Press.

Larson, Gerald James (2012) "Hindu Cosmogony/Cosmology." In James Haag, Gregory Peterson, and Michael Spezio (eds.), *The Routledge Companion to Religion and Science*. New York: Routledge, pp. 113–123.

Larson, Gerald James (2016) "Myth as History and History as Myth: The Instructive Case of India." In Knut Jacobsen, ed., *Routledge Handbook of Contemporary India*. New York: Routledge, pp. 313–328.

Mahaprashasta, Ajoy Ashirwad (2015) "Irfan Habib: 'Nation's Mental Make-up May Suffer Grievously'." *Frontline* (October 16). Available at: www.frontline.in/the-nation/ nations-mental-makeup-may-suffer-grievously/article7698404.ece (accessed January 21, 2016).

Make In India (2016) Official website. Available at: www.makeinindia.com/home (accessed February 21, 2016).

Marx, Karl ([1844] 2002) "Critique of Hegel's Philosophy of Right." In John Raines, (ed., *Marx on Religion*. Philadelphia, PA: Temple University Press, pp. 170–182.

Mukunda, H.S., S.M. Desphande, H.R. Negendra, A. Prabhu, and S.P. Govindaraju (1974) "A Critical Study of the Work 'Vymanika Shastra'." *Scientific Opinion* 5: 5–12.

Nanda, Meera (2003) *Prophets Facing Backward*. New Brunswick, NJ: Rutgers University Press.

Nanda, Meera (2006) "How Modern Are We? Cultural Contradictions of India's Modernity." *Economic and Political Weekly* 41(6): 491–496.

Nanda, Meera (2007) "Secularism without Secularisation: Reflections on God and Politics in US and India." *Economic and Political Weekly* 42(1): 39–46.

Narasimha, Roddam (2015) "The 'Historic' Storm at the Mumbai Science Congress." *Current Science* 108(4): 471–472.

Narlikar, Jayant (2003) *The Scientific Edge*. New Delhi: Penguin.

Nath, Vijay (2001) "From 'Brahmanism' to 'Hinduism': Negotiating the Myth of the Great Tradition." *Social Scientist* 29(3/4): 19–50.

Nye, David (2003) *America as Second Creation: Technology and Narratives of a New Beginning*. Cambridge, MA: MIT Press.

Ornella, Alexander (2015) "Towards a 'Circuit of Technological Imaginaries': A Theoretical Approach." In Daria Pezzoli-Olgiati, (ed.), *Religion in Cultural Imaginary: Explorations in Visual and Material Practices*. Baden-Baden: Nomos, pp. 303–332.

Parry, Jonathan (1985) "The Brahamanical Tradition and the Technology of the Intellect." In Joanna Overing, ed., *Reason and Morality*. New York: Tavistock, pp. 200–225.

Perera, Sasanka (2015) *Debating the Ancient and Present: A Conversation with Romila Thapar*. Delhi: Aakar Books.

Prakash, Gyan (1999) *Another Reason: Science and the Imagination of Modern India*. Princeton, NJ: Princeton University Press.

Quack, Johannes (2012) *Disenchanting India: Organized Rationalism and Criticism of Religion in India*. New York: Oxford University Press.

Raman, Varadaraja V. (2011) *Indic Visions in an Age of Science*. New York: Metanexus.

Saraswati, Dayanand (1908) *Satyarth Prakash*, translated by Durga Prasad. Lahore: Virjanand Press.

Shankar, Aranya (2015) "Indian Definition of Secularism Is Incomplete, Says Romila Thapar." *The Indian Express* (August 20). Available at: http://indianexpress.com/article/cities/delhi/indian-definition-of-secularism-is-incomplete-says-romila-thapar/ (accessed September 1, 2015).

Sharma, Ritu (2014) "Science Lesson from Gujarat: Stem Cells in Mahabharata, Cars in Veda." *The Indian Express* (July 27). Available at: http://indianexpress.com/article/india/gujarat/science-lesson-from-gujarat-stem-cells-in-mahabharata-cars-in-veda/99/ (accessed June 15, 2015).

Singer, Milton (1972) *When a Great Tradition Modernizes: An Anthropological Approach to Indian Civilization*. New York: Praeger.

Soni, Vikram and Romila Thapar (2014) "Mythology, Science and Society." *The Hindu* (November 7). Available at: www.thehindu.com/opinion/op-ed/mythology-science-and-society/article6571525.ece? (accessed November 8, 2014).

Thapar, Karan (2014) "The Two Faces of Mr. Modi." *The Hindu* (November 1). Available at: www.thehindu.com/opinion/op-ed/comment-the-two-faces-of-mr-modi/article6553304.ece (accessed November 2, 2014).

Thapar, Romila (2014) "History Repeats Itself." *India Today* (July 21). Available at: http://indiatoday.intoday.in/story/romila-thapar-smriti-irani-old-history-baiters-of-bjp/1/370799.html (accessed July 12, 2015).

Tiwari, Vishwamohan (2013) "Aircraft Design in Ancient India," presentation at the Indian Institute of Science, January 30.

Trivedi, Lisa (2007) *Clothing Gandhi's Nation: Homespun and Modern India*. Bloomington, IN: Indiana University Press.

Tyagi, B.K. (2014) "Fostering Scientific Temper." *VIPNET NEWS* 12(2): 1–3.

Vahia, Mayank (2015) "Evaluating the Claims of Ancient Indian Achievements in Science." *Current Science* 108(12): 2145–2148.

3 Visualizing Sikh warriors, royalties, and rebels

Photography in colonial Punjab

Kristina Myrvold

Photography arrived in India quickly after the daguerreotype process had been invented and made public in 1839. Thacker, Spink and Co. in Calcutta advertised imported cameras in the paper *Friends of India* already in 1840 and the first known lithograph based on a daguerreotype in India appeared the same year, portraying the "Sans Souci" theater in the city (Pinney, 1997: 17; Khan, 2002: 14; Thomas, 1979: 216). The first commercial photographic studio began operating in Calcutta by the end of the 1840s and photographic societies were established during the 1850s in Bombay (1854), Calcutta (1856), and Madras (1856) to disseminate photographic knowledge through meetings and annual exhibitions (Allana, 2014: 34; Thomas, 1979: 218). It remains uncertain when photography was introduced in the province of Punjab but some of the first images with the photographer identified was taken by John McCosh, a British surgeon in the East Indian Company who was stationed at Ferozepur. During the second Anglo-Sikh War (1848–1849) he prepared calotypes depicting Sikhs and places in Lahore and also created a portrait of the 10-year old Maharaja Dalip Singh in profile (Bance, 2009:22, 175; Khan, 2002: 14; Kumar, 2012; McKenzie, 1987; Patel, 1999: 194). Although there were early European and Indian enthusiasts for the new technology, photography during the mid-nineteenth century involved experimenting with bulky cameras and chemicals that were not accessible to all. In Punjab the practice initially relied heavily on travelling government officers in the British civil and military services as well as visiting European photographers in search of the picturesque who captured the landscape, buildings and people from colonial imagination. Another early photographer to represent the Sikhs in images was the Italian Felice Beato who traveled through northern India to document the aftermath of the Mutiny in 1857. His catalogue from the 1850s includes, for instance, images of Sikh soldiers, Nihangs, British and Sikh officers in the Hodson's Horse Regiment as well as different views of the Golden Temple in Amritsar (Patel, 1999, 196–198; *The Last Empire*, 1976: 13). Among the photographers that followed especially the Golden temple was eternalized through the lens whether the purpose was to record historical buildings, sell images for the commercial market, or preserve visual tourist souvenirs (see Table 3.1; Madra, Singh and Singh, 2011).

Table 3.1 Some photographs of the Golden Temple in the nineteenth and early twentieth centuries (year and photographer/company)

1856, Charles Waterloo Hutchinson
1858–1860, Felice Beato
1865, Samuel Bourne
1860s, John Edward Saché
1863–1864, Samuel Bourne
1864–1866, William Baker
1868–1870, James Craddock
1870, Captain W. G. Stretton
1872, Baker & Burke
1880s, Bourne & Shepherd
1890, Bourne & Shepherd
1900, General A. Skeen
1906, Hannah P. Adams
1906, Herbert G. Ponting
1908, Underwood & Underwood
1908, Stereo Travel Co.
1910, Colonel H. Templar

This chapter presents an overview of how the practice of photography evolved and transformed in colonial Punjab in relation to technological developments during the nineteenth century with special emphasis on Sikh interests and uses of the camera. Furthermore, the chapter illustrates how the Sikhs were visualized in colonial photographic representations that were underpinned by orientalism and racial ideologies and continued to be reproduced long into the twentieth century. This is firstly done by a selected focus on the predominant anthropometric photography that evolved to identify the Indian population through racializing categorization. Meanwhile the Sikh aristocrats in Punjab developed a keen interest in photography and adjusted the genre of portraiture to Indian aesthetics by blending the imported inventions with indigenous traditions of portrait painting. If photography in Punjab was initially under patronage of the military, the colonial administration, and Indian nobility, new technological developments by the end of the nineteenth century transformed the access and practice of photography. The final sections of the chapter provide examples of how technological advancements opened up for commercial opportunities among both European and Indian photographers and enabled the creation of new visual representations and agency that would eventually challenge the colonial power. As scholars have highlighted, the academic study of photography in India have generally focused on the colonial elite and renowned commercial photographers, while Indian photographers and provincial studios have received less attention (see e.g. Whitehall, 2014: 15). Except for studies on famous photographers and colonial initiatives, photography in Punjab and especially among the Sikhs remains a largely unexplored field. Based on research of surviving photographic material and colonial records on Punjab, this chapter can be approached as a preliminary study that elucidates how the new technology provided shifting possibilities with European and Indian interests intersecting and eventually became an agent for change with societal effects far beyond the visual reproductions.

Colonial anthropometric photography

Early photography in colonial India was embedded in an empiricism which presumed the camera could be used as a positivist device to collect scientific material for imperial knowledge and control of colonial subjects. Photography was considered to provide a new kind of indexicality of the reality and scientific prestige for documentation and identification of people in political and ideological projects that supported evolutionary and imperial theories. Christopher Pinney suggests that photography in nineteenth-century India was primarily conducted within the two paradigms of "salvage" and "detective," according to which the former aimed to document fragile communities before their presumed extinction and the latter map out vital communities that could be used as guides to identify colonial subjects. Characteristic for both was an orientalism preoccupied with typicality of the Indian subjects, who were categorized by generalizing collectivities, such as "races," "castes," "natives," "criminals," and so on, and unlike representations of Europeans kept anonymous (Pinney, 1997: 45, 53).

Many of the earliest photographs of Sikhs were part of ethnographical studies that aimed to identify and record the physical characteristics of human races. When travelling in India during the late 1850s the German ethnologist Andreas Fedor Jagor captured front and side portraits of a male Sikh in Lahore that were used for his studies of the Indian "tribes" (*völkerstämme*). The photographs, in which the man stands bare-chested without the turban that is associated with status and honor, but with his hair bound and exposed before the camera, illustrate the disturbing power relations between photographers and their subjects that were typical for anthropometric photography up to the mid-twentieth century. Undressing colonial subjects to make their bodies open to investigation through the lens, or dressing them up in exaggerated traditional costumes, underscored their vulnerable and powerless positions (Evans, 2004: 236).

Collections that aimed to represent the Indian people and cultures existed before photography. According to John Falconer, the foundation for ethnographical studies was laid already by the oriental scholar William Jones and the Asiatic Society of Bengal established in 1784, but it was during the 1840s and

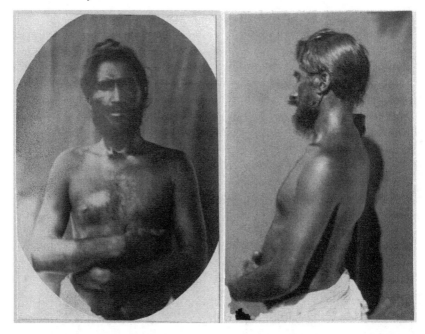

Figure 3.1 Photographs of a Sikh in Lahore by Fedor Jagor. © Ethnologisches Museum der Staatlichen Museen zu Berlin – Preußischer Kulturbesitz

1850s physical comparisons between different groups became predominant when people within the colonial regime interacted more closely with the population and illustrative material was considered an important source of information (Falconer, 2002: 56). The manuscript "Seventy-two Specimens of Castes in India," for instance, was produced for American missionaries in 1837 and contained hand-painted images of men and women on mica. The Sikhs were represented by drawings of a "Sikh chief" and his "female"—the male dressed in traditional long shirt (*chola*) in blue color and holding an arrow, and the female wrapped in a blue scarf with a bird sitting on her right hand. Photography, however, was believed to provide new means for creating more "realistic" depictions of various groups that were not dependent on artistic interpretations. From the 1850s it became increasingly popular to produce specific albumen prints that depicted people in costumes and with objects identifying their particular religious, caste or trade group. The purpose of these publications was to illustrate the racial and regional "typicality" of different people. One of the earliest albums was made by William Johnson and William Henderson in Bombay who published portraits of Indian people in a series titled *The Indian Amateurs Photographic Album* between 1856 and 1859 and which later was published as the ethnographic work "The Oriental Races and Tribes, Residents and Visitors of Bombay" (see Johnson, 1863, 1866; Falconer, 2002: 58).

Since important markers of typicality of the "natives" were regional and religious costumes, the Nihang Sikhs with their dresses and weaponry attracted early colonial attention and portraits of them came to represent the Sikhs in general. Colonel Willoughby Wallace Hooper in the 4th Regiment of the Madras cavalry is one photographer who in the 1860s was seconded from his military duties in Secunderabad in order to collect portraits of people in the central provinces. Together with the veterinary surgeon George Western he captured several portraits of Nihangs that were copied for exhibitions and a wider market. Some of the Sikhs portrayed in these photographs, posing in studio settings with different weapons in their hands, might have served in the irregular force of the Nizam of Hyderabad (see Falconer, 1983; Johnson, 2003: 51; Nihang and Singh, 2008: 169, 177, 181). One portrait depicting a Nihang with a high *dumala*, decorated with the large metal object (*gajgah*), was apparently included in a photographic collection of different "native heads" in India and displayed in the London International Exhibition in 1871 (Victoria and Albert Museum, 2016). Several portraits of Nihang Sikhs from the nineteenth century, which were widely reproduced and later used by Sikhs themselves for identity projects and commemoration of their history, were initially created for colonial anthropometric projects that tried to identify, represent and appropriate the native races and tribes of India.

Especially after the Mutiny in 1857, visual information about people and societies became a matter of political and military interest for the colonial government. In a pilot project to test new security techniques, the Inspector General of Police in Punjab, George Hutchinson, initiated photography in Lahore Central Jail from 1868 and also brought the new method to register criminals before the Home Secretary. Punjab became a pilot province for a broader implementation of photography in jails in British India (Sauli, 2006: 230; Anderson, 2004: 146). Portraits of prisoners were to be taken when they were entering and leaving jail, along with personal identification sheets that informed about name, origin, crime and sentence, and physical characteristics (Pinney, 2008: 63). The photographs were numbered and preserved in the Central Police Office, while the negatives were retained at the jail (Ball, 1868: 101). Later, in 1893, the Lahore Central Jail further adopted the Bertillion system of anthropometric measurement with full-face and profile photographs of the perpetrators and during the first year of implementation took measures of 80 prisoners in Lahore (Report on the Administration of the Punjab, 1894: 58).

A larger governmental project was the collection *The People of India*, which was published in eight volumes between 1868 and 1875 with John Forbes Watson and John William Kay as the editors and contained 468 albumen prints of races, tribes and castes annotated with descriptions. The project was an official attempt to document characteristic "likeness" of different people in an organized manner by collecting photographs with assistance from the provincial administration. As Christopher Pinney has explained, the concern was "not with individuals but with categories" of people (Pinney, 1997: 44; see also Falconer, 2002). During the year 1861 the government of Punjab sent directives to the commissioners of the different divisions with a request to submit photographs of "remarkable tribes" with "photographic likeness" along with information about their names and terms in Urdu and the vernacular language of the districts (*Press lists of old records in the Punjab Civil Secretariat*, 1926: 317, 341, 348). Amateur photographers, many in civil or military employment, were commissioned and submitted photographs from various districts. Amritsar was, however, excluded as the responsible commissioner was unable to obtain photographs and consequently the government decided to dispense with the "natives" of Amritsar since they were deemed to "resemble the people of Lahore" of whom photographs were already available (*ibid*: 359). The photographers were instructed to submit 20 copies of each negative that were forwarded to the India office in London, as well as provide one copy each for the museums at Delhi and Lahore (*ibid*: 349, 383). When the photographs were edited and entered in *The People of India* the Sikhs were represented in totally eight portraits of individuals and groups (see Table 3.2).

The portraits and annotations reflected the colonial assumptions and ethnocentrism that were implicit to the project. Two descriptions of the Nanakshahi fakir and the Sikh jat in Lahore used quotations of stories about the Sikhs that had previously been narrated in Henry Steinbach's book about Punjab (Steinbach, 1846) and in Lepel Griffin's work on the Punjab chiefs (Griffin, 1865). The Udasins and the Nihangs (termed Akalis) were described to be on the extreme sides of Sikh practices, the former presented as followers of Guru Nanak with an "ascetic spirit" and the latter as "fanatical soldiers ... always armed to the teeth" (Vol. 4). Loyalty to British power and regulations was used a device to measure the moral condition of the Sikhs. The Sodhi Sikhs, represented through two images, were described as descendants of the Sikh gurus who were supposed to act as teachers within the community, but instead had adopted an idle lifestyle in moral decay, being notorious for female infanticide and intoxication (Vols. 4 and 5). With the access to camera in Lahore Central Jail, the portrait of the three Mazbee Sikhs, representing "outcaste Sikhs" in *The People of India*, was a photograph depicting interns

Table 3.2 Photographic representations of Sikhs in *The People of India* (1868–1875)

Name	Place	No.	Vol.
Nanukshahee Fakir	Bareilly	123	3
Oodassees	Delhi	196	4
Sodhee Sikh	Trans-Sutlej states	219	4
Akalee	Lahore	225	4
Sikh jat	Lahore	233	5
Muzbee Sikhs	Lahore	237	5
Sodhee	Lahore	240	5
Sikh Akali	Sindh	324	6

Figure 3.2 Photo of the 14th Ferozepur Sikhs under Captain Claye R. Ross with a "Sikh priest." The photograph was supplied by Captain Lovett and published in *The Illustrated London News* on April 13, 1895. © Illustrated London News Ltd/Mary Evans

who were confined with life-sentences for murder and robbery. The annotation labeled their "class" to be athletic, industrious, and loyal to the colonial power during the Mutiny, but due to bad influences they had adopted criminal behaviors (Vol. 5).

Consistent with predominant essentialistic ideas, the British increasingly perceive the Sikhs as one of the "martial races" in India, being specially loyal and well-suited for military service after the Mutiny. From the 1880s the colonial power initiated a "Punjabization" of the British Indian Army and recruited about half of the army from this province (Omissi, 2012: 37; Talbot and Thandi, 2004: 1). As Heather Streets illustrates, "race" in the martial race ideologies was initially used more flexible to morally and hierarchically differentiate people and their progress towards a civilized state based on religion, language and technological advancement. In the end of the nineteenth century, however, "race" was increasingly understood in terms of inborn and physical characteristics that could be scientifically measured and studied and, simultaneously, used as a manipulating performative tool to rule and secure the empire from internal revolts. Since many Sikhs had proved loyalty to the British during the Mutiny, they were strategically presented as having natural proclivity to the arms which could justify a selective recruitment along racial terms (Streets, 2004: 7–9). The ideas of martial races with the Sikhs deemed as especially "warlike" were reproduced extensively in visual representations up to the Second World War and continued to echo in identity projects among the Sikhs long after independence.

One typical colonial example of martial race ideologies in photography was the large-format collection titled *Types of the Indian Army, Illustrating the Races Enlisted in the Bengal, Punjab, Madras and Bombay Armies* which was published in 1897 by the Scottish photographer Frederick Bremner. After having worked at the photo studio of his brother-in-law in Lucknow in the 1880s, Bremner established his own firm with branches in Karachi, Quetta, Lahore and Rawalpindi, and later also a summer studio in Simla where he eventually took over the place of Bourne and Shepherd (the "Talbot house" named after the W.H. Fox Talbot who invented the calotype process). While photographing army officials in Rawalpindi he observed the characteristics of different ranks and decided to conduct a three-month tour to prepare a photographic series (Sharma, 1989: 295–297). The album on the martial races in the Indian Army was intended to be used as companion to military recruitment manuals and contained 60 carbon prints with the Sikhs well represented. The group photographs portrayed uniformed soldiers in front and side positions, standing and sitting on horses in museum-like poses that indicated their orders of dress in relation to each other. As the publication was purchased by Queen Victoria, Bremner come to claim royal patronage of his work. Sheila Asante suggests that Bremner's photographic project can be placed within the framework of a British "re-territorialisation" of India after the Mutiny when the native "races" were to be represented in a new colonial structure (Asante, 2013: 90). Within this structure, and through the ideological lens of martial races, the Sikh population was widely visualized through images of ideal masculine warriors within the British Empire. For example in October 1907, 50 years after the Mutiny, *The Illustrated London News* published a photomontage (prepared by the photographer Thiele) with the heading "Our hundred million dusky fellow-subjects: Representative races of His Majesty's Indian Empire" that was to symbolize the population in India. The Sikhs were represented through a picture of a Nihang with a high *dumala* and a man who wore a high turban like soldiers in the army. All "races" were deliberately placed in front of the Cashmere Gate in Delhi, "the scene of the fiercest fight of the Mutiny," which can be interpreted as an attempt to project visions of the British recapture and control of India. The photomontage illustrates how the hegemonic power manipulated the technical practice of image-making to create fake representations that suited orientalist ideologies.

Portrait photography among aristocrats

The art and technology of photography attracted early attention of the ruling families in northern India who considered it fashionable and had the means

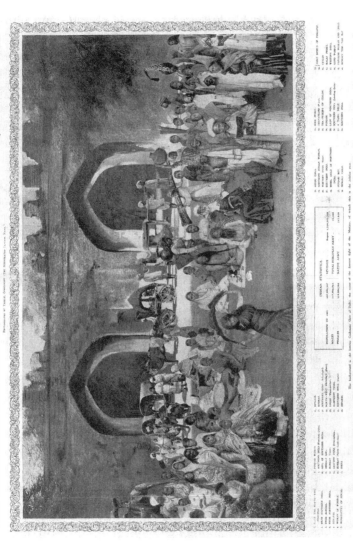

Figure 3.3 Photomontage of the Indian population published *The Illustrated London News*, October 12, 1907. © Illustrated London News Ltd/Mary Evans

to patronize photographers and purchase the required paraphernalia. The photographer Samuel Bourne informed through his travel reports in 1866 that even the Raja of the princely state Chamba in the Punjab hills was a photographic enthusiast and had procured expensive cameras, lenses and chemical equipment that was termed "spices" (*masalas*) (Dehejia, 2006: 226). Writing in his typical self-satisfied style, often intolerant towards Indians, Bourne interpreted the raja's camera possession as just an "outward show" for status and recognition rather than for taking pictures of high quality (Ollman, 1983: 12). The Maharaja Dalip Singh is similarly reported to have developed a keen interest in photography especially after his exile from Punjab in 1854. According to narratives of contemporaries and portraits preserved in the British Royal Collection he photographed when visiting the royal family at Windsor and Osborne and even made portraits of the young princes sometimes dressed up in Indian costumes. Because of his "craze" for photography visitors to Castle Menzies, where he stayed between 1855 and 1858, were persuaded to "leave their 'shadow' behind" in the photographs he took (Login, 1890: 348, 398, 404). Other preserved images demonstrate that Dalip Singh and his family members posed for several renowned photographers in Europe, such as Antoine Claudet, John Mayall and John W. Clarke, whose portraits were published in luxury publications and reproduced in engravings for the wider press (Bance, 2009: 175–187). Original portraits of Dalip Singh were for instance included in the 1864 edition of John Mayall's "New Series of Portraits of Eminent and Illustrious Persons" (*The Athenaeum*, 1864).

With a well-established tradition of miniature painting in Punjab and the popularity of realistic portraiture among Sikh artists during the early nineteenth century (Goswami, 1999: 109), photography became widely used for portrait making of dignitaries and was soon combined with painting to enhance their status and appearance. After albumen print was introduced from the 1850s and paper copies could be made from glass negatives it became a vogue among royalties to have photographs taken when visiting larger cities with photographic studios and make larger cabinet cards or smaller visiting cards, so-called *carte de visites*, with portraits mounted on hardboard (see Harris, 2001). Both the firm Bourne & Shepherd in Simla as well as Baker & Company with studios in Peshawar, Murree and Rawalpindi began publishing these cards already in the 1860s and included them in various albums (Khan, 2002:144). In the *Album of cartes de visite portraits of Indian rulers and notables* by Bourne & Shepherd in the 1870s, for instance, the rajas of Faridkot, Nabha and Patiala were posing in their courtly costumes (The British Library, n.d.).

The Sikh royal houses of Punjab patronized both European and Indian artists and photographers for portraiture that came to provide a continuation of the traditional miniature painting through the use of photography. If paintings required hours of sittings before the artist while the portrait was made, the new technology made it possible to use photographs as the artistic base for quicker reproductions (see Sharma, 1988). Many of the portrait paintings from the royal houses of Patiala, Nabha and Kapurthala in the late nineteenth century were in this way created from photographs (Grewal, 2013: 83). Furthermore, the practice to paint and color photographs by different techniques became increasingly popular in the royal courts. Although it was early common to tint and paint daguerreotypes and the subsequent photographs by hand to improve the visual quality of images, painted photographs among Indian royalties developed into an aesthetic style and practice that melded photography with portrait painting (Pinney, 2013a: 21). A studio portrait of Hira Singh, the Raja of Nabha, from Bourne & Shepherd in the 1880s, for example, illustrates how an anonymous painter have used white watercolor to enhance the appearance of details in the raja's turban, dress and sword (Dewan, 2012: 49). Photographs in the courts of Sikh nobility were sometimes painted to the extent that they transformed into paintings (Grewal, 2003: 77). An illustrative example of this is a photograph of prince Balbir Singh of Faridkot, taken by John Blees in 1892, that was embellished with watercolor by an artist to the extent that the photographic dimension and depth became flat (Alkazi and Allana, 2008: 23).

Because of the emerging intermediary art of portraiture under royal patronage, several artists adopted photography just as photographers engaged in painting to sustain and operate their businesses. Historiographies of painting traditions in Punjab assert that Kapur Singh, a famous Sikh painter who received patronage of the Kapurthala court, was one of the first painters to learn photography in the province, even if the sources do not provide information about when this happened (Hasan, 1998: 157; Srivastava, 1983: 28). Jagtej Kaur Grewal has exemplified how the court of Nabha was early enthusiastic about photography and patronized artists for photographs, painted photographs, as well as paintings based on photographs. Trained as miniaturist and renowned for his illustrations in Max Arthur Macauliffe's work on the Sikh religion, the artist Lal Singh worked both as a photographer and painter for the Nabha court and in a context-sensitive manner continuously adjusted his artistic abilities to the changing taste of his patrons (Grewal, 2013: 86). Given the increasing popularity of painted photographs, studios in Bombay, Calcutta, Simla, and Lahore competed for commissions in painting by advertising themselves as "photographic artists" and employed artists to both color and paint portraits (Grewal, 2003: 172). It is perhaps noteworthy that the Census of 1891 reported about 2024 painters and photographers in Punjab, grouped in a shared category, and close to half of them (45 percent) were females (Maclagan, 1891). If portrait photography initially was used in the royal circles of Punjab, it began attracting a broader clientele from the 1870s onwards, often with colonial and aristocrat patronage. Individual and group portraits of members of the royal courts, Sikh scholars, religious specialists, and other luminaries from the ending decades of the nineteenth century have been preserved in various collections. For instance, when Thakur Singh Sandhawalia, the first president of the Singh Sabha association in Amritsar (1873), was invited to England by his cousin Maharaja Dalip Singh in 1884, a group photo of his entourage was taken in Amritsar before leaving (Bance, 2007: 25; 2009: 180; Saini, 2015).

A Sikh artist who developed his own style of portraits with the use of camera was Umrao Singh Sher-Gil (1870–1954). As the eldest son of Raja Surat Singh of the Majithia clan, Sher-Gil led an aristocratic life and officially worked as an independent scholar of Sanskrit and Persian. Already in the 1880s he took up photography and during the subsequent 60 years created around 80 self-portraits and several hundred portraits of family members. His production generated over 2,500 vintage prints along with glass plates and film negatives (Sher-Gil Sundaram Arts Foundation, n.d.).With access to the latest technology he experimented with autochromes, an early coloring process, and stereoscopy, a technique to create illusion of depth in photographs. After his first Indian wife passed away in 1907 he married Marie-Antoinette Gottesmann-Baktay, a Hungarian opera singer, and in 1912 the couple moved to Budapest where they received their two daughters, one of whom was Amrita who became a famous painter. The couple returned to India and settled in Simla after the First World War. Although Sher-Gil was drawn to socialist values and supported the Congress Party, he distanced himself from all political involvements after the war when the colonial power in India confiscated his property because of suspected involvements with the Ghadar Party. His interest for photography was primarily artistic with attempts to set up self-fashioned scenes that could capture a presence of himself and his family. The self-portraits, created both in India and Europe, depict him both as a yogi, only dressed in loincloth (*langota*) or drawers (*kachera*) with the beard, hair and body displayed, and as a man of letters garbed in Indian clothes and turban while contemplating before his musical instruments or typewriter, surrounded by papers and books (Amrita Sher-Gil, 2007: 28–29, 157). Unlike the practice of undressing colonial subjects in anthropometric projects to create representations of collectivity or the studio staging of dignities in regalia to convey their status and power, his artistic work was individual and private in character and has been interpreted as attempts to create a new modern self-fashioning through photography in the early twentieth century (Ananth, 2008).

Commercial photography

The growth of commercial photography in Punjab and elsewhere was made possible by different inventions during the nineteenth century that transformed the practice and accessibility of photography. The arrival of albumen positive paper prints in the 1850s enabled reproduction from glass plate negatives. The collodian wet plate process that was used by many photographers in India up to the 1880s, however, required long exposure times and an immediate processing of the photographic material. Photographers would thus bring chemicals, developing tents, and glass plates with them when taking pictures. Significant inventions were the Kodak system with photographic film, portable cameras, and machine-coated papers from the late 1880s which made photography easier and paved the way for mass production and a new type of amateur photography as the technology became accessible to a broader clientele (Khan, 2002: 15, 135; Whitehall, 2014: 25). As Greame Whitehall argues, if many spaces in colonial India were divided between Europeans and Indians, the photo studios became open to anyone who could afford to take or have a picture taken. As a result the significant demarcation was consequently decided by wealth and class belonging rather than "race" (Whitehall, 2014: 75). Portraiture had been predominant in early photography because of the technical limitations, but with the new advancements it remained the most popular type of photography in India and was further boosted by the emergence of mass-produced photo-postcards from the 1890s.

The earliest Europeans to launch commercial photography in Punjab after the British annexation in 1849 were men, often with a history in military and civil services, who had access to the equipment and sought colonial and military patronage. The first photographic studios were accordingly created in Simla, the summer capital of British India from 1864, and Murree, the summer headquarter of the Punjab Government up to 1876 (when transferred to Simla), as well as in Peshawar and Rawalpindi with permanent cantonments for the army. In addition to the reliance on colonial residents and military to maintain businesses, the early European photographers were engaged in commissioned work for the wealthy rulers of Punjab, including the Sikh princely states. The English-born James Craddock established his first photographic studio in Simla in 1859 and expanded to Peshawar in the 1860s. During the following decades he also opened studios in Lahore, Rawalpindi and Ambala with his son George Craddock who took over the business (Khan, 2002: 165; Patel, 1999: 207). Craddock claimed his firm to be appointed by the Lieutenant Governor of Punjab and was one of the photographers for the *darbar* between Viceroy Lord Mayo and the Amir of Afghanistan at Ambala in 1869 (Falconer, 2004: 343). Another renowned photographer in Simla was Samuel Bourne who left Nottingham in 1863 and went to India to photograph picturesque sceneries during several excursions in the Himalayas. Bourne went into partnership with the photographer Willam Hower in Calcutta and moved to the British summer capital where he created the commercial portrait studio Bourne & Shepherd together with Charles Shepherd who had worked as a photographer in Agra. When Bourne left India in 1871, Shepherd continued to run Bourne & Shephard in Simla until his departure eight years later (Sampson, 2006: 163–175). The firm, which retained its name, engaged many photographers and managed to retail extensively through agents and wholesale distributors in India and Europe. The firm's photographs from Punjab were widely reproduced for the postcard market (see Dehejia, 2006: 220–221). At Peshawar, William Baker, an Irish sergeant who was discharged from the army in 1859, is credited for having established the first photographic business in 1861 which he combined with auction activities and later expanded with branches in Murree, Rawalpindi, and Lahore. His firm Baker & Company also claimed official patronage of the Lieutenant Governor of the Punjab. Baker was joined by the assistant apothecary John Burke and together they changed the firm to W. Baker & Burke in 1871. Gradually Burke took over the firm and worked in Punjab until the early twentieth century. Some of the most famous photographs in the Burke collection portray the infantry regiment the 45th Rattray's Sikhs during the Second Anglo-Afghan war (Khan, 2002: 11, 20, 40, 147, 163).

Although it is more challenging to retrieve detailed information about Indian photographers in Punjab, available sources indicate that new techno-logical developments in the late nineteenth century encouraged Indians to take up photography as a profession and develop businesses for photographic goods in different towns of Punjab. In January 1885, for instance, the journal for the society *Anjuman-i-Punjab* in Lahore reported that Lala Parma Nand had opened a "Punjab Photographic Studio" on the premises opposite to the Mayo hospital. During a visit in England he had acquired "the science and art of Photography in all its details" and was offering the service of taking, copying and enlarging single and group photos of any size (*Journal of the Anjuman-i-Punjab and Punjab University Intelligencer*, 1885: 7). In a report on the art industries in Punjab from 1888 John Lockwood Kipling, the principal of Mayo School of Arts and the curator of Lahore Museum, remarked that "[t]here are a few native photographers and several European who practice the art" (*Papers relating to Technical Education in India, 1886–1904*, 1906: 140). Five years later the Gazetteer for Lahore district informed that photo-graphy "has become a very popular amusement with natives and they show remarkable aptitude for mastering the technique of the science. About half a dozen men have taken to it as a profession and doing fairly well" (Walker, 1894: 190). Although little is known about his person, the Indian landscape photographer Jadu Kissen left behind a legacy of photographic reproductions that have been preserved in various collections. In the 1890s he became an archaeological photographer for the Government of India in Lahore and Simla and worked for the Archeological Survey of India. His photographs were, among other things, published in "Simla: Past and Present" (Buck, 1904; Whitehall, 2014: 237). In the early twentieth century he established the firm "Archaeological Photographic Works of India" with branches in Kashmir and Delhi.

One historical source that provides a hint of the various commercial pho-tographic activities in Punjab during the second half of the nineteenth century and the early twentieth century is *Thacker's Indian Directory* by Thacker, Spink & Co. in Kolkata which listed British and Indian merchants, manu-facturers and industries in the colonized areas. It was initially published as a post office directory primarily for the Bengal Presidency, but also included information about the *mofussil*, the regions outside the capitals of the East India Company (Bombay, Calcutta and Madras). From 1885 it was called *Thacker's Indian Directory* and covered the whole of British India. Although the annual directories were suited for colonial needs and did not embrace all commercial activities consistently, an examination of photographers, photographic studios, and dealers in photographic material that were registered for the towns in Punjab (Delhi excluded) during the period 1864 to 1920 suggests that European photographers initially established photographic studios and companies at the colonial administrative and military centers of the province (see appendix 3.1). From the 1860s European photographers were registered for Simla and Peshawar and from the 1870s also in Lahore, Murree, Rawalpindi and Ambala. From the 1890s onwards, however, *Thacker's Indian Directory* registered several Indian photographers and stores selling cameras, chemicals, and other photographic goods that were run by Indian families. For instance, *The Egerton Frontier Photo and Stationery Depot* in Rawalpindi, later renamed to *N.D. Thapur Brothers*, between 1891 and 1898 advertised as dealers in photographic material. The business was owned by a Thapur family who also managed the Egerton Press, which similarly was registered to provide photographing and photographic goods between 1891 and 1916. Another business in Rawalpindi was Edward Art Studio that might have operated earlier but was registered between 1903 and 1915 with different owner constellations created by J.J. Jamasjee, F.R Unvala, Jamasji J. Boga, and D.N. Bali. Among its output the studio published the photographic book *The 1st Battalion Cameronian Regiment* with group photos of militaries. In *Thacker's Indian Directory* Edward Art Studio was the first photographic business to advertise itself with samples of photographic reproductions in 1906.

Although the sources do not elucidate religious or ethnic belonging of the commercial photographers, the names recorded in *Thacker's Indian Directory* during the selected period suggest that it was primarily Sikhs and other Indians who developed photographic ventures in Amritsar. The first to be registered as a photographer and merchant in the city between 1892 and 1900 was Bishen Singh. Later a company called Bishan Singh and Sons advertised as dealers in photography, watches, clocks and harmonium. Both the firms G. Darashaw & Co. and Baness Brothers operated as photographers in Amritsar from the early 1890s. Lahore, on the other hand, which hosted European photographers since the 1870s, seems to have provided business opportunities for Indian photographic firms from the early twentieth century. Like colleagues in Amritsar and at the hill stations, many of these combined their businesses with other work as chemists, opticians, dentists, general merchants, portrait painters, and so on. The company B.N. Kapoor, for instance, besides selling photographic goods, was also a manufacturer of rubber stamps in Lahore between 1908 and 1911. The firm Satwalkar & Co. operated both as photographers and portrait painters from 1913, and the manager S.D. Satwalkar apparently entered into cooperation with an H.R. Subbarwal to start The Fine Arts Studio in 1919. The increasing transnational links in the early twentieth century are also evident from advertisements of agents in Europe, usually in London, with whom the Punjabi companies were cooperating.

In addition to photographers and firms mentioned in colonial directories it is likely that many Europeans and Indians worked as photographers or assistants and took up photography as a hobby or side work. At the branch office of the firm J. Burke & Co. in Murree, for example, 24 assistants were employed in the 1890s (Khan, 2002: 186). The Census tables of 1901 recorded 477 persons to be earning their livelihood on photography in Punjab, the Native states, and the North-West Frontier Province. Out of these, 173 were registered as "actual workers" while the remaining was categorized as "dependents" that included family members as well as workers of both sexes. The distribution by districts suggests that most male photographers worked in Amritsar (36), Jalandhar (29), Peshawar (26), Rawalpindi (16), and Lahore (10). While women were frequently reported as dependents to their husbands, the Census indicates that about ten female photographers were operating in Rawalpindi (3) and Ferozepur (7) (Rose, 1902: xlvi, clxxxvii).

One example of a European hobby photographer is the Italian Federico Peliti who was a café owner, hotel proprietor and chocolatier in Simla and documented the life in the colonial summer capital. His collection includes, among other things, three plates with close-up portraits of Sikh carpenters who worked in Simla for the ruling elite in the 1890s as well as one photograph from a lunch event with his wife Judith and unidentified Sikh individuals. Greame Whitehall argues that Peliti's photographic production exemplifies a viewpoint different from the colonial visualization along racial types since his pictures had a personal character and portrayed inter-communal relationships with Europeans and Indians interacting in different social activities (Peliti Associati, 1993: 28–29, 40; Whitehall, 2014: 172, 176, 330–331). Another example of a Punjabi photographer is G.L. Nanak Chand, who was not mentioned in the directories but in the early twentieth century took pictures for the private family album of Elinor Tollington in Simla. Even if little is known about Chand, his photographs indicate that he operated under colonial patronage and documented the new infrastructure (railways, hospitals, post office, etc.), sometimes by including Sikhs as supernumeraries to establish scale (Whitehall, 2014: 206, 208, 226, 231).

Although photography was primarily learnt through practice, one of the earliest educational institutions to provide instruction in photography was the Mayo School of Art in Lahore, which was founded in 1875 to train sons of craftsmen to develop the industries.

An administrative report for 1878 showed that of the 58 pupils attending the Mayo School that year 26 were Sikhs. Even if the photographic class was small with only six pupils, the students were able to "copy from still life, enlarge and reduce drawings, maps, etc" (Holroyd, 1880: 73–74). In 1902 the school established a "photo-lithographic" studio which attracted students even when the training was at intervals reduced to theory, especially during the First World War, because of expensive supplies and chemicals ordered from England. During the period 1916 to 1921, for instance, between 19 and 30 students participated in the training at the department of photo-lithography (*Gazetteer of the Lahore District*, 1916: 158; *Report on the Department of Industries*, 1921: xxii, xxiv; *Report on the Progress of Education*, 1917: 39–40).

Indian women were typically absent in early photographs because it was by many considered improper to pose before male photographers (Thomas, 1979: 222). It is perhaps illustrative that one of the first known pictures of the Golden Temple in Amritsar with women included was taken by the British photographer Herbert G. Ponting in 1907, more than 50 years after the first photographs of the Sikh pilgrimage center appeared (Singh, 2012). From a British perspective a notice in the *Women's Gazette* of 1878 observed the women's photographic interest and barriers: "There is a growing desire amongst Indian ladies to have themselves and their children photographed; but owing to the domestic institutions of their country, they cannot have this done except their husbands and brothers happen to be amateur photographers" (Taylor, 1878: 11). Several commercial photographers in India opened so-called *zenana* studios, that is, ateliers adjusted for women with females behind the camera. Already from the 1860s European women in Calcutta ran studios of this kind and also offered to take portraits at the women's houses and teach them photography (Ghosh, 2014). In Hyderabad the famous photographer Lala Deen Dayal opened his popular *zenana* studio in 1892 with Mrs. Kenny-Levick, the wife of the editor of *Deccan Times*, as photographer (Sinha, 2006: 69; Welch, 1985: 445).

Although no distinct *zenana* studio seems to have been established in Punjab, the commercial companies offered similar services, and the practice of photography seems to have opened up opportunities for work and business ventures to both European and Indian women. Elizabeth Baker, the wife of William Baker, worked as a merchant for her husband's photographic business in Punjab (Khan, 2002: 24). According to *Thacker's Indian Directory* the photographer T. Winter had a Miss Vockers working as his assistant in the photographic studio in Rawalpindi from 1887. In Jalandhar Mrs. E. Wilkinson (probably the wife of a soldier in the cantonment) was reported to be the proprietress of the Cheltenham Hotel and worked as an independent photographer between 1887 and 1895. Both the wives of the photographers Frederick Bremner and John Blees with studios in Lahore and Simla were actively engaged in the photographic businesses of their husbands, even partners of the companies, and photographed (see also Asante, 2013: 91; Sharma, 1989: 298). In the early twentieth century Bremner advertised the service of portrait photographs adjusted for women and wrote in his memoir that his wife Emily Anton was "applying her hand to use of the camera on the occasion of photographing a Purdah [i.e. 'behind-the-veil'] lady whose face … men are not allowed to look upon" (Sharma, 1989: 298). The first Indian woman to be mentioned in *Thacker's Indian Directory* is a Mrs. S.R. Kathju, probably of a Kashmiri family, who was registered as the proprietress of *The Indo-European Trading Company* which manufactured cameras and other photographic apparatus in Rawalpindi from 1896 onwards. With the turn of the century, and especially when amateur photography spread, Sikh and

Punjabi women also began appearing more frequently in portraits of couples and families.

With the growth of commercial photography, postcards with printed photographic images emerged and created a new business that became highly transnational. The number of letters and postcards that were received annually for delivery in the postal circles of Punjab and the North-West Frontier Province increased from 53 to 99 million between the years 1897 and 1907 (*Statistical Abstract Related to British India*, 1908: 90). From the early twentieth century, Indian and European postcard companies published old and new photographs of Sikhs, ruling families, buildings, with several photo reproductions portraying the Golden Temple in Amritsar in black and white as well as in color. A renowned postcard company in Punjab was Moorli Dhur & Sons of Ambala which operated from 1899 and collected photographs that were reproduced in black and white and tinted with collotype print in Germany and Britain (Petrulis, 2006–2016; see also Mathur, 2007: 115). In line with anthropometric projects and in response to a growing interest among collectors, publishers in India and Europe issued thematic sets of photographs that were suited to albums. Examples of this were postcard series such as "Beauties of India," which included a "Punjabi Beauty," and "Types of India Women," with a portrait of two "Jat Sikh Women" spinning cotton. The notable Indian photographer D.A. Ahuja, who likely originated from Punjab and ran a firm in Rangoon from 1885, created a series that encompassed two hand-colored portraits of a young woman with the titles "A Punjab Lady (before marriage)" and "A Punjab Lady (after marriage)" (Johnson, 2003: 50; Pandhi, 2015; Sadan, 2014: 294–296). As Saloni Mathur highlights, the postcard industry "transformed the fascination with exotic native types that shaped the photographic collection *The People of India* by making the images available in a portable and more accessible form" (Mathur, 2007: 119). The postcards on Indian women can certainly be seen as projections of exotic and erotic imaginations of the time, but yet the genre did not portray women in sexualized poses or dresses, like the pictures of dancing girls (*nautch*), but rather as dressed and veiled in a traditional way.

Amateur and documentary photography

When new technologies transformed the photographic practice, the established photographers in Punjab were offering photographic knowledge to amateurs, probably as business strategies addressing a new clientele. In Lahore, John Burke advertised that "development, re-touching and printing [is] done for amateurs at moderate rates and lessons if required" in 1886 (Khan, 2002: 165). John Blees, who published a manual on photography in India (*Hindostan: Or Reminiscences of a Travelling Photographer*, 1877) and ran a photographic warehouse in Lahore from 1894, promoted his firm as "The Amateur Photographers Friend" and more generously offered "darkrooms free to all" (*British Journal of Photography Annual*, 1895: 1239). The

A Type of Punjab Beauty

Figure 3.4 Postcard "A Type of Punjab Beauty," printed in Saxony, early twentieth century. Author's collection

increasing access to the practice in the early twentieth century encouraged new types of image-making and representations in the private and public spheres that were also used for propaganda and resistance.

An understudied field in the visual culture of Punjab is the "snapshots" that were not intended to be art work or commercial items but more casual images to capture moments in time. Preserved photos of Sikh families, gurdwaras, religious leaders, ceremonies, associations, and so on, testify to the spread and popularity of amateur photography in the Sikh community. Sikhs who migrated to distant locations and documented their new homes and lives constitute another category. The photographers behind many of these pictures have remained anonymous but their images tell stories from different times and places. One Sikh amateur photographer whose production was recently rediscovered by Punjab Digital Library is Dhanna Singh who combined his interest for photography with religious pilgrimage in Punjab and termed himself a "cycle yatru" (cycle pilgrim). When working as a driver in the royal garage of Maharaja Bhupinder Singh in Patiala he set out on a pilgrimage tour on bicycle in the 1920s to visit historical gurdwaras in different states during three years. After the first tours he purchased a camera and learnt photography to document his continued travels in writing and picture. His collection gathered from 25,000 miles of travels on bicycle encompasses eight diaries and several hundred snapshots from the gurdwaras he visited in the early 1930s as well as articles he wrote for newspapers (Sethi, 2015). In relation to the many artistic and commercial pictorialization of the Golden Temple in Amritsar, often devoid of people for the enhancement of architectural splendor, Dhanna Singh's snapshots provided a different personal and subaltern narrative of the lived Sikh religion in India.

One category of well-preserved visual representations of Sikhs is the photographs of soldiers who served with the British Army during the First World War. Although several war pictures that were publicly distributed claimed to document soldiers at war, many images were staged imitations of real war situations for propaganda. Photographers were generally excluded in the war and official restrictions on taking pictures in war zones were implemented from 1916, but officers and soldiers would still bring pocket cameras along and several professional photographers achieved the required permission to work for the military (Badsey, n.d.). The Canadian Hilton DeWitt Girdwood was in the late 1914 appointed as the official photographer for the Indian Expeditionary force and is behind many of the preserved images of the Sikhs on the Western Front and in British military hospitals. Since he was not permitted to photograph on the front line he staged many scenes for the camera that were to look like documentation of the troops in action (Roberts, 2016). During the Gallipoli campaign 1915–1916 officers in the 14th Sikhs also took several snapshots to document their daily life which were included in a collection called *The Sikh Album* (Stanley, n.d.). The American photojournalist Ariel Varges was given the post as an official photographer for the British Army in Mesopotamia and documented the 45th Rattray's Sikhs when organizing a festival and setting up a temporary gurdwara in 1918. The images, portraying a procession for the Sikh scripture Guru Granth Sahib, were published in the propaganda magazine *The Great War* the following year and were later widely copied to illustrate how the Sikhs honored their sacred scripture during the war. Photographs of Sikh prisoners in German and Austrian camps were also used for German war propaganda. Audio recordings, films and photographs of interns were produced for the media and projects in physical anthropology and oriental studies (see e.g. Evans, 2004, 2010; Roy, Liebau and Ahuja, 2011). Especially the "Half-moon camp" (*halb-mond lager*) in Wünsdorf-Zossen, with many Indians detained, became an important propaganda camp. Sikh prisoners in camps of Münster were likewise photographed for the production of postcard series on different "völkertype" (folk types) in which the prisoners were typically portrayed in profile and frontal views to display racial typicality (Evans, 2004: 229). Based on detailed body measurements and photographs of 76 Jat Sikhs in the "Half-moon camp" the anthropologist Egon von Eickstedt published in 1920/21 his work *Rassenelemente der Sikh* (Racial elements of the Sikhs) which aimed to identify five different racial "types" among the Sikhs (von Eickstedt, 1920/21).

In the political climate of India after the war, the colonial view on photography transformed during the events following the Jallianwala Bagh massacre in Amritsar 1919, when a large crowd of non-violent protesters was fired upon by troops of the Army on the order of General Dyer. Christopher Pinney argues that a "civil contract" of photography was mobilized and undermined the British power and control of the technical practice (Pinney, 2013b: 43–44). The photographer Narayan Vinayak Virka from Maharashtra arrived in Amritsar shortly after the massacre and captured the aftermath in images which appeared like documentation of a crime scene. His photographs challenged official explanations of the events and were later used in the Punjab Inquiry report of Indian National Congress (Pinney, 2008: 83; 2013b: 43–44). Three years later, in 1922, Amritsar was again in focus when Sikhs were arrested and severely beaten by the police for trespassing on a piece of land of the gurdwara *Guru ka bhag*. This time there were many cameras to document the events as they unfolded. The photographer Ariel Varges was present and indiscriminately captured the protesters in procession and the police brutality, with the result that much of his work was later censored. The incidents in Amritsar marked the beginning of a new type of photojournalism which the colonial power perceived as threatening and tried to control by different measures, even if the new access and practice of photography had already made these attempts futile. Photography was attributed the quality of having an evidential potential and could therefore be used to prove colonial oppression and to mobilize resistance and support of nationalist politics (Pinney, 2008: 92–93; 2015: 26).

Another example of how photography was utilized for Indian nationalism and also spurred traditions of martyrdom is the images of the Sikh socialist and revolutionary Bhagat Singh who was executed in 1931 for the Lahore

Conspiracy Case and the assassination of a British police officer. Two portraits of Bhagat Singh were elevated to an iconic status and gained more popularity and spread than images of Mahatma Gandhi (Pinney, 2004: 117). The first appears like a documenting snapshot, often annotated with information that is was taken secretly, and depicts Bhagat Singh in the Lahore Railway Police Station during his first arrest in 1927 when he sits on a bed with his hair displayed and bound in a knot. While escaping a capture the following year he had his hair cut and assumed the dress of a European "sahib" (Maclean, 2011: 1054). The second photo, in which he is wearing mustache and a Western hat in a European style, has been presumed to be a studio portrait taken for a security pass or by the police. As Kama Maclean shows, however, the photo was arranged in the studio of Ramnath photographers in Delhi just a few days before the 1929 bombing in the Central Legislative Assembly that led to his final arrest. Knowing that he would be captured, Bhagat Singh wished to have the photograph distributed after the attack and it was consequently secretly sent to Indian newspapers by his comrades. The first to publish the portrait in April 1929 was the Urdu newspaper *Bande Mataram* in Lahore (Maclean, 2016). Maclean argues that Bhagat Singh understood the process of martyr-making and from his previous experiences as a journalist used photography to bring texture to his story. The studio portrait was spread and replicated in paintings and posters all over India and even inspired the young to dress up with hats for photographing (Maclean, 2011: 1061–1073). For generations of Sikhs and Indians, Bhagat Singh represented a bold revolutionary against the oppressive power and reproductions of his portraits were etched into national historiographies and martyrdom traditions that were kept alive until the twenty-first century.

Concluding remarks

As theorists of photography suggest, photography needs to be read through the lens of the performative forces and meanings that are involved in the technical practice. A photograph is not merely an aesthetic object to view but an "interlocution" that can and do transform things in the social world when produced and used (see e.g. Levin, 2009: 329). From this perspective photographs are not merely visual representations that display norms and attitudes of cultures but active agents that can shape discourses and history, activate emotions, and motivate social and political change. This chapter has illustrated that photography in colonial Punjab was initially under patronage of the military, the colonial administration, and Indian aristocrats. While the earliest photographers in Punjab were Europeans from the military and civil services and travelling visitors who portrayed the Sikhs and their religious traditions from colonial imagination, the Sikh princely states of Punjab adopted the technology early and patronized both European and Indian artists for a new kind of portraiture that blended photography with local art traditions of miniature paintings to enhance their public appearance and status. The colonial visualization of the Sikhs can be approached as a part of performative uses of photography that not only attempted to control the native subjects by identifying their religious and regional typicality but also functioned as imperial strategies to reterritorialize and soothe colonial anxieties after the Mutiny. From the perspective of ideologies of martial races that could justify a selective recruitment to the Indian British Army, the Sikhs were widely and enduringly represented in photographic projects as masculine warriors within the empire. The technological advancement in the late nineteenth century opened up for new performative forces that provided tools to critique colonial representations and afford opportunities for counter-hegemonic narratives and representations. The growing access to the technical practice enabled the crossing of social and ethnical borders as Sikhs and Indians were increasingly engaged in commercial ventures of photography in Punjab and in their own image-making that eventually created new religious and cultural representations and political resistance to the imperial power.

The performative uses of many photographs that were taken during the colonial period have continued in transformed versions up to the twenty-first century. Several of the nineteenth-century images portraying the Nihangs in traditional dresses and the Sikhs as ideal warriors in British service have been lifted from the original context of colonial racial ideologies to assume new religious meanings in various contemporary identity projects, commemorations of collective history, and martial traditions among the Sikhs. The studio portrait of Bhagat Singh is still widely reproduced in printed posters, on webpages, and in social media and has been integrated in hagiographical traditions that honor him both as an Indian revolutionary and a Sikh martyr. Further studies of Sikh uses of photography in Punjab and in the diaspora could illustrate that especially various types of portraiture became well integrated in religious practices. Photographic portraits of ancestors, religious leaders, and martyrs are decorating the walls in Punjabi homes, shops, and various institutions in the private and public sphere and through the images the people depicted are honored, commemorated, and sometimes worshiped in rituals. The Central Sikh Museum at the Golden Temple in Amritsar, for instance, displays photographs of martyrs who sacrificed their lives during the Operation Bluestar in 1984 when the Indian Army stormed the temple complex. The photographs portray their dead bodies or faces and have been attached with studio portraits from when they were alive to contrast life with death. Several rooms of the museum are also dedicated to painted portraits of male Sikh leaders and politicians in history which strongly resemble the nineteenth century realistic portraiture based on photography. Similar to colonial performative uses of photography to represent restored political control, many Sikh gurdwaras across the globe exhibit photographs of the Akal Takht ("the eternal throne") in Amritsar representing the Sikh seat of power when it was devastated during the Operation Bluestar. These are often placed beside images of the later renovated building to indicate the restored power and control of the Sikh community. As Lily Kong observes with reference to new technologies in the twenty-first century, the politics of space, identity, and community that occur when technology and religion intersect in new spaces is only "new insofar as new technologies are involved" (Kong, 2001: 405) The conditions of how technologies intersect with religion and are employed in performative uses over time reveal ongoing processes of change. The patterns of contemporary approaches to technology are certainly different from those that can be traced to the colonial period but yet very similar to the same.

Acknowledgment

I am grateful to the helpful staff at Asian and African Studies at the British Library and Mr. Harpreet Singh for valuable assistance with the collection of archival material. The work has been prepared with support from the Swedish Research Council (www.vr.se) under Grant 2014–2956 and within the Centre for Concurrences in Colonial and Postcolonial Studies at Linnaeus University.

Table 3.3 Photographers and dealers with photographic material in Punjab (Delhi excl.) according to *Thacker's Indian Directory* between 1863 and 1920 (arranged by location)

Lahore

- J.A. Bartholemy, photographer and photographic artist, 1870–1886.
- J. Saché, photographic artist, 1881.
- J.A. Bartholemy & A. Saché & Co., photographers, 1887–1888.
- J. Craddock & Co., photographers, 1890–1891.
- John Burke, photographer/photographic artist (from 1899 J. Burke & Co.), 1890–1903.
- G. Craddock & Co., photographers and photographic artists, 1890–1911.
- The Punjab Medical Shop, importer of photographic chemicals, 1892–1907.
- Jadu Kishen, archaeological photographer to the Government of Punjab, 1892, 1896–1912.
- John Blees, photographic warehouse, 1894–1898.
- E. Plomer & Co., dealers in photographic and artists materials &c., 1895–1920.
- Basant Ram & Sons, photographers and photographic engravers, 1902–1905.
- Sarkar & Co., photographic artists, dentists and rubber stamp manufacturers, 1903.
- H. Seymour & Co., photographers, 1903–1909.
- Frederick Bremner, photographer, 1904–1919.
- Girdhar Roy, photographer &c., 1905.
- P. Girdhar Roy & Sons, photographers, dentists and opticians, 1908–1920.
- Girdhari Lal, photographer and enlarger, 1908–1909.
- B.N. Kapoor, dealers in photographic goods and rubberstamp manufacturers, 1908–1911.
- Shanker Dass & Co., dealers in photographic goods, 1908–1920.
- Kesho Ram & Sons, photographers and dealers with photo materials, 1913–1920.
- Satwalkar & Co., portrait painters and photographers, 1913–1918.
- Imperial Photo Engraving Company, photo and general engravers, 1917–1920.
- The Fine Art Studio, photographers, 1919–1920.
- Half Tone Photographic Company, photo-engravers and photographers, 1919–1920.

Simla

- C.W. DeRussett, photographer and photographic artist, 1863–1872.
- James Craddock (from 1885 Craddock & Co.), photographer, 1864–1889.
- Howard, Bourne and Shepherd, photographers, 1865–1868.
- Bourne & Shepherd, photographers and artists (in the "Talbot house"), 1870–1911.
- G. Craddock & Co., photographers and photographic artists, 1890–1897.
- Johnston and Hoffman, photographers, 1890.
- R. Hotz, photographer, 1892–1915.
- Jadu Kishen, archaeological photographer to the Government of Punjab, 1894–1916.
- J. Cowell (Cowell & Co.), photographer, 1898–1902.
- E. Plomer & Co., dealers in photographic and artists materials &c., 1899–1920.
- C.K. Polacek, photographer and artist, 1904–1907.
- A. Jeakins, photographer and fine art dealer, 1904–1920.
- Frederick Bremner (Bremner & Co.), photographer, 1911–1920.
- J.H. King & Co., photographers, 1912–1919.
- H. Moller & Co., photographers, 1913–1915.

Amritsar

- Bishen Singh, photographer and merchant, 1892–1900.
- G. Darashaw & Co., photographers and general merchants, 1892–1900.
- Baness Bros., photographers and photographic artists, 1894–1907.
- Bishan Singh and Sons, photographers and dealers in watches, clocks, harmoniums &c., 1905.
- B. Sewa Singh & Sons, photographers, 1908–1910.
- Punjab Photographic Company, photographers, auctioneer &c., 1908–1914.
- Punjab Photographic and Enamel Iron Sign Manufacturers, 1910–1916.
- S.R. Suksena & Co., photographers, photo goods dealers, bankers, 1908–1914.
- Noshir & Co., chemists and dealers in photographic goods, 1913–1916.

Murree

- W. Baker and Co., photographers, 1870–1872.
- John Burke, photographer/photographic artist (from 1894 J. Burke & Co.), 1874–1899.
- E.G. Ganley, photographer, 1879.
- T. Winter, photographer, 1887–1897.
- George Dean, photographer, 1907–1912.
- W. Wilson, chemist and importer of photographic goods, 1903–1920.
- Jagat Singh & Bro., chemists, photo chemists, photographic goods dealers, 1910–1920.
- Didar Singh & Bros., chemists, druggists and photo goods dealers, 1917–1919.
- Jai Chand & Co., chemists, druggists, photo goods dealers, 1920.

Peshawar

- W. Baker and Co., photographers, 1864–1875.
- James Craddock, photographer, 1867–1869.
- John Burke, photographer/photographic artist, 1876–1878.
- Mela Ram and Holmes, photographers, 1904–1911.
- Jagat Singh & Bro., chemists, photo chemists, photographic goods dealers, 1910–1920.
- Didar Singh & Bros., chemists, druggists and photo goods dealers, 1917–1919.

Rawalpindi

- W. Baker and Co., photographers, 1871–1875.
- John Burke, photographer/photographic artist (from 1894 J. Burke & Co.), 1874–1899.
- E.G. Gauty, photographer, 1879–1880.
- T. Winter, photographer, 1886–1911.
- H. Browning, photographer, 1887–1890.
- J. Craddock & Co., photographers, 1890–1898.
- Dossabhoy J. Devacha, photographer, 1890–1911.
- Brown & Hogan, photographic artists, 1890–1892.
- N. Pandeth, photographic and medical stores, 1890–1892.
- The Egerton Frontier Photo and Stationery Depot, dealers in photographic material, 1891–1898.
- Frederick Bremner, photographer, 1895–1898.
- The Indo-European Trading Company, manufacturers of photographic cameras and other photographic apparatus, and photo chemists, 1896–1920.
- R.E. Shorter, photographer, 1903.
- D.N. Bali, photographer, 1900–1915.
- D.J. Divacha, photographer, 1900–1902, 1906–1911.
- The Frontier Photographic Company, F.R. Unvala, 1900–1901.
- George Dean, photographer, 1901–1912.
- H. Seymour & Co., photographers, 1901–1902.
- Edward Art Studio, photographers and dealers in photographic goods, 1903–1915.
- W. Wilson, chemist and importer of photographic goods, 1910–1915.
- Hussain M., marble merchant, sculptor, and photographer, 1905.
- W.J. Jones, photographer, 1905.
- K.P. Kacher, photographer, 1905–1911.
- Jagat Singh & Bros., chemists, photo chemists, photographic goods dealers, 1910–1920.
- Didar Singh & Bros., chemists, druggists and photo goods dealers, 1917–1919.
- Jai Chand & Co., chemists, druggists, photo goods dealers, 1920.

Jalandhar

- Mrs. E. Wilkinson, photographer, 1887–1895.
- E. Wilkinson, photographer, 1896–1902.
- Daulat Ram, photographer and general merchant, 1900–1903.
- Punjab Medical Hall & Hospital, chemists and druggists, importers of photographic goods in Jalandhar, 1911–1915.

Ambala

- J.R. Serrot, photographer, 1877–1878.
- Hobson Ball & Co., pharmaceutical and photographic chemists, 1902–1904.
- F.R. Unvala, late N.K.B. Modi, artist, photographer, and picture framer, 1908–1914.
- Nehal Chand & Co., dispensing and photographic chemists, 1912–1920.
- R.S. Bindra & Son, photographers and dealers with photographic goods, 1913–1915.
- Ghosh & Co., opticians and photographic chemists, 1914–1920.
- Modi & Co., photographic artist, general contractor, an insurance agent, 1915–1920.
- Nand Ram, photographer, 1915.
- Basheshar Nath & Co., druggists and photographic chemists, 1917 and 1919.
- Ball & Co., photo chemist, 1918–1920.

Sialkot

- R.E. Shorter, photographer, 1895–1912.
- M. Imtiazaly & Co., sculptors, engravers, and photographers, 1901.
- P.N. Handa and Karim Bux, photographers, 1905.
- Jai Chand & Co., chemists, druggists, photo goods dealers, 1920.

Ferozepur

- Bateman and Cripps, chemists and photographers, 1905–1913.
- Nand Lal Son & Bros., dealers in photo goods and army contractors, 1918–1920.

Hoshiarpur

- M.L. Jaini & Bros., dealers in photographic goods, 1915–1920.

Appendix 3.1

Bibliography

Alkazi, Ebrahim and Rahaab Allana (2008) *Painted Photographs: Coloured Portraiture in India*. New Delhi: Mapin Publishing.

Allana, Rahaab (2014) "Early Landscape Photography in India." In Rahaab Allana and Davy Depelchin, (eds.), *Unveiling India: The Early Lensmen 1850–1910*. New Delhi: Mapin Publishers and The Alkazi Collection of Photography, pp. 14–43.

Amrita Sher-Gil: An Indian Artist Family of the Twentieth Century (2007). Munich: Shirmer/Mosel.

Ananth, Deepak (2008) *Umrao Singh Sher-Gil: His Misery and His Manuscript*. Delhi: Photoink.

Anderson, Clare (2004) *Legible Bodies: Race, Criminality and Colonialism in South Asia*. Oxford and New York: Berg.

Asante, Sheila (2013) "Lucknow to Lahore: Fred Bremner's Vision of India." *Asian Affairs* 44(1): 89–96.

Ata-Ullah, Naazish (1998) "Stylistic Hybridity and Colonial Art and Design Education: A Wooden Carved Screen by Ram Singh." In T. Barringer and T. Flynn, (eds.), *Colonialism and Object: Empire, Material Culture and the Museum*. London: Routledge, pp. 68–81.

The Athenaeum: Journal of English and Foreign Literature, Science, and the Fine Arts (1864) No. 1913. Saturday June 25.

Badsey, Stephen (n.d.) "Photography." World War One, British Library. Available at: www.bl.uk/world-war-one/articles/photography#sthash.lePiv8G9.dpuf (accessed November 14, 2016).

Ball, W.E. (1868) *The Punjab Record: Or, Reference Book for Civil Officers: Containing the Reports of Civil and Criminal Cases Determined by the Chief Court of the Punjab and Decisions by the Financial Commissioner of the Punjab*, Vol. 3, part 2. Punjab Printing Company.

Bance, Peter (2007) *The Sikhs in Britain: 150 Years of Photographs*. Stroud: Sutton Publishing.

Bance, Peter (2009) *Sovereign, Squire and Rebel: Maharajah Duleep Singh*. London: Coronet House.

Bance P. Bhupinder Singh, Sukhbinder Singh Paul and Gurpreet Singh Anand (2008) *Khalsa Jatha British Isles 1908–2008*. London: The Central Gurdwara (Khalsa Jatha) London.

British Journal of Photography Annual (1895). London: Henry Greenwood & Co. Ltd.

The British Library (n.d.) Photographs Album details for Shelfmark Photo 127. Available at: www.bl.uk/catalogues/indiaofficeselect/PhotoShowDescs.asp?CollID=286 (accessed November 14, 2016).

Buck, Edward J. (1904) *Simla: Past and Present*. Calcutta: Messrs. Thacker, Pink and Co.

Colonial and Indian Exhibition 1886. Empire of India. Special Catalogue of Exhibits by the Government of India and Private Exhibitors (1886). London: William Clowes & Sons.

Dehejia, Vidya (2006) "Maharajas as Photographers." In Vidya Dehejia, (ed.), *India through the Lens: Photography 1840–1911*. Washington, DC: Freer Gallery of Art and Arthu M. Sackler Gallery, Smithsonian Institution, pp. 209–229.

Depelchin, Davy (2014) "Pioneering Photography in India: The Continuation of a Pictorial Tradition." In Rahaab Allana and Davy Depelchin, (eds.),*Unveiling India: The Early Lensmen 1850–1910*. New Delhi: Mapin Publishers and The Alkazi Collection of Photography, pp. 44–52.

Desmond, R. (1977) "19th Century Indian Photographers in India." *History of Photography* 1(4): 313–317.

Dewan, Deepali (2012) *Embellished Reality: Indian Painted Photographs*. Toronto: Royal Ontario Museum Press.

Evans, Andrew D. (2004) "Capturing Race: Anthropology and Photography in German and Austrian Prisoner-of-War Camps during World War I." In Eleanor M. Hight and Gary D. Sampson, (eds.), *Colonialist Photography: Imag(in)ing Race and Place*. London and New York: Routledge, pp. 226–256.

Evans, Andrew D. (2010) *Anthropology at War: World War I and Science of Race in Germany*. Chicago, IL: University of Chicago Press.

Falconer, John (2004) "Craddock and Co., James." In John Hannavy, ed., *Encyclopedia of Nineteenth-Century Photography, Vol. 1*. London: Routledge, p. 343.

Falconer, John (1983) "Willoughby Wallace Hooper: 'A Craze about Photography'." *The Photographic Collector* 4(3):258–285.

Falconer, John (2002) "'A Pure Labor of Love': A Publishing History of the People of India." In Eleanor M. Hight and Gary D. Sampson, eds., *Colonialist Photography: Imag(in)ing Race and Place*. London and New York: Routledge, pp. 51–83.

Gazetteer of the Lahore District, 1916 (1916). Lahore: Superintendent Government Printing, Punjab.

Ghosh, Siddhartha (2014 [1988]) "Zenana Studio: Early Women Photographers of Bengal, from Taking Pictures: The Practice of Photography by Bengalis" (Translated by Debjani Sengupta). *Trans Asia Photography Review* 4(2). Available at: http://quod.lib.umich.edu/t/tap/7977573.0004.202/-zenana-studio-early-women-p hotographers-of-bengal?rgn=main;view=fulltext (accessed November 14, 2016).

Goswami, B.N. (1999) "Painting in the Panjab." In Susan Stronge, (ed.), *The Arts of the Sikh Kingdoms*. London: V&A Publications, pp. 93–113.

Grewal, Jagtej Kaur (2013) "Presentations of Kingship: Portraits in Princely Courts." *The Panjab Past and Present* 44(2): 83–90.

Grewal, Jagtej Kaur (2003) "Oil Painting in Punjab: Circa 1840 A.D. to Circa 1930 A. D." Unpublished thesis, Panjab University, Chandigarh.

Griffin, Lepel H. (1865) *The Panjab Chiefs: Historical and Biographical Notices of the Principal Families in the Territories under the Panjab Government*. Lahore: Chronicle Press.

Harris, Russel (2001) *Maharajas at the London Studios*. New Delhi: Roli Books.

Hasan, Musarrat (1998) *Painting in the Punjab Plains (1849–1949)*. Lahore: Ferozsons Ltd.

Holroyd, W.R.M. (1880) *Report on Popular Education in Punjab and its Dependencies, for the Year 1878–1879*. Lahore: Punjab Government Press.

Johnson, Robert Flynn (2003) *Reverie and Reality: Nineteenth Century Photographs of India from the Ehrenfeld Collection*. San Francisco, CA: Fine Arts Museum of San Francisco.

Johnson, William (1863) *The Oriental Races and Tribes, Residents and Visitors of Bombay. A Series of Photographs, with Letter-Press Descriptions, Vol. I*. London: W.J. Johnson and Bolton and Barnitt.

Johnson, William (1866) *The Oriental Races and Tribes, Residents and Visitors of Bombay. A Series of Photographs, with Letter-Press Descriptions, Vol. II*. London: W.J. Johnson.

Journal of the Anjuman-i-Punjab and Punjab University Intelligencer (1885), 5(1), January 7.

Khan, Omar (1997) "John Burke, Photo-Artist of the Raj." *History of Photography* 21 (3): 236–243.

Khan, Omar (2002) *From Kashmir to Kabul: The Photographs of John Burke and William Baker 1860–1900*. New Delhi: Mapin Publishing.

Kong, Lily (2001) "Religion and Technology: Refiguring Place, Space, Identity and Community." *Area* 33(4): 404–413.

Kumar, Pramod (2012) "Portrait of an Era." *The Tribune*, June 24.

Levin, Laura (2009) "The Performative Force of Photography." *Photography & Culture* 2(3): 327–336.

Login, Lady (1890) *Sir John Login and Duleep Singh*. London: W.H. Allen & Co.

Maclagan, E.D. (1891) *Census of India, 1891: The Punjab And Its Feudatories, Volume XX, Part 2*. Calcutta: Government of India Central Printing Office.

Maclean, Kama (2011) "The Portrait's Journey: The Image, Social Communication and Martyr-Making in Colonial India." *The Journal of Asian Studies* 70(4): 1051–1082.

Maclean, Kama (2016) "That Bhagat Singh Hat." *India Today*, March 30. Available: http://indiatoday.intoday.in/story/bhagat-singh-kama-maclean-a-revolutionary-histor y-of-interwar-india/1/631177.html (accessed December 10, 2016).

McKenzie, Ray (1987) "The Laboratory of Mankind: John McCosh and the Beginnings of Photography in British India." *History of Photography* 11(2): 109–118.

Madra, Amandeep Singh, Parmjit Singh and Juga Singh (2011) *The Golden Temple of Amritsar: Reflections of the Past (1808–1959)*. London: Kashi House.

Mathur, Saloni (2007) *India by Design: Colonial History and Cultural Display*. Berkeley and Los Angeles: University of California Press.

Nihang, Nidar Singh and Parmjit Singh (2008) *In the Master's Presence: The Sikhs of Hazoor Sahib, Vol. 1: History*. London: Kashi House.

Ollman, Arthur (1983) *Samuel Bourne: Images of India*. Carmel, CA: The Friends of Photography.

Omissi, David E. (2012) "Sikh Soldiers in Europe during the First World War, 1914–1918." In Knut A. Jacobsen and Kristina Myrvold, (eds.), *Sikhs across Borders: Transnational Practices of European Sikhs*. London: Bloomsbury, pp. 36–50.

Pandhi, Nikhil (2015) "Do You Feel Jealous, Old Girl? Personal Histories and Postcards from Burma." Scroll.in. Available at: http://scroll.in/article/720691/do-you-feel-jealou s-old-girl-personal-histories-and-postcards-from-burma (accessed November 14, 2016).

Papers Relating to Technical Education in India, 1886–1904 (1906). Calcutta: The Superintendent of Government Printing.

Patel, Divia (1999) "Photography and the Romance of the Panjab." In Susan Stronge, (ed.), *The Arts of the Sikh Kingdoms*. London: V&A Publications, pp. 193–207.

Peliti Associati (1993) *Federico Peliti (1844–1914): An Italian Photographer in India at the Time of Queen Victoria*. Manchester: Cornerhouse Publications.

Perrill, Jeffrey Price (1976) "Punjab Orientalism: The Anjuman-i-Punjab and Punjab University, 1865–1888." Unpublished doctoral thesis, University of Missouri, Columbia.

Petrulis, Alan (2006–2016) "D-Publishers," metropostcard.com. Available at: www. metropostcard.com/publishersd.html (accessed November 14, 2016).

Pinney, Christopher (1997) *Camera Indica: The Social Life of Indian Photographs*. Chicago, IL: The University of Chicago Press.

Pinney, Christopher (2004) *Photos of the Gods: The Printed Image and Political Struggle in India*. London: Reaktion Books.

Pinney, Christopher (2008) *The Coming of Photography in India*. London: The British Library.

Pinney, Christopher (2013a) "Stirred by Photography." In Christopher Pinney, Beth Citron and Rahaab Allana, eds., *Allegory and Illusion: Early Portrait Photograph from South Asia*. Ahmedabad: Mapin Publishing, pp. 12–29.

Pinney, Christoper (2013b) "What's Photography Got to Do with It?" In Ali Behdad and Luke Gartlan, (eds.), *Photography's Orientalism: New Essays on Colonial Representation*. Los Angeles, CA: Getty Research Institute, pp. 33–52.

Pinney, Christopher (2015) "Civil Contract of Photography in India." *Comparative Studies of South Asia, Africa, and the Middle East* 35(1): 21–34.

Press lists of old records in the Punjab Civil Secretariat, Vol. XVIII: From 1859 to 1863 General Department (1926). Lahore: Superintendent Government Printing Punjab.

Report on the Administration of the Punjab and Its Dependencies for 1893–1894 (1894). Lahore: Punjab Government Press.

Report on the Department of Industries, Punjab, for the Year ending 31st March 1921 (1921). Lahore: Superintendent Government Printing.

Report on the Progress of Education in the Punjab during the Quinquennium ending 1916–1917 (1917). Available at: http://dli.ernet.in/handle/2015/102016 (accessed November 14, 2016).

Roberts, Hilary (2016) "Photography." *1914–1918-online: International Encyclopedia of the First World War.* Available at: http://encyclopedia.1914-1918-online.net/article/p hotography (accessed November 14, 2016).

Rose, H.A. (1902) *Census of India, 1901. Imperial Tables, I-VII, X-XV, XVII and XVII for the Punjab, with the Native States under the Political Control of the Punjab Government, and for the North-West Frontier Province.* Simla: Provincial Superintendent of Census Operations.

Roy, Franziska, Heike Liebau and Ravi Ahuja (2011) *'When the War Began We Heard of Several Kings': South Asian Prisoners in World War I Germany.* New Delhi: Social Science Press.

Sadan, Mandy (2014) "The Historical Visual Economy of Photography in Burma." *Bijdragen tot de taal-, land- en volkenkunde* 170: 281–312.

Saini, Neha (2015) "Duleep Singh's Descendants for Memorial to Him in City." *The Tribune,* March 10.

Sampson, Gary D. (2006) "Photographer of the Picturesque: Samuel Bourne." In Vidya Dehejiua, (ed.), *India through the Lens: Photography 1840–1911.* Washington, DC: Freer Gallery of Art and Arthu M. Sackler Gallery, Smithsonian Institution, pp. 163–175.

Sauli, Arnaud (2006) "Circulation and Authority: Police, Public Space and Territorial Control in the Punjab, 1861–1920." In Claude Markovits, Jacques Pouchepadass and Sanjay Subrahmanyam, eds., *Society and Circulation: Mobile People and Itinerant Cultures in South Asia.* London, New York, Delhi: Anthem Press, pp. 215–239.

Sethi, Chitleen K. (2015) "A Sikh Pilgrim's Chronicle of Gurdwaras across the Nation in the 1930s." *Hindustan Times,* August 20.

Sharma, Brij Bhushan (1989) "Fred Bremner's Indian Years." *History of Photography* 13(4): 293–301.

Sharma, Brij Bhushan (1988) "Artist and Photography: Some Indian Encounters." *History of Photography* 12(3): 247–258.

Sher-Gil Sundaram Arts Foundation (n.d.) "Umrao Singh Sher-Gil (1870–1954)." Available at: www.ssaf.in/thegrant.html (accessed November 14, 2016).

Singh, Parmjit (2012) "Celebrating Sikh Women." Sikh Culture GT1588, March 13. Available at: http://gt1588.com/celebrating-sikh-women/ (accessed November 14, 2016).

Sinha, Gayatri (2006) "Women Artists in India: Practice and Patronage." In Deborah Cherry and Janice Helland, eds., *Local/Global: Women Artists in the Nineteenth Century.* Aldershot: Ashgate, pp. 59–76.

Srivastava, R.P. (1983) *Punjab Painting: A Study in Art and Culture.* New Delhi: Abhinav Publications.

Stanley, Peter (n.d.) "Photographs." *Anzacs & Indians on Gallipoli.* Available at: www.indiansongallipoli.com/sources/photographs/ (accessed November 14, 2016).

Statistical Abstract related to British India (1908). Vol. 42.

Steinbach, Henry (1846) *The Punjaub: Being a Brief Account of the Country of the Sikhs.* London: Smith, Elder and Co.

Streets, Heather (2004) *Martial Races: The Military, Race and Masculinity in British Imperial Culture, 1857–1914.* Manchester and New York: Manchester University Press.

Talbot, Ian, and Shinder Thandi, (eds.) (2004) *People on the Move: Punjabi Colonial and Post-colonial Migration.* Karachi: Oxford University Press.

Taylor, Helen B. (1878) "Art and Science Notices." *The Woman's Gazette; or, News about Work*, January to December. London: Hatchards.

Thacker's Indian Directory (all annual directories between 1863 and 1920). Calcutta: Thacker, Spink and Co. Retrieved from the British Library, London.

The Last Empire: Photography in British India, 1855–1911 (1976). New York: Aperture Inc.

Thomas, G. (1979) "The First Four Decades of Photography in India." *History of Photography* 3(3): 215–226.

Victoria and Albert Museum (2016) "The Costumes and People of India." Available at: http://collections.vam.ac.uk/item/O72319/the-costumes-and-people-of-photographs-w-w-hooper/ (accessed November 14, 2016).

von Eickstedt, Egon (1920/21) "Rassenelemente der Sikh: Mit einem Anhang über biometrische Methoden." *Zeitschrift für Ethnologie* 52/53: 317–394.

Walker, G.C. (1894) *Gazetteer of the Lahore District, 1893–1894.* Lahore: Civil and Military Gazette Press.

Watson, J. Forbes and John William Kay (1868–1875) *The People of India: A Series of Photographic Illustrations, with Descriptive Letterpress of the Races and Tribes of Hindustan, Originally Prepared under the Authority of the Government of India, and Reproduced by the Order of the Secretary of State for India in Council.* London: India Museum.

Welch, Stuart Cary (1985) *India: Art and Culture 1300–1900.* New York: The Metropolitan Museum of Art.

Whitehall, Greame (2014) "The Import(ance) of History and Modernity: Home; Parish, and Imperial Order in the Photographic Representation of Simla 1860–1920." Unpublished doctoral thesis, University of the West of England, Bristol.

4 From the great goddess to everywoman

Western naturalism and the Durga *murti* in West Bengal

Moumita Sen

A wide-eyed goddess with ten arms, bright yellow in color, flanked by her children on both sides, with a white horse-like lion at her feet lightly biting the arm of a sap-green colored "demon"—this was the traditional Durga *murti* (image) in the early twentieth century in Bengal. The traditional caste-based craftsmen of Bengal—*Sutradhar*s (carpenters), *Patua*s (scroll-painters) and *Kumbhakar*s (pot-makers)—modeled the goddess's face in the shape of a betel leaf, her eyes like bamboo leaves, a hooked nose like the beak of a parrot, and a small red mouth. From the nineteenth century, however, there was a growing taste for Western objects and styles among the native elite. With colonial patronage and the institution of colonial art academies in Calcutta, traditional craftsmen received education in Western art (particularly naturalism) and some of them even traveled to parts of Europe to demonstrate their craft in the great colonial exhibitions and learn classical sculpture in European academies. The education and enthusiasm in Western naturalism soon began to affect the making of god images all over Bengal.

In the 1940s, Gopeshwar Pal, a young clay-modeler from Ghurni (West Bengal)[1] began to experiment with the form of the traditional Durga image. Pal had trained with his uncles and brothers in the traditional workshop or *karkhana* system[2] of the Kumbhakars of Bengal. However, after being noticed by a British general in a village, he found an opportunity to demonstrate his skill in the British Empire exhibition at Wembley in 1924 and subsequently studied sculpture at an Italian art academy. He applied the principles of naturalism to create a more lifelike Durga. For the first time, the sculptor brought to life the scene of the fight between Mahishasura and Durga in the goddess image of Bengal.[3] Other artists praised his work by saying that his representation of the goddess is a picture of a real, living woman, like a mother, sister or wife. Following this intervention, the Durga image has been experimented with in several ways, particularly in contemporary Bengal. This chapter locates the shift from the traditional Durga to Gopeshwar Pal's Durga, which came to be known as "*Art'er Durga*" ("Art Durga" or "Artistic Durga").

When Gopeshwar Pal created his image, there were reactions from the middle-class Bengali society deriding it as a "Western *memsahib*[4] Durga" who is used more for satire than *bhakti*.[5] However, 75 years later in contemporary

Durga *puja*, spectacular goddesses appear in theme *pandal*s as "African," "Mexican," or as a character in the Hollywood film *Avatar* (2009). Often, the Bengali Brahmin priests do not accept them, but demand a small, "traditional," more "natural" looking Durga for the ritual treatment. Interestingly, these natural looking mass-produced small *murti*s that are used for religious worship today take after Gopeshwar Pal's Durga. I argue that the mixture of pre-colonial image-making technologies and Western naturalism created a hybrid form for the Durga image in the 1940s, which was eventually "naturalized" in popular perception. In other words, the colonial visual regime, especially naturalism, affected the native imagination so extensively that images which were once considered too Western for a devotional icon became the most readily acceptable and "natural" form of the goddess in Bengal.

One of the etymological roots of the term "technology" is the ancient Greek *techne* (τέχνη) which related to making and doing things, and to art and craft. The dominant contemporary understanding of technology is related to a "scientific" way of doing things, whereas the idea of *techne* pertains to ways of making and doing things[6] in a context not specific to modern science. The chapter approaches the techniques of clay-modelling in the sense of *techne* and then shows how they negotiated the visual technologies of the west and created remarkable changes in the visual worlds of postcolonial West Bengal. These changes are examined by focusing on the most popular Hindu goddess of the region at the present: the body of goddess Durga, Mahishasura and her *vahana* (mount), the lion.

The chapter is based on my ethnographic study of the clay-modelers of West Bengal conducted between 2010 and 2016 (Sen, 2016). The study focused on three sites of making at Kumortuli and Kalighat in Kolkata and Krishnanagar in Nadia, and the respondents belonged to the *Kumbhakar* (pot-maker) and the *Patua* (scroll-painter) castes. Several of them were middle-class, art academy-trained, and well-respected visual artists, while some were struggling for livelihood or status. I refer to their forefathers, who were important clay-modelers from these areas in Bengal, in order to show how the image of the goddess transformed in their hands around the mid-twentieth century. The chapter is based on ethnographic data, historical accounts, and a Bengali scriptural text. In addition, the oral narratives from my respondents have been used to point out how they interpret their own tradition.

I will first introduce the festival of publicly worshipping Durga in Bengal and then continue with a discussion on the contradiction in the two technical manuals used by the clay-modelers: one is provided by their caste-masters, the Brahmins, and the other is provided by their colonial masters. Then, I will show how the changes in the appearance of the goddess illustrate the hybridization of "ways of making" from the Sanskrit manual texts or *Shilpasutra*s and naturalism, a Western visual technology. My main objective is to show how a craft which is rooted in a traditional knowledge system (which I have understood as *techne* in this piece) has been changing since the twentieth century in a remarkable way. One of the major catalysts of this change has been the introduction of naturalism in the colony. This chapter traces the first change from the traditional image to the "naturalistic" image and its implications. While this image was loved by many, it was contemporaneously considered somewhat contentious by Bengali Brahmin priests. In the final section, I show this contentious naturalistic image is transformed into the "natural" and the most acceptable image of the goddess in contemporary Bengal. I will show how an image which was once considered far too "Western" by the priestly classes became normalized in relation to other creative even provocative images in contemporary Bengal.

The Durga *Puja* of Bengal

The history of the public festival forms the context in which the goddess images, or *murtis*, are commissioned, worshipped, gazed at, photographed, fetishized, sometimes vandalized and finally discarded or immersed. The anthropomorphic form of the goddess, which has been used since the mid-eighteenth century, has a longer history than her public worship, which only began in the twentieth century (Guha-Thakurta, 2015: 39–70, McDermott, 2011). The beginning of the worship of the anthropomorphic Durga of Bengal has been ascribed to the kings and landlords of Bengal such as Raja Kangshanarayan of Tahirpur, Raja Lakshmikanta Majumdar of the Sabarna Raoychoudhuri family of seventeenth century and Raja Krishnachandra in the eighteenth century (Guha-Thakurta, 2015: 161–162). Before the practice of making anthropomorphic models, Durga used to be worshipped in the form of *patachitra*, which was a painted image (Guha-Thakurta 2015: 161), and a *kumbha* (pot) which was called *ghatey-patey puja* (McDermott, 2011: 105–106).[7] In the nineteenth century, in addition to the continuation of the private elite *pujas*, a new form of organizational structure for worship emerged that was known as the *barowari puja*, when five to six Brahmins would get together, raise a subscription, build a shed, construct an idol, invite singers, and worship the goddess. The nineteenth century was the heyday of the *barowari* festivals, which were not entirely public even though anthropometric, temporary images were being made for these "sheds." It was only in the twentieth century with the establishment of *sarbajanin puja* that the festival culture became public and the goddess traveled from the parlor to the streets. Both Tapati Guha-Thakurta and Rachel McDermott argue that the transformation of the *barowari puja* into the *sarbajanin puja* was related to the communal relations between Hindus and Muslims, the maturing of a new *bhadralok* public sphere and nationalist politics among the elite of Calcutta (Guha-Thakurta, 2015: 94; McDermott, 2011: 60–64). The *sarbajanin pujas* of the early twentieth century introduced a new organizational structure of the worship. Youth clubs or civic organizations of mainly male members represented different neighborhoods of Calcutta. These youth clubs collected subscriptions from the residents of the neighborhood which they represented in order to finance the *murtis*, the *pandal* (the temporary marquee in which

Figure 4.1 An example of a theme Durga *puja*, Rupchand Mukherjee Lane Kolkata 2013

the goddess is worshipped), and other related expenses. *Murti*s were commissioned from *Patua*s (scroll-painters) and *Kumbhakar*s (pot-makers) (Banerjee, 1989: 133).

There have since then been significant changes in the scale and format of the *sarbajanin puja* in West Bengal. At least from the 1980s in Calcutta, spectacular *pandal*s were being constructed from cloth, and then decorated with lights. The monopoly of the large, spectacular, many-turreted cloth *pandal*s and the traditional *pandal*-makers was broken by a breed of designers and visual artists who began to create art-like installations as the *pandal* around the 2000s. This new format, popularly called "theme *puja*," became the most attractive format for the festival revellers (see Figure 4.1). However, this is not to suggest that the aristocratic *puja*s are no longer performed. The zamindari *puja*s still hold their own importance because of their long tradition, authenticity and aristocracy as opposed to the so-called "kitschy" theme *puja*s. For example, in the traditional Jagatdhatri *puja* of a small town in Hooghly district called Shantipur, the local landlord (*zamindar*) family still brings their patronized drum-players (*dhaki*s) and fly hot-air balloons (*fanush*) in a parade, marking their erstwhile status and aristocracy on the day of the immersion, as the local people gather on two sides of the street. But the spectacle of LED light dioramas, gigantic *murti*s, big budgets and the crowds of the Jagatdhatri *puja* of the neighboring town of Chandannagar in the same district far outshines the pomp of aristocracy in Shantipur. As the organization of *puja*s shifted from the aristocracy to the middle class, the technologies also changed in order to capture the popular taste. The drums gave way to the cassette and then CD players with powerful loudspeakers. The lamps and hot-air balloons gave way to bulbs and then elaborate light displays. Alongside traditional material like clay, cloth and wood, new materials such as thermocol, fiberglass, plastic, among other things cheap packaging material, are now used in creative ways. The *murti* of the goddess has altered along with the changing technology of the various components in the larger structure of the festival culture.

Between Sanskrit and English: the manual texts

While there is significant disagreement on the subject (see e.g. Robinson, 1983),[8] both P. C. Ghosha (1871) and K.M. Varma (1970) have argued for the relevance of the *Shastra*s in the craft of clay-modelling. My study suggests that it is not possible to assert that there is no influence of guidelines from Brahmanical texts even in the contemporary field. Alongside influences from folk and high Art, it is not implausible to argue that during the early twentieth century in Bengal, at least two types of technical knowledge were available to a clay-modeler. The first is influenced by manual texts from the *Shastra*s which tells the image-maker how to make a *murti* fit for consecration. The second is derived from Western naturalism. These were general principles of naturalistic representation in European visual art, a body of knowledge informed by enlightenment values of science and reason.

Let me begin with the first kind of technical knowledge. In the 1970s, K.M. Varma compiled the techniques of clay-modelling from a set of Agama texts, namely *Kashyapashilpa* (12th century CE), *Vimanarchanakalpa* (8th century CE), *Kashyapagyanakanda* (16th century CE) and *Atrisamhita* (17th century CE) (Varma, 1970) and compared them to contemporaneous practices of making among clay-modelers of Bengal. Varma compellingly shows parallels between the theory and the contemporaneous practice. He explains in minute detail the material and the technique for building an image that is fit for consecration. Prior to Varma, Pratap Chandra Ghosha's account (1871) of the Durga *puja* of Bengal gives us a list of the duties of the artisan who makes the image. He also elaborates on the material, technique and the time (as per the lunar calendar) when these procedures must be carried out in order to make a ritually correct image. But Ghosha's artisan was part of a semi-feudal social order where he made one image for each festival in lieu of rent-free land from his *jajman* (patron) (Ghosha, 1871: 3). In contemporary West Bengal, the clay-modelling industry is a free market in the informal sector where business-minded men try to maximize profit in every way possible. Therefore, it is not feasible for the clay-modelers to observe the rules their forefathers followed.

Now, let me come to the second set of rules. Naturalism has been understood as one of the most important aspects of the regime of visuality that went hand in hand with colonization and imperial values. Ernst Gombrich has pointed to the capacities of naturalism as "the technological aspect of art" (quoted in Mitter, 1994: 7). The art educators in the colonial academies not only privileged the scientific and technological superiority of perspectivalism and naturalism, they did so by denigrating native forms as "incorrect" or "unscientific" (Mitter, 1994: 7, 32–33). However, naturalism was also appropriated by the nationalists and proto-nationalists – a process Kajri Jain has called "reterritorialization" (Jain, 2007: 246–249). The allure of this picture-form has been used as a means to fascinate, capture and mobilize people both by colonizers, native elite, bazaar painters and nationalists (see Pinney, 2002). One of the major interventions in the history of clay-modelling in West Bengal is the influence, or "infiltration," to quote one of my respondents (interview with Debdulal Pal, Krishnanagar, 2012), of Western art forms such as naturalism and illusionism, broadly understood as Western Academic Realism. This form heavily influenced the native elite with its power to show reality *as it is*. The larger history of Indian art shows how the encounter with European art forms such as illusionism, realism and naturalism led to dramatic changes under the spell of the real. It is not clear if these art forms charmed the non-Western forms of visuality simply by their power of showing life *as it is*, or if they were enforced by economic and political forces of imperialism[9]— or both. Be that as it may, the history of clay-modelling is very closely linked to the coming of Western visual forms to the colony (see Sen, 2016). The intervention of Gopeshwar Pal, the first clay-modeler to study sculpture in Italy, is understood as a turning point for this craft. Subsequently, others who formally trained with him or followed him changed the traditional image of the goddess to a more realistic or human-like form.

The body of the goddess, although molded by the clay-modelers, was always at the mercy of the elites, whether it was the taste of the patrons or Brahmanical rules. The clay-modelling industry produced images to cater to the demands of various patrons and not according to their free creative will. The shift in imagery I am concerned with is not only a result of the encounter between traditional rules of image-making with other image-worlds, particularly that of naturalism, it is also intimately related to the changing taste among the elites in colonial and postcolonial India. In the words of Partha Mitter: "When European naturalism replaced traditional aesthetics in the last [twentieth] century, the English-educated [native elites] accepted Renaissance naturalism as the acme of perfection" (Mitter, 1994:10).

The law of the gods and the contemporary clay-modeler

As per Varma's argument, the traditional technical knowledge system of the clay-modelers of Bengal is based on the *Shilpasutra* texts (Varma, 1970). These texts state the anthropometry, iconography, and methods for constructing a *murti* which is fit for the consecration. But as we observe in traditional and folk arts all over South Asia, the demands of the modern market have created several changes in their production (Singh, 1996; Bundgaard, 1999; Hauser, 2002). So, in the throes of modernity, do the clay-modelers still follow these scriptural guidelines? Do they even know of these? Is the body of the goddess still created along the scriptural lines? In this section, I will show how certain rules for making *murti*s are still present in contemporary practice while others are broken in the interest of the business.

Let us begin with a simple question: do the practitioners know about the *Shastra*s? I quote a conversation with a painter and clay-modeler from the *Patua* community, Bhaskar Chitrakar, regarding the technical manuals. I began by asking him about what he knows about the role of *Shastra*s and if it was evoked when he started training with his father and grandfather as a child. To this he said:

BC: This I don't know of. Maybe the older men who have more experience might be able to tell you about the *Shastra*s. I know nothing of it. You could ask my father – maybe he knows something. I feel like I don't know many details of the books. I am doing the work – but I don't know many things.

MS: From what I have read, it seems that the *kathamo* works like a skeleton.

BC: That's true – the *kathamo* is like a skeleton.

MS: The book says that the clay is like flesh. The ropes are like nerves and the color is like life.

BC: (Thinks) This is true – the rope is like nerve – it runs all over the body. And we call clay flesh.

MS: In the book, it says that there are seven kinds of substances used for the *murti* and they correspond to the material of the human body respectively.

BC: That is a wonderful idea! It's good I learnt about this.

Clearly Chitrakar did not know of these books but the ideas immediately resonated with him. But as a creative practitioner, he immediately grasped the metaphorical nuance of the *Shilpasutras*. What is obvious is that Bhaskar, like several other clay-modelers I have spoken to, does not claim to know anything about these books. Bhaskar Chitrakar's father could not tell me anything about the *Shastra*s either. Chitrakar's ascription of traditional wisdom to the older men or the ancients of the community is telling. The clay-modelers by no means learn the craft by reading the 'holy books;' a sizeable part of my respondents did not finish secondary school. They train at home with their fathers, brothers, uncles and grandfathers. These rules, if at all, are part of the traditional training they receive from their male family members at home. Therefore, we must complicate what constitutes "knowing the books" in order to understand the influence of the Brahmanical texts on their traditional knowledge. In other words, we need to observe practice in order understand the place of theory in this craft.

The ritual procedure to create an image fit for consecration is as follows: The entire body of the goddess is measured out in precise terms and the basic unit of measurement is the finger of the maker in this "*Talamana* system" (Varma, 1970). In addition, the *Sri Sri Chandi*, a vernacular version of *Devi*

Mahatmya spells out in metaphorical terms the appearance of the goddess (Jagadishwarananda, 1976: 384–394). This text, referred to as "Chandi" by my respondents, came up in my interviews with organizers, priests and clay-modelers as the correct manual for the ritual treatment of Durga. In the chapter entitled "*Murti Rahashya*" (The secret of *murti*), the text details the iconographic features of the different avatars of goddesses, along with descriptions such as: "The goddess has hair like the river, eyes like flames, high breasts and she sits on a lotus" (Jagadishwarananda, 1976:386). There descriptions are consequently interpreted as rules for the production of the images. Later in the chapter, we will see how some of the most important clay-modelers used to inscribe lines from "*Sri Sri Chandi*" at the base of their Durga *murti*.

In addition, there is a detailed list of material and its ritual significance in K.M. Varma's account of clay-modelling (1970). Each of the seven materials used for image-making has a metaphorical relationship to the living human body. The clay stands for flesh, the ropes for nerves, the armature for the skeleton, cloth for skin, chalk-glue for blood, and color for life, and so on. A closer look at the practice of contemporary clay-modelers, gives us a clue about the relevance of *Shastric* knowledge to the method. As I mentioned, in the metaphorical system in the *Shilpasutras*, clay symbolizes flesh (Varma, 1970: 7). In contemporary sites in Kolkata, two kinds of clay-dough of different consistencies are referred to as "*harer mati*" (clay of the bones) and "*mangsher mati*"(clay of the flesh). For larger images of the goddess, a very fine cloth is applied on the arms to consolidate the structure, which in the *sutras* signifies skin (Varma, 1970: 7).

Alongside some such similarities, we also find several changes in ritual gestures and the lack of adherence to ritual guidelines which demonstrate the way the clay-modelers negotiate the tradition of the craft and its modern demands. For example, the agamic texts prioritize the use of unfired clay for the goddess image. This is because it contains life in terms of earth and water; firing kills this life, attracting divine wrath in the form of fire (Bean, 2011: 607–608). However, firing the *murti*s is a common practice in the clay-modelling communities. The high demand for images forces the clay-modelers to work on *murti*s till the last minute before delivery. And this means they must fire the *murti*s to dry them before they paint, attach hair, and drape clothing on it. The other reason is the scale of *murti*s. Large *murti*s – taller than 10 or 15 feet – do not dry adequately in the sun. For primarily these two reasons, the clay-modelers use hand-torches to fire the *murti* (see Figure 4.2).

In these sites, the practice of unfired clay-modelling among the Kumbhakar community has changed in several ways, and it is constantly shifting according to changes in patronage. If there were influences of the Shastras in the traditional knowledge system of the clay-modelers remains an open question. In some cases, we see the persistence of practices while in other cases we see clear divergences. It is certain, however, that the craft has changed drastically and the adherence to the Brahmanical rules is on the decline. In my study, the

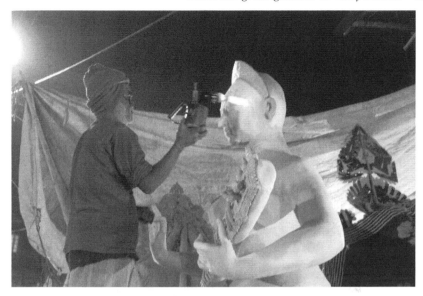

Figure 4.2 A clay-modeler drying a Sarasvati murti with a torch on the eve of Sarasvati puja, Kumortuli 2014

shift in patronage from *jajmani* system to the contemporary uncontrolled market appeared to be the fundamental factor behind this change.

The great goddess of the holy books

In the following sections, I will focus on the changing appearance of the goddess from an aesthetic perspective. In my study, it was quite clear that contemporary clay-modelers no longer observe a standardized anthropometry. The oeuvre of the modern clay-modeler – in terms of method, material and style – is a rich, complex, hybrid space. Let me lay out the types of Durga images that are commonly used by makers and patrons in the marketplace. Nimai Chandra Pal, one of the most respected, so-called "old school" makers, says that there are four kinds of Durga *murti: debi murti, putul murti,* oriental *murti* and modern *murti* (interview, Nimai Pal, 2015).

In order to understand the number of styles that contemporary claymodelers work with, let me briefly describe the oriental and modern murti. The oriental murti borrows from the style of the relief sculptures of Ajanta and Ellora. Broadly, it is closer to the pre-modern traditions of Indian sculpture with highly stylized, twisted bodies. This type of Durga was in vogue in the 1950s, echoing the revivalist Bengal Art School movement. This kind of Durga with more dynamic postures, was not fully clothed (Agnihotri, 2001: 84). Typically, Durga was pictured as a Yakshi or a feminine version of Shiva with loose, matted hair with dreadlocks, bare breasts, a skirt of tiger hide and decorations all over her body in the form of snakes or climbers. Shrish Pal of

Kalighat specialized in recreating the images of Abanindranath Tagore and Nandalal Bose, artists of the Bengal school, in his Durga images (Guha-Thakurta, 2015: 165). On the one hand, it reflected the nationalist revivalist movement in the visual arts of the time, returning to the pre-modern Indian forms. But on the other hand, it attracted the ire of the traditionalist conservatives who critiqued the uncovering of Durga's body as essentially Westernized, sexualized and incommensurate with Bengali values (Agnihotri, 2001: 85). However, the entire *murti* was made of clay and the hand-molded hair, dress, and ornamentation took more time and labor, driving up the cost of production. This economic factor also resulted in the eventual drop from popularity of this style.

The modern *murti* is an umbrella term employed to encompass the large variety of styles which are innovated routinely every year in the zest for novelty, spectacle, even gimmickry in the field of contemporary Durga *puja* in Kolkata. The theme *puja*s which started roughly in 2002 followed earlier traditions of making *pandal*s and *pratima*s in novel material like nails, iron, dried chilies, and plastic bottles, and so on. The theme *puja*s effectively intervened in the Durga *puja* scene to create a more artistic visual language with the use of folk art and crafts under a new group of professionals who did not emerge from artisanal backgrounds but were designers, artists and other visual art practitioners from media and film industry (see Guha-Thakurta, 2015). It is impossible to enumerate with any detail the plethora of styles that the "modern *murti*" signifies. But the idea of themes and this drive towards novelty, spectacle and gimmickry is inextricably tied to the neo-liberalization of Indian economy and the influx of advertising imagery and consumerism in popular culture since the 1990s. The commodification of Durga *puja* has been highly debated in both print and electronic media (see Guha-Thakurta, 2015). The attraction of advertising revenue and awards lies at the heart of this drive towards finding a new startling image of the goddess annually. McDermott effectively quotes Arjun Appadurai to bring out the connection between the viral growth of novel imagery and neo-liberalism: "The much vaunted feature of modern consumption – namely, the search for novelty—is only a symptom of a deeper discipline of consumption in which desire is organized around the aesthetics of ephemerality" (McDermott, 2011: 141).

Let me now focus on the *debi murti* (also known as the "Bangla *murti*") in relation to the *putul murti* (literally, "doll *murti*") to discuss the significant shift in the 1940s which rendered the great goddess as the lifelike everywoman in the popular discourse of the time. The *debi murti*, roughly speaking, is the goddess from the pages of *Chandi*, whose skin is yellow as the sunflowers. Nimai Pal is one of the last few clay-modelers of Bengal who specializes in the making of the *debi murti*. He laments that those who are still making this image do not follow the correct procedures which are labor-intensive, time-consuming and tedious. "To create a goddess who will inspire real bhakti," he says, "you need to learn so much ... small details ... and you need to be patient. These days, young boys don't want to learn the old art – the real art. They only want to make a quick buck. So their Durgas are wrong and fast, like fast food" (interview, Nimai Pal, 2015).

The most "traditional" image we know of from photographic sources and paintings in the nineteenth century are closer to what is now called *debi murti*, or the "Bangla" *murti*. With large eyes like the leaves of bamboo plant, face like a betel leaf, nose like a bird's beak, a small mouth and a vacant gaze called "*shunyo drishti*" (vacant gaze) so the goddess could return the gaze of the devotee. The gaze of this type of *murti* extended till the *naat-mandir* (the outhouse of the temple) which was the limit of visibility of the icon for the devotee in Hindu temple architecture (Agnihotri, 2001: 82).

The *debi murti* is an image of power, grace and peace. The killing of Mahishasura, therefore, is not performed in the tableaux. The *asura* rests, demolished and fallen, at the feet of the goddess. In the traditional image, Mahishasura was painted sap-green. The story of the lion and the *asura* is crucial to my analysis (see Figure 4.3). The lion here does not really resemble the animal. It has an elongated arched back almost like a dog, its face resembles that of a *hilsa* fish, according to some (Agnihotri, 2001: 80), and its snout had a painted thin, twirled moustache like humans in *pata* or scroll paintings. An interesting idea I have heard among several respondents is that since the lion is not a native animal to Bengal, this idea of the lion springs from the creative imagination of the artisans. In that sense, it becomes a composite animal which borrowed features from aquatic animals such as a *makara* (mythical crocodile-like animal) or *hilsa*, a fish commonly known in Bengal, a horse, and a dog. I will soon return to this image of the lion and the *asura*.

Figure 4.3 Archival undated image of Durga, ascribed to 1920s, Satyen Mandal's collection, Krishnanagar

Figure 4.4 Durga *murti* at Baghbazar Sarbajonin Club, Kolkata, 2013

This *murti* (see Figure 4.4) is still considered to be the most authentic, tra-ditional representation of the goddess. It is quite naturally assumed by the devotees and revellers during the festival that this icon truly inspires *bhakti* (devotion). It is also common among the older generation or the elites to have a marked disdain for the new styles of Durga. They would only take the pains to travel across the crowded festival city to gaze at and pray to the looming *debi murti* of Baghbazar Club in North Kolkata. However, the different ver-sions of *debi murti* in the contemporary city vary from the archival images of the nineteenth century *murti* (see Figure 4.3). The face of the goddess has become more rounded with time. But the most crucial difference in the figure is the lion and the *asura* (see Figure 4.4).[10] In the next section, I demonstrate the difference between these two images. In addition, I talk about the attempts of clay-modelers to bring alive the drama of the battle in the majestic, awe-inspiring but static icon that is the *debi murti*.

From great goddess to everywoman

In the mid-twentieth century in Calcutta, we encounter a generation of East Bengali clay-modelers who thought of vitality and life in an image not simply

Figure 4.5 Debi murti (left) and *putul murti* (right), Kumortuli, 2012

in theological terms of consecration, but in aesthetic terms. They wanted to show and to bring alive the static icon. They wanted to make the image perform the drama of the battle with the dynamic, valiant human body of the goddess, the rage of the lion and the fallen, anguished body of the powerful *asura*. For this, they applied principles of naturalism to the body of the goddess. This type of *murti*, also called *"Arter murti"* (Art image), refers to the naturalistic Durga *murti* which came about in the 1930s, changing the format of the tableau and the body of the goddess in a decisive manner. This shift has been ascribed to two stalwarts of the clay-modelling community, Gopeshwar Pal and Ramesh Pal, both of whom were educated in Italian art academies and practiced painting, sculpting and clay-modelling simultaneously. Between 1930s and 1970s, these two artists conceptualized the body of the goddess, the iconography, the balance, the style, the color, and the space occupied by the tableau. Anita Agnihotri argues that all contemporary Durgas are either copies or variants of the naturalistic Durga that was conceived between the career spans of these two artists (Agnihotri, 2001: 89–90).

> The artist was looking for inspiration and in a flash of genius; he gathered his straw, wood, bamboo, ropes and clay. And with the final strokes of his brush, he created a goddess who was also our mother, sister or the girl next door.
>
> (Das, 1998: 68)

Popular opinion, media reportage and historical accounts reflect the claim that the naturalistic Durga truly reflected the coming of the goddess from her abode in the Himalayas to our earth, her paternal home, in the form of everywoman (See Das, 1998; Agnihotri, 2001). They also pointed out that Western naturalism found a lyrical marriage with traditional clay-modelling in the work of Gopeshwar Pal. Despite the rhetoric around the representation of Durga as "everywoman," the actual *murti*s were far from being strictly naturalistic. G. Pal mixed pink with the chrome yellow hue of the goddess's skin to create a more lifelike appearance. The eyes of the goddess were still rather large in comparison to "correct" human anatomy and her face was meant to reflect a kind of other-worldliness, even though she looked closer to a real woman in these *murti*s. G. Pal's *murti*s sharply intervened with the *debi murti* of the time in two ways. Firstly, he took the rather staccato, frozen form of the tableau and brought out the inherent drama of the situation. What he essentially showed was a mono-scenic narrative where Durga is represented at the very moment where she kills the *asura* by piercing his chest with her trident. Tapati Guha-Thakurta likens him to the celebrated nineteenth century painter Ravi Varma such:

> Like his far more celebrated predecessor, the painter Ravi Varma, he also became the conduit through whom the skills of Academic realism entered and dramatically transformed the world of popular devotional iconography, except that he never acquired anything akin to Ravi Varma's artistic stature or nation-wide fame.
>
> (Guha-Thakurta, 2015: 167)

G. Pal had left out Durga's children as he sought to dramatize the battle-scene as a mono-scenic narrative. However, the priests of the time and the public in general were reluctant to accept the individuation of Durga. Ramesh Pal, armed with his technical sophistry in sculpture from the Italian Academy of Fine Arts, found a way to incorporate all the children of Durga in the tableau that we still see in *pandal*s all over Bengal. The face of Ramesh Pal's Durga has been variously described in scholarly writing, media reportage and fiction in metaphorical terms to connote that it was the perfect coming together of the traditions of the East and the West to create a paradigm of feminine beauty and grace (Agnihotri, 2001: 90). While the body of the goddess has been understood to be a beautiful hybrid of Western naturalism and traditional clay-modelling, G. Pal and Ramesh Pal completely transformed the earlier forms of the lion and the *asura* in the *debi murti* format (see Figure 4.3).

In an interview with Ramesh Pal's son, several issues regarding this mixture of Western naturalism with traditional clay-modelling comes to fore. Prasanta Pal, Ramesh Pal's son, sets apart the modelling of divine *murti*s and "sculpture" in a crucial way. The making of Durga *murti*s, according to Prasanta Pal, has to do with ritual precepts of *Sri Sri Chandi* and the arousal of devotion in a beholder. It is not about novelty of theme or excellence of what he calls "new types of design." Inspiring *bhakti* appears to be the primary concern for Prasanta Pal even as he speaks for his father's work. He says,

> We worship her [Durga] even though we cannot see her in reality. But there is an image of this goddess in our minds. My father could somehow give a real form to this spiritual idea we have of Durga in our minds. In his images, Durga appeared as more than a woman, as super-woman. My

father always followed Chandi to make the *debi murti*. He often had *sloka*s from Chandi inscribed under his images. The *debi-murti* is impossible without the Chandi ... The super-human quality in my father's Durgas inspires *bhakti*. This is the specialty of our *gharana* [worship/lineage].

Prasanta Pal says that in their school of making there are no "styles." There is only one universal Durga image. He disagrees with those who claim there are four kinds of Durga *murti*. But he agrees that there was an effect of naturalism on Ramesh Pal's work. In his words:

> The Western aspect in his [Ramesh Pal's] work is not reflected in the *debi-murti*. My father made the *asura* in the form of a human being. In his *asura* figure there was a clear influence of Italian art. He studied Italian sculpture very closely. His *asura* bears resemblance to Michelangelo's sculpture in terms of musculature and anatomical perfection.
>
> But if you speak about Western realism, you have to think of the lion. The lion you see in my father's Durga *murti* is very different from lions that you see around us – the real one in the zoo, or the ones on top of pillars and buildings. The lion that you see in the zoo—the real lion and the ideal lion—are mixed together in a strange [*adbhut*] way to make up a new form which is my father's lion!

I asked him the difference between the *real* lion of the zoo and the lion in the *murti*. His answer was that the lion Ramesh Pal made was far more expressive than the *real* lion in the zoo. He said, "Let's imagine a lion is grabbing something with its paw; in real life, there is not much force in that movement. But when a sculptor expresses that movement (gesticulates again), it seems as if the lion is more fiercely and forcefully digging all its claws into something! When sculpture is involved, there is more pressure in his muscles; there is more force in the movement." Therefore, according to him, the techniques of sculpture (by which he means Western techniques) aim at heightening the effect of real or natural beings and objects. "Sculpture," he says, is more than the skill to represent things *as they are* – the basic tenet of Western naturalism. Here, we see a reference to ideals of Expressionists (in European modernism) for the lion alongside the emphasis on anatomical correctness for the body of the *asura*.

The hybridization of the form was not necessarily harmonious– there were dissonances in the act of bringing together these forms. The story of the *asura* elucidates the dissonance between traditional values and the ideals of Western art. Rumors in both Krishnanagar and Kumortuli state that the Bengali upper caste people of Calcutta were outraged because G. Pal controversially used non-Hindu or so-called "*mlechcha*"[11] models for his *murti*. This is understandable because both Dalit (low-caste) and Muslim communities belonged to the working class serving the elites of the city, and intensive manual labor gave them naturally toned, well-sculpted musculature. One of respondents reported that he used a Muslim man as a model for the figure of the *asura*. Brahmins, at the time, accused the artist of blasphemy. Later, Ramesh Pal is known to have used body-builders and wrestlers as models for the *asura* figure.

This convention of making *manush-rupi* (human-like) goddesses started gaining ground soon after Ramesh Pal and eventually monopolized the market, but there was dissonance in the taste of the patrons, the common people and the Brahmin priests. I was told in an interview with a club that there were priests who did not worship these Art/*putul murtis*– they claimed that the new Durgas looked like "memsahibs" of the West. This comment tied together with the term "Art *murti*" reflects on the anxiety felt by the traditionalist conservatives regarding the rampant Westernization of the Bengali way of life. Irrespective of this rejection of the Westernized Durga, a floodgate had already opened in the history of changing styles of the Durga image.[12]

I wish to juxtapose an anecdote from 2013, which reveals the process of naturalization of naturalism. It is common in several theme *pujas* these days to have two *murtis*—one for public display and *darshan*, and the other for ritual treatment by the priest. In 2013 a youth club in South Kolkata club had designed a *pandal* based on a song by a popular poet. Surrounded by painted sceneries, there were two Durgas (see Figure 4.6). The *pandal* and *murti* were built by a local resident who is a professional designer and interior decorator for showrooms, upper-class homes and shopping malls. The two *murtis* at a *pandal* typically means that the goddess on display was not deemed ritually correct

Figure 4.6 Two Durgas, Gariahat, Kolkata 2013

because of form and/or material. Often, priests refuse to worship *murti*s made in fiberglass or stone because unfired clay is the ritually prescribed material in the *Shastra*s. My surprise at two *murti*s in this *pandal* stemmed from the fact in this case both *murti*s were made of clay. The organizers explained that the artist did not want traces of rotten flowers, vermillion or other ritual offerings to "soil" the *murti*. And the priest explicitly asked for a cheap, small *murti* because "he wanted a natural Durga." As we see in the image, the small *murti* replicates an "Arter *murti*" or naturalistic *murti*. It is striking that decades later, the naturalistic *murti* which was once thought to be "Westernized," "memsa-hib"- like has now gained ground as the natural appearance of the goddess.

Let me now return to the *debi* Durga of Baghbazar. If we look closely, we will notice while the Durga is traditionally portrayed in the chrome yellow and abstract features, the lion and the *asura* are made along the conventions of the naturalistic Durga. I argue that this contemporary image, more than any other, truly embodies the coming together of Western naturalism and traditional clay-modelling.

Conclusion: reterritorialization

Research on popular visual cultures of India has convincingly demonstrated the powerful influence of naturalism. This influence worked through networks of colonial pedagogy and a proliferation of Western art objects. The changing appearance of the Hindu pantheon in images – painted, printed and sculpted (see Pinney, 2004; Jain, 2004; Jain, 2007) – is a result of the allure of naturalism. What Ravi Varma achieved in terms of rendering fleshly, real gods on canvas and oleographs for the first time (see Kapur, 2000; Mitter, 1994), G. Pal and Ramesh Pal achieved in the area of clay-modelling in Bengal.

However, if we return to the issue we started with, what does it mean for the "memsahib" Durga to transform herself into the Bengali everywoman? Christopher Pinney argues for a phenomenon of reterritorialization by which colonized and postcolonial Indians appropriated naturalism, realism and allied forms of visual technologies which were instituted as part of the colonial visual regime (Pinney, 2002). They subverted these forms towards nationalist ends to counter colonial hegemony. They appropriated it to picture their own gods and great men in their own way. With the intervention of an individual artist followed by several other ruptures and interventions by this group of clay-modelers, the two visual technologies of the scriptures and the Western art academy were both intertwined, vernacularized and transformed.

Colonial perspectivalism and naturalism with values of European enlightenment related to science and reason is the technology the native craftsmen were faced with. In the journey of this living craft, we see that the craftsmen preserved some of their traditional knowledge system, imbibed some aspects of the colonial visual technology in addition to being influenced by other ways of "making and doing things" to borrow a phrase from Jacques Rancière (2013).

The term of the Greeks, *techne*, does not refer to principles of science and reason. It refers to the knowledge of "making and doing things." By using this term instead of "technology," we are not only free from the teleological moorings of Western art history, we are also free from the Enlightenment discourse of science and its Other. *Techne*, to my understanding, best describes the hybridized, vernacularized knowledge system of contemporary clay-modelers of Bengal.

Technology, related to notions of science, is understood in terms of progress and hence outmodedness. Another reason to prefer the idea of *techne* over that of technology is the fact that these ways of making and doing things do not become outmoded as they often do in the world of technology. As we saw, the style of Durga has changed drastically over time. But it is still possible to find all the styles in one festival season. It is not possible to establish that any of the images of the goddess have become outmoded or obsolete.

I have shown how the clay-modelers of Bengal have borrowed and incorporated different visual styles they were acquainted with, like any other intelligent visual artist. But they were taught about how to represent their subject by two manuals of style: one from their caste-masters, the Brahmins and the other from their colonial masters. The Sanskrit *sutra*s were the manuals from those who claimed to know matters of the other-worldly. And another one came from the art educated elites who spoke in English – the language of power for matters of the this-worldly. They bended, twisted and vernacularized both technical guidelines to create their own aesthetic grammar and a series of hybrid goddess images in Bengal.

Notes

1 Ghurni is still a prominent center for clay-modelling in West Bengal. Located near the river Jalangi in Krishnanagar in the Nadia district of contemporary West Bengal, Ghurni has a group of award-winning clay-modelers who make religious, political and decorative statues for patrons in India and abroad.

2 The system of dissemination of knowledge is similar to but not the same as the *gharana* system which pertains to Classical Indian musicology. The *guru* or the teacher is not revered in the same capacity and the students are technically free to move between *gharana*s. This system is neither as formalized as the guild system of early modern Europe as we learn from Michael Baxandall (1974). I therefore call this a *karkhana* (workshop) system after Susan Bean's suggestion (Bean, 2016).

3 On the contrary, Jayanta Das argues that Gopeshwar Pal did not invent this human-like form; in fact he was echoing the larger stylistic oeuvre of the so-called "east Bengali" clay-modelers who were experimenting with the naturalist form (Das 1998: 68).

4 The term *Memsahib* was used by natives of the service class to refer to British women. It is still used for an elite woman, particularly a Caucasian one.

5 Rachel McDermott argues that popular cultural critique of goddesses as *memsahib*s (white, foreign women) based on Westernized attire or behavior, which exploded in the eighteenth and nineteenth centuries, is part of a longer tradition of satire stretching back to medieval literature (McDermott, 2011: 151).

6 The term *technique* will be used frequently in relation to both these ways of understanding technology. Technique is defined as individual small ways of doing things manually or solving problems individually while technology is understood to be a larger, "scientific" framework. I will complicate this understanding by looking at technique as a set of manuals that connects the larger technological systems with the small-scale everyday tasks.

7 According to my informants, this practice is still prevalent in parts of Bengal, especially in the villages.

8 Jim Robinson (1983) fundamentally disagrees with Varma, arguing that the Bengal region was not influenced by the Agamic texts. Instead we should understand clay-modelling in this region in terms of folk art. I am however somewhat persuaded by Varma's argument, given the links between theory and practice I noticed in my field study of the clay-modelling neighborhoods in West Bengal.

9 Partha Mitter argues that it was not the inherent aesthetic quality of Western art forms that captured the imagination of native elites and eventually postcolonial worlds (1994). He argues, alongside other postcolonial scholars, that naturalism conquered the world through various economic and political moves such as the institution of art academies, the denigration of native visual crafts and a larger "planned epistemic violence of the imperialist project" (Gayatri Chakravarty Spivak quoted in Jay and Ramaswamy, 2014: 7).

10 The Baghbazar club has religiously commissioned the same model of the *debi murti* from the same clay-modeler in Kumortuli. In 2013, I was told in an interview that after their "*bandha* (tied) *shilpi* (artist)" passed away, the task was passed on to his son. But interestingly, the Baghbazar club has been the sole custodian of the original mold of the face of the goddess for generations. They claim that this particular authentic face is unparalleled in contemporary *sarbajanin puja*. I was told that the clay-modeler works within the premises of the club. And that the club trusts him to not stealthily make a copy of the original mold.

11 The term *mlechcha* in Bengali means impure in a colloquial sense. The term has been used for non-Hindus such as Muslims or Catholics living in a dominantly Hindu society. According to the Samsad Bengali English dictionary, a *mlechcha* is a "nonHindu [sic] or anti-Hindu; wicked, sinful, given to unscriptural practices" (Biswas, 1982: 862).

12 One such example is that through the 1960s to the 1980s, there was a vogue of heroines from Bengali and Bombay cinema portrayed as goddesses (McDermott, 2011; Guha-Thakurta, 2015).

References

Agnihotri, Anita (2001) *Kolkatar Protimashilpira*. Kolkata: Ananda Publishers.

Banerjee, Sumanta (1989) *The Parlour and the Streets: Elite and Popular Culture in Nineteenth Century Calcutta*. Calcutta: Seagull Books.

Baxandall, Michael (1974) *Painting and Experience in Fifteenth Century Italy: A Primer in the Social History of Pictorial Style*. Oxford: Oxford University Press.

Bean, Susan S. (2011) "The Unfired Clay Sculpture of Bengal in the Artscape of Modern South Asia." In Rebecca M. Brown and D.S. Hutton, (eds.), *A Companion to Asian Art and Architecture*. Chichester, West Sussex; Malden, MA: Wiley-Blackwell, pp. 604–628.

Bean, Susan S. (2016) "Opponent's presentation." Presented during a public defense of the doctoral dissertation of Moumita Sen, "Clay-modelling in West Bengal: Between Art, Religion and Politics." University of Oslo, May 20, 2016.

Biswas, Sailendra (1982) *Samsad Bengali-English Dictionary.* Calcutta: Sahitya Samsad.

Bundgaard, Helle (1999) "Contending Indian Art Worlds." *Journal of Material Culture* 4(3): 321–337.

Das, Jayanta (1998) "Kumortulir charsho bachhorer bibartan," *Desh Patrika.* Calcutta: Anandabazar Publishers Ltd.

Ghosha, Pratapacandra (1871) *Durga Puja.* Calcutta: Hindoo Patriot.

Guha-Thakurta, Tapati (2015) *In the Name of the Goddess: The Durga Pujas of Contemporary Kolkata.* Kolkata: Primus books.

Hauser, Beatrix (2002) "From Oral Tradition to 'Folk Art': Reevaluating Bengali Scroll Paintings." *Asian Folklore Studies* 61(1):105–122.

Jagadishwarananda, Swami (1976) *Sri Sri Chandi.* 12th ed. Kolkata: The Indian Press Private Limited.

Jain, Jyotindra (2004) *Indian Popular Culture:"The Conquest of the World as Picture".* New Delhi: Ajeepay Press.

Jain, Kajri (2007) *Gods in the Bazaar: The Economies of Indian Calendar Art.* Durham, NC: Duke University Press.

Jay, Martin and Sumathi Ramaswamy (2014) *Empires of Vision: A Reader.* Durham, NC: Duke University Press.

Kapur, Geeta (2000) *When was Modernism: Essays on Contemporary Cultural Practice in India.* New Delhi: Tulika.

McDermott, Rachel Fell (2011) *Revelry, Rivalry, and Longing for the Goddesses of Bengal: The Fortunes of Hindu Festivals.* New York: Columbia University Press.

Mitter, Partha (1994) *Art and Nationalism in Colonial India, 1850–1922: Occidental Orientations.* Cambridge: Cambridge University Press.

Pinney, Christopher (2002) "A Secret of Their Own Country: Or, How Indian Nationalism Made Itself Irrefutable." *Contributions to Indian Sociology* 36(1–2): 113–150.

Pinney, Christopher (2004) *"Photos of the Gods": The Printed Image and Political Struggle in India.* London: Reaktion Books.

Rancière, Jacques (2013) *The Politics of Aesthetics.* London: A&C Black.

Robinson, James Danter (1983) "The Worship of Clay Images in Bengal." Unpublished doctoral thesis submitted to the University of Oxford.

Sen, Moumita (2016) "Clay-modelling in West Bengal: Between Art, Religion and Politics." Unpublished doctoral thesis submitted to Department of Culture studies and Oriental Languages, University of Oslo.

Singh, Kavita (1996) "Changing the Tune: Bengali Pata Painting's Encounter with the Modern." *India International Centre Quarterly* 23(2):60–78.

Varma, K.M. (1970) *The Indian Technique of Clay Modelling.* Santiniketan: Proddu.

5 Indian TV soaps and gender roles
Hindu widows in historical texts and contemporary TV serials

Xenia Zeiler

In many parts of India, a *vidhava* – "widow"[1] – is perceived as a danger (Chen, 1998: 19–59). Because she outlives her husband, a widow is not safeguarded and is unsupervised. But India is by no means alone in perceiving widows as society's "anomalies" (Chen, 2000: 30); in fact, many cultures temporarily separate widows from married women. Ever since approximately the tenth century, parts of Hindu society have permanently excluded widows, especially those of high caste. These widows are forced into "perpetual mourning" (Chen, 2000: 30). Around 10 percent of all women, as well as about 55 percent of all women above the age of 50 and five percent of all women below 35 were widowed in India during the 1990s, and less than one percent of them remarried (Census of India, cited in Chen, 2000: 366, 370). For more than 26 million widows in India, only one lifestyle is available to them: asceticism. The textual sources from ancient India give another picture of widowhood; the practices of levirate, *niyoga*, and widow remarriage seem to have been common. Asceticism was advised only for widows so inclined before it was rigorously promoted for all.

Levirate, the practice of marrying a woman to the brother of her deceased husband, was found in many ancient cultures; references to it occur, for example, in ancient Sparta and in the Old Testament. There were a number of reasons for levirate, among them the desire to protect widows both materially and socially, and as joint family property. While levirate is likely to have existed in ancient India, the sources speak more often of *niyoga*, a custom in which a substitute for the husband was delegated to insure a woman's child. This practice was meant to insure explicitly male offspring, who are needed in a Hindu context for religious reasons, among other things. *Niyoga* was practiced until approximately 300 BCE (Fisch, 1998: 331, n.6). For example, several heroes of the Sanskrit epic Mahabharata, among them the five Pandava brothers, were the progeny of *niyoga*. There is evidence for a later countermovement, headed by Apastamba, Baudhyayana, and Manu (Altekar, 1973: 146). The ancient treatise on statecraft *Arthashastra*, dating from the 2nd century BCE to the 3rd century CE and attributed to Kautilya, mentions *niyoga*. Until around 200 BCE, restrictions were increasingly placed on the custom, and after 600 BCE, there is a complete absence of any mention of the practice in the sources (Kane, 1974: 599–607). Narada and Parashara were among the last to acknowledge *niyoga*. The entire Puranic literature condemns *niyoga* as not befitting the *kaliyuga*.

A similar development can be seen for widow remarriage (Gidumal, 1989: 315–337). The *Dharmasutra*s that date from the fourth century BCE to the first century CE and several *Jataka*s allow remarriage, and both Indian epics *Ramayana* and *Mahabharata* mention it (Jayal, 1966: 183–188). Manu did not refer to such remarriage as illegal, but did recommend lifelong asceticism as the best practice for widows (Winternitz, 1920: 94–95): Kautilya, Narada, and Parashara all permitted widow remarriage. Even early opponents to widow remarriage saw exemptions for young, childless widows. From around the sixth century CE, more and more voices were raised in opposition to the practice, and from the tenth century on, that opposition was extended to child widows (Kane, 1974: 608–619). During the nineteenth century, efforts were made to reform the tradition, which by then had been established for centuries (Basu, 2004: 67–84). But it should be noted that this practice, which was consistently and specifically set forth in basically all texts, was probably relevant only for the upper levels of society. In contemporary India, a number of communities permit widow remarriage.[2]

Asceticism for widows was advised in older Hindu books of law, Manu's being among the first. Yet in the beginning, only if a widow felt so inclined did she need to live in such a way. It has been only since the tenth century that sources have rigorously ordered widows to live an exclusively ascetic lifestyle. Even in the *"suttee* debate" of the nineteenth century, the strict opponents to *suttee*, such as Rammohan Roy, who founded the Brahmo Sabha movement, never doubted the necessity of asceticism for widows (Fisch, 1998: 335). Widowhood *is* asceticism and is often related to the asceticism of *samnyasin*s and *brahmacari*s (Leslie, 1989: 299–300; Ojha, 1981: 256–257). For example, widows, ascetics, and *brahmacari*s share certain prohibitions: they are not allowed to use betel, body oils, or copper or brass dishes (Leslie, 1989: 299; Kane, 1974: 584). Often, they are permitted only one meal per day, consisting of fruits or vegetables, and they must take regular *vratas* or vows (which may include a vow to fast at specific times, a vow to perform certain rituals, and so on) (Olivelle 1991: 23–29). Widows are strictly advised to sleep on the ground and avoid all contact with men.

Unlike male ascetics, widows do not have the option of renouncing house-hold life. A woman's asceticism is based on worship of and loyalty to her deceased husband and the desire to liberate him (and thereby herself). Only in a certain form of asceticism, widows leave their own families. This usually happens when families do not take their economic responsibilities for a widow seriously. In her fieldwork, Martha Alter Chen found that as many as 85 percent of all widows depend economically on themselves or their sons (Chen, 1998: 23–24, 38–43). In a number of pilgrimage centers, both historically and still today, there are clusters of widows who are without funds and who live an ascetic, religious life by depending on the charity of others. The city of

Kashi plays an important role among these centers, mainly because it is believed that to die in Kashi means instant liberation from the cycles of birth and death (Saraswati, 1988; Parry 1994: 50–52).

Another essential factor defining widows' position in Indian society, a factor that has changed substantially over time, is economic status. Guaranteed property rights are the basis for the economic independence of widows and their autonomy, since their material dependency is also used as a means of influencing and controlling their way of life. Property rights for widows have changed greatly over the centuries; in addition, such rights have always been and still very much are defined by local laws. Chen summarizes this situation:

> In considering the rights of Widows under Hindu law, we have to distinguish between modern legal rights (those guaranteed under modern statutory Hindu law), traditional legal rights (those guaranteed in traditional Hindu texts), and customary rights (those recognized under prevailing local norms), and actual practice. (Chen, 2000: 261)

The *Dharmashastra*s are not consistent in their depiction of property rights for widows (Altekar 1973: 251–259). In the twelfth century, two commentaries, *Mitakshara* and *Dayabhaga*, gained importance. Both granted widows ownership rights under certain conditions: in essence, these restricted property rights largely included administrative rights to widows' properties and rights of use to the estate of the deceased husband. For centuries, local traditions were influenced by law schools, which relied on both of these texts. Since the beginning of the twentieth century, formal inheritance and property rights for widows have mainly been based on the Hindu Women's Property Act of 1937 and the Hindu Succession Act of 1956 (Nandwana and Nandwana, 1998: 228–240). Yet in practice, local law is often applied arbitrarily, and widows rarely make use of their rights (Chen, 2000: 273–274). Thus, in many cases, widows are excluded from owning any (land) property that would ensure them economic control and significant independence.

"Karmic crime" and the potential danger of widows

Widows are often made responsible for the death of their husbands. Their "guilt" is attributed either to bad deeds in a previous life or to a lack of worship of the husband in this life, but in any case to a "karmic crime" (Chen, 2000: 118). This is the main reason that widows are considered potentially dangerous. Their very existence disturbs the social order. Some communities in both North and South India go so far as to believe that widows devoured their husbands and eat human beings as a general practice (Harper, 1969: 90–91; Chen, 2000: 118; Sharma et al., 1988: 75, n.342). Hindu mythology does not give widows a prominent role. The only widow with at least some mythological significance in ancient and medieval Hindu literature is Kunti in the *Mahabharata* (Chakravarti, 1998: 70, 89, n. 27).

Widows are also often associated with death. Childless widows especially are frequently related to black magic or witchcraft because they are considered frustrated, maligned, and envious, especially of happily married women with sons. Widows are constantly regarded as symbols of all inauspiciousness, and one consequence is that they are kept away from festivals, especially weddings, since it is believed that persons associated with happiness and prosperity, such as bridal couples, must avoid even looking at a widow. It is feared that widows will transfer their misfortune. These women are permanently trapped in a transitional stage between two auspicious states: marriage and reunion with their husbands after the widows' death (Sharma et al., 1988: 80). They are also regarded as dangerous because of this lifelong entrapment in a transitional stage.

Along with inauspiciousness and misery, widows are associated with impurity. Women ritually die at the death of the husband, i.e. they are excluded from almost all rituals from this point on. Marriage, however, is also their "most important purity measure" (Michaels, 1992: 118); many excluding practices base on the belief that when a woman's husband dies, her inherent impurity re-surfaces. Widows are furthermore regarded as ritually impure because of their connection with death and feared for their alleged potential to pollute others. For that reason, society takes precautionary measures, usually by segregating them.

Various attempts have been made to explain Hinduism's numerous negative associations with widows. To some extent, the explanations are probably related to the outsider positions of widows and to attempts to exclude them from social life. Many cultures regard persons in marginal positions as being particularly threatening; such persons are accused and distinctively identified, probably also to facilitate control over them (Douglas, 1994: 99). Studies in South India, for example, indicate a close link between feelings of guilt for the relentless behavior toward widows and the exaggerated fear of their (magical) reactions to this behavior (Harper, 1969: 81–95). In general, many factors contribute to the negative perceptions. However, throughout Hindu societies, widows are not only confronted with various, partly very restrictive, rules and prohibitions, but also are externally marked, because of their perceived inauspiciousness and impurity.

The danger attributed to widows is explicitly often connected to their uncontrolled sexuality:

> While there are many elements of the widow's existence that are symbolized there is an overwhelming concentration on the profound danger represented by the sexuality of the widow ... The theme that dominates the ceremonies and rituals of widowhood is the sexual death of the widow. (Chakravarti, 1998: 65–66)

Young widows in particular are sexually feared because they desire and are desirable, yet they remain unprotected and uncontrolled by a husband. Some of the regulations on food for widows are aimed, among other things, at restricting their sexual passion. In the widespread Hindu Indian classification of food into hot (meat, eggs, alcohol, onions, garlic, and other things) and cold (rice, milk, honey, and so on), widows are expected to restrict themselves to cold food. The mere presence of widows potentially endangers the moral structure of society, less because of their supposed sexual dissoluteness (Leslie, 1986: 40) than because of the possible consequences of their behaviors. Through sexual activity or progeny, it is feared, a widow could contaminate the lineage of the deceased husband's family. Widows, especially those of child-bearing age, must thus be de-feminized and transformed into a neuter gender. The removal of all ornaments, plus regulations on hairstyle, which in some areas have reached the point of tonsure, and clothing restrictions all contribute to transforming a widow into a sexless, asexual being. Since women in primarily orthodox communities are regarded primarily as a medium for reproduction, the sexual death of a widow effectively means her social death.

Markers of widowhood and their symbolism: dress, jewelry, hair

The most important external markers used to distinguish widows are clothing, jewelry, and hairstyle. All of these change significantly compared with the widow's previous married status. On the one hand, these markers were specifi-cally selected because they are instantly visible and thus indicate immediately the status of the person concerned. On the other hand, these modifications can be made without much effort. However, Hindu society also assigns certain religious and social symbols to widows. For the transition from the status of married woman to that of widow, a rite of passage is crucial, meaning the ritual removal of all bridal clothing, jewelry, and other symbols of marriage (which vary according to local traditions, but often include bangles; *sindur*, the orange-red mark in the hair-part worn only by married women, which is often made of turmeric; or the *mangalsutra*, the necklace declaring a woman to be married). All external signs of well-being and joyfulness must be discarded. The *Mahabharata* mentioned white clothing for widows, and later texts agreed, prescribing colorless clothes. Up to the present time, the most usual clothing for Indian widows has undoubtedly been an unadorned white *sari*.

As revealing of social status as clothing is hairstyle. Among women, widows especially are set apart by their altered hairstyle. Like clothing and jewelry, hair is external, a readily visible feature that is effortlessly changed. However, unlike clothing and jewelry, hair is an inseparable part of the body and thus is significantly more closely associated with widows and their purported danger-ousness than are materials that only temporarily touch the body. The impurity of widows is often considered to be present in their hair. And in Hindu contexts, hairstyles per se carry additional symbolism.

Hair in general is believed to be closely connected to the current purity of the wearer. For example, where death is concerned, the worst possible con-tamination occurs, and therefore shaving the head completely is essential.

Head shaving for widows is of relatively recent origin. *Grihyasutras* and *Dharmasutras* and all older *Smrtis* remain silent on the topic; up until the ninth century, there are no literary or epigraphic references – quite unlike the numerous references condemning the use of hair oil, hair ornaments, or hair braiding. Widow tonsure was probably a Tamil custom initially (Chakravarti, 1998: 76), adopted by different communities in North India (Fisch, 1998: 335, n.18). By the twelfth century at the latest, the custom of widow tonsure began to spread. Almost without exception, medieval advocates refer to the *Kashi-khanda* of the *Skandapurana*, which gives lengthy instructions for widows prescribing tonsure (Kane, 1974: 585–586). The custom remained alive until the end of the nineteenth century, especially in South India. The reasons why complete tonsure for widows arose and was maintained in certain Indian regions and communities are not entirely clear, but possibly the measure was based on an attempt to bring the outward appearance of widows into line with (Buddhist or Jain) nuns or to express the ascetic aspiration of widows. Hair is also seen as the seat of energy and vitality and, where women are concerned, of sexual energy and radiance. Widow tonsure must thus also be interpreted as a symbolic clipping of the life force and sexuality. In addition, shaving the head causes visual deformation and loss of attractiveness and is a clear and public symbol. In South Asia, hair as a culturally defined symbol in general is strongly linked to sexuality, which is why it plays an important role in various rites of passage. The hairstyle is changed as a symbol of the formal transfer of a person to another socio-sexual status (Obeyesekere, 1981: 45–50; Leach, 1958: 157), and a shaved head indicates celibacy.

The symbolism of opened, unrestrained, and unbraided hair in Hindu traditions stands diametrically opposed to that of controlled, restrained, and dressed hair. The latter is generally associated with social control and, for women, is an outward mark of the auspicious status of marriage. Unrestrained hair on women always indicates separation from society, exceptional social and ritual states, and dissolution in general. As Alf Hiltebeitel in his studies on Draupadi has put it:

> The untying of Draupadī's braid represents the potential untying of the universe. For the universe itself is a braid, composed of the three *gunas* or strands of *prakriti*, nature. (Hiltebeitel, 1981: 210)

In sum, widows were and are exposed to varying degrees of observation and control in Hindu society. Their behavior is often regulated by various psychological, social, or physical punishments in the event of transgression. In order to uphold the social and moral order of society, control measures in the form of regulations are imposed on widows. But it should also be stressed that the rules outlined above need to be regarded as prototypical. Of course, not all widows were and are treated in the same way, varying with family contexts. While the prototype certainly was partially lived, especially in orthodox families with sufficient financial resources, the overwhelming number of widows has probably always been less restricted, in milder ways than in some of the extreme forms discussed above. Economic reasons play some role here: many women, including widows, must contribute to household finances or even provide for themselves and their children.[3] In addition, women in general and widows in particular are often less subject to strict religious rules in non-Brahman contexts, where they are more mobile and independent (Chakravarti, 1998: 63–92).

Renegotiating widowhood in contemporary Indian TV serials

In parts of contemporary India, the information contained in classical texts and prescribed by local traditions, which developed mainly on the basis of the texts, still defines how society deals with widows. Nevertheless, in recent years, the position of widows in Hindu society has been discussed with increasing openness, with television and film being highly important means for generating such discourse. A number of Bollywood movies, such as *Rajniti* (2010), *Kahani* (2012), and *Dor* (2006), have made widows the center of their narrative. These films are often part of a "New Bollywood" (Stafford, 2014: 289), which, among other things, emphasizes social themes. Not surprisingly, at the center of narratives that discuss gender roles in general and widowhood in particular, we frequently find representations and discussions of colliding worldviews, tensions between more or less traditional contexts, and social changes in globalized, urban contemporary Indian spaces (see e.g., Anujan, Schaefer, and Karan, 2004; Biswas, 2002; Bose, 2008; Datta, 2000; Gokulsing and Dissanayake, 2004).

Such discussions and negotiations are not restricted to Indian films. Increasingly, they are also shaping Indian soap operas (e.g. Gokulsing, 2004; Mankekar, 1999). While a number of studies have researched Indian soap operas (e.g. Chakrabarti, 2011; Deprez, 2009; Munshi, 2010), with some focusing especially on women (e.g. Fazal, 2009; Jensen and Oster, 2009; Somani and Doshi, 2016),[4] no study so far has highlighted the representation and discussion of widows in Indian soap operas. Nevertheless, in the last decade, some Hindi TV serials have focused on a widow as a leading character and her life in society as the main narrative, such as *Ishq Ka Rang Safed* ("White is the Color of Love," 2015–2016), *Gangaa* (2015, ongoing), or *Balika Vadhu* ("Child Bride," 2008–2016).[5] The topics highlighted in these serials are controversial in part and, compared to the historical texts, may be regarded as provocative. They include especially, though not exclusively, topics that broach the issue of love or marriage, for example, posing questions about widow remarriage or about a widow's right to fall in love and be loved. In these cases, the narrative often centers on emotional aspects and seems to be intended to trigger emotions in the viewers. But other topics even less acceptable in the historical texts are taken up, such as widows actively taking part in religious rituals. All of the topics mentioned can be integrated into the serial narrative in various ways, ranging from passing mention to placing them at the center of a program or even promoting them.

In portraying a new or (partly) reformed picture of widows, such media depictions, not surprisingly, are also finding their way into debates and reflections beyond media, and actively contributing to processes of renegotiation and transformation in contemporary Indian society. Today, in times of "deep mediatization," media are inseparable from all aspects of social life (Hepp, 2016), and media use shapes and reshapes perceptions of what is acceptable (or not), desirable (or not), and so on. Media narratives are powerful vehicles for negotiations and constructions of beliefs, opinions, and social life in general. Media such as TV serials are thus becoming instrumental in constructing new representations of widowhood in contemporary India.

Ishq Ka Rang Safed

The most recent serial on Indian television to stage a widow as a main character premiered on August 10, 2015, on the private channel Colors TV. *Ishq Ka Rang Safed* was directed by Uttam Ahlawat, Shahwanaz Khan, and Nitin Mahesh Chaudhary and produced by Amit Chandra, Rupali Guha, and Kalyan Guha. It was aired in 342 episodes, running until August 26, 2016. Throughout its year on TV, the serial had high viewer numbers and a dedicated fan base, making it a popular show among the numerous daily soap operas on Indian TV. This was due in part to the popularity of the leading male actor, Mishal Raheja (as "Viplav"), who portrayed a young man falling in love with the leading female actor – the young widow "Dhani" (originally played by Eisha Singh, who left the show and was replaced by Sanjeeda Sheikh).

The story is set in Benares. Some places of pilgrimage (*tirtha*s) in India have traditionally drawn large numbers of widows and still do today, especially widows without funds of their own who depend on charity and who live an ascetic life dominated by religion. Among these *tirtha*s, Benares holds a unique position. Because of the city's alleged power to grant liberation from the cycle of birth and rebirth to a person who dies there,[6] and also because of the assumed overall pure and devotion-centered character of Benares, which is of great significance to many traditional Hindus, houses of refuge and shelters for widows (*ashrama*s) have thrived there for centuries. The exceptionally dense concentration of widows in Benares, the so-called *kashivasi* widows ("living-in-Benares widows")[7] are still legendary in contemporary India.

Thus, it is not without significance that the TV serial begins by portraying a traditional picture of the main female character. Dhani and her mother live in a widow's refuge and follow a traditional way of life as prescribed by the classical texts. But, even at this early stage, some controversial topics related to society's treatment of widows are crucially embedded in the plot. Several instances of how Dhani or her housemates are ridiculed or even beaten up in public spaces are shown and used to develop the lead male role, Viplav, as a protective character who outspokenly defends the widows, especially Dhani. His role is consolidated by depicting him as successfully fighting a court case on behalf of the widows, who had been in danger of losing their shelter to one of the program's main antagonists. Dhani begins to trust Viplav, who has repeatedly stood up for her and others, and they become friends.

Not surprisingly, especially given the serial's title, the friendship turns into love. Viplav confesses his love to Dhani who needs longer to accept her feelings than he, but in the end they agree to marry. Viplav especially continues to fight the orthodox views of society as depicted in the serial and begins actively promoting widow remarriage. The couple's wedding plans are strongly opposed by just about everyone, including Viplav's parents and grandparents, and numerous conspiracies and schemes to undermine the wedding of the leading characters dominate the storyline for a long time. Throughout this strand of the narrative, the episodes with emotional sequences supporting the husband-and-wife-to-be openly promote widow remarriage.

Ishq Ka Rang Safed, which is the most recent in a number of Indian daily soap operas to discuss widows and their position in society, makes use of narrative and visual elements that have been employed before, but it also introduces new ways of showing the struggles of widows in Indian society today. Some of these are bolder than anything taken up before on Indian TV. For example, a mob in Benares which not only beats up Dhani, but even threatens to kill her because she wears colored clothes instead of a plain white *sari* is graphically depicted as blood-thirsty and hateful, in sharp contrast to Dhani's character, which throughout the serial is shown as loving, caring, and helpful. It is especially the setting of *Ishq Ka Rang Safed* in Benares that enabled the producers to highlight the extreme contrasts between the classical Indian texts with their sanctified expectations of how widows should behave and contemporary, more open approaches to widowhood, which are not (exclusively) based on religiously motivated regulations. While the older traditions are noticeably shown as being restrictive on individuals and hindering personal happiness, the new approaches are promoted throughout the serial's episodes as viable alternatives.

Gangaa

Premiered on March 2, 2015, *Gangaa* continues to run. The daily soap opera broadcast on &TV, a channel owned by Zee TV, not only has a strong fan base, but also has been officially honored by the Indian film community. For example, the serial won several awards specifically for its content and embedded message, including the award for "Best Programme with a Social Message" at the Indian Telly Awards 2015 and "Best Child Actress" at the Indian Telly Awards 2015 and 2016. It is directed by Yusuf Ansari and produced by Sunjoy and Comall S. Waddhwa, Vivek Budakoti, and Rajita Sharma. Like *Ishq Ka Rang Safed, Gangaa* is set in Benares. But it stresses another controversial issue regarding widowhood: It focuses on the life story of Ganga, who was widowed on her wedding day at the age of five. The serial also allows the main female character to stand up for herself more than does the leading female role in *Ishq Ka Rang Safed. Gangaa* focuses on a young girl's struggle for her individual right to happiness, including her opposition to social restrictions on widows.

The narrative begins by briefly mentioning Ganga's childhood marriage and the deaths of her husband and father. During an attempt to live in a widow refuge where she is mistreated, she meets Niranjan, accidently bumping into him on the banks of the river Ganges, when she is chased by her housemate widows who are trying to cut her long hair. Niranjan not only assists her in her resistance against having her hair cut at that time, but even decides to provide a home for the orphaned Ganga.

A father-like figure, Niranjan provides a home and continuous support. But even in this seemingly sheltered space, she has to fight for her rights, which are violated by family members and friends; for example, she has to resist being forced to work as a maid and has to struggle to be allowed to study. The contrast of traditional versus contemporary views is symbolized in the serial mainly by two main characters who represent two different generations: Niranjan's mother Kanta, a widow herself, represents orthodox views of widowhood, while her son Niranjan is pictured as progressive. In this household, Ganga tries to find her place, and in time she succeeds. Moreover, a close friendship develops between her and Niranjan's son Sagar.

The most striking plot development involves a ten-year leap. Sagar, who has been in London, returns and eventually, he and Ganga fall in love. The narrative now moves from focusing on the universal rights of widows, such as safety, shelter, and education, to more specific personal rights, namely, love and (re)marriage. Several complications arise, as the couple fights for this right, including a rival for Sagar, who is also in love with Ganga. The storyline culminates in a tragic twist: shortly before the wedding, Ganga becomes pregnant by Sagar, who has been (unwillingly) intoxicated and does not remember the night they spent together. The wedding does not take place, and Ganga raises her daughter alone. She leaves the family she has been living with since childhood and moves to Delhi with her daughter. After several other twists, the plot line attempts to reunite the couple.

More universal rights of widows, such as the right to education or to make individual decisions, are discussed during the serial, but these are more prominent in the episodes that depict the child Ganga. While the issue of child marriage is also broached, it is never the focal point. Rather, the entire narrative centers on aspects of widowhood in today's society (exemplified by Benares' traditional surroundings and later, a more urban space in Delhi). The serial stands out for presenting and discussing these issues, interweaving them into a complex narrative. As an example, there is the introduction of a rival for Sagar, who also wants to marry the widow Ganga; rather than simply depicting one suitor, the program shifts the focus – from a view of men who fall in love with widows as rare exceptions to the presentation of a more complex reality. Although it is, of course, typical of soap operas worldwide to work with extreme plot twists and complicated story lines, *Gangaa* uses these soap opera style elements in a distinctive way in an emotional narrative of a young widow to create public awareness of the position of widows living in traditional Hindu contexts, even in contemporary India, and to promote widows' right to self-determination.

Balika Vadhu

Balika Vadhu differs from the two previous soap operas in a number of ways, especially with regard to its popularity, running time, and narrative. Premiered on July 21, 2008, the serial ran for eight years in 2,248 episodes until the final episode, on July 31, 2016. The serial's great popularity is indicated not only by its running time, but also by the fact that it was dubbed in two South Indian languages – Telugu (airing as *Chinnari Pellikuthuru* on MAA TV) and Tamil (airing as *Mann Vasanai* on Raj TV). The serial was directed by Sidharth Sengupta and Pradeep Yadav and produced by Zakir Shaikh, Sachin Chavan, and Fuzel Khan. It won numerous Indian Television Academy Awards and Indian Telly Awards, including in such prominent categories as Best Drama Series, Best Actor(s), Best Story, and Best Teleplay.

Formally, the serial is divided into two seasons – the first, significantly longer, which centers on the main characters, Anandi and Jagdish, and their lives from marriage as children to death, and the second, which focuses on the life stories of their children. Like *Gangaa, Balika Vadhu* begins with a child marriage plot. But here, the main female character, Anandi, is not widowed for very long. Rather, as its name suggests, *Balika Vadhu* centers on child marriage and the potential complications this custom may create for all of the families involved. Anandi and Jagdish are married in rural Rajasthan, and the serial depicts at great length Anandi's struggle to adapt to her new family and establish her role in it at the age of eight. As a teenager, Anandi indeed falls in love with her husband, who not only rejects her, but also divorces her to marry his new love. Even though her in-laws refuse to accept the new marriage, Anandi is left on her own and of necessity begins to build a new life. Her identity struggles are part of the serial's narrative as much as her practical struggles. Anandi remarries and adopts an orphaned boy with her new husband, Shivraj. After two years of happily married life, Shivraj is killed in a terrorist attack and Anandi is widowed. Shortly thereafter, she gives birth to twins. In a complicated plot spanning several years, her daughter Nandini's story is then recounted. Nandini is kidnapped and married to her kidnapper's son, and only after twelve years of searching for her mother's first husband, Jagdish, does she find her mother and the two are reunited. The successful trial against the kidnapper by Anandi and Jagdish leads to an arrest, but at the very end, the kidnapper vengefully kills Anandi.

In its storyline, *Balika Vadhu* conveys many traditional views – more so than the two serials discussed above. For example, child marriage is discussed critically only up to a point; for a large part, it is relativized and thus partly sanctioned. For example, Anandi's childhood in-laws are depicted as being supportive and family oriented, and the love and support of the new in-laws from the second husband are also depicted. But this love and support within the family by no means points at a general disapproval of social restrictions for widows in the serial: rather, it is conditional. For example, in a scene showing a gathering of Shivraj's family and friends immediately after his death, a dialogue takes place when Anandi enters in a pale yellow and slightly embroidered, but not entirely white, *sari*; with simple gold jewelry, thus not entirely unadorned; without the marriage mark in her hair-part, but rather with a small decorative mark on her forehead. This way of dressing and adorning herself with jewelry is immediately and harshly contested by some guests. The grandfather then sanctions the situation by explaining that because Shiv has given his life for his country and thus is respected and remembered by all his widow Anandi is considered to remain married.

In the episode, the grandfather's speech brought tears to the eyes of the listeners and approval from most of those present. What started out as a narrative that began to criticize traditions of marking and socially excluding widows ended in praise for the heroic death of the husband, which is given as the *only* reason why, in this specific case, traditions should be overthrown. As with most other potentially relevant social aspects in the serial, *Balika Vadhu* in its representation of widows stays traditional, uncontroversial, and unprovocative. Thus, for serials like *Balika Vadhu*, which address more conservative and possibly rural audiences, the observations by Shehina Fazal apply: While the deregulation of TV in India in the early 1990s led to a proliferation, especially on private TV, of more and more representations of women, the images depicted are often bound by patriarchal considerations (Fazal, 2009).

Conclusion

As in many cultures worldwide, widows have been given a particular position in South Asian society since early times. What is specific or even unique in the case of Hindu society is that from around the tenth century onwards, parts of society favored excluding widows permanently from most aspects of social togetherness and constrained them to a state of "perpetual mourning" (Chen, 2000: 30). One means of defining a widow's position in society is by her economic status, which changed over time and place in South Asia, but often included highly restrictive property rights. Even though property ownership would support economic self-determination and independence, widows are more often than not excluded from owning (land) property. In practical terms, this has led to a widow's material dependency on her in-laws and has restricted her autonomy.

Overall, widows' position in society, especially since the tenth century, has been formulated in very strict rules and regulations based on the belief that an austere, ascetic lifestyle was the only acceptable way of life for a widow. This has included restrictions on food, clothing, and adornment. Easily identifiable visual markers for widows were introduced, the most important being in dress, jewelry, and hairstyles. The rigorous restrictions and the almost complete exclusion of widows from social life promoted in several sacred Hindu texts were based on the underlying perception of a widow as personally guilty for her husband's death, either because of her bad deeds in a previous life or because of a lack of worship of and for the husband in this life. Consequently, widows were believed to be disruptive to the social order, to be inauspicious, impure, and polluting, even potentially dangerous. The danger attributed to them was connected in part to their presumed uncontrolled sexuality, especially in the case of young widows of childbearing age. The ban on ornaments, hairstyle regulations, and clothing restrictions were surely also aimed at de-feminizing widows and marking them as neutered, asexual beings.

The information from these classical texts are deep-rooted in Indian society. This has led to a fear of widows and uncertainty in dealing with them, which still persists in parts of contemporary India. Nevertheless, in recent years the position of Hindu widows has been increasingly discussed, with television and film being highly important for generating such discourses in society. A number of Hindi TV serials, such as *Ishq Ka Rang Safed* (2015–2016), *Gangaa* (2015, ongoing), and *Balika Vadhu* (2008–2016), as well as Bollywood films have taken up the subject of widows and their social life as central to their narratives. In portraying a new picture of widows, or even a partly reformed one, such media depictions also find their way into debates and reflections beyond media, and thus actively contribute to processes of renegotiation and transformation in contemporary Indian society.

Compared to the prescriptions in historical texts, representations of widows in contemporary Indian soap operas range from rather conservative and traditional to increasingly controversial, even provocative. One of India's most popular and currently its longest running soap operas, *Balika Vadhu*, is set in rural Rajasthan and for that reason possibly attracts more conservative and rural audiences; it stays largely traditional in its representations of women. Yet other serials have taken a much more tolerant approach. Especially the newer daily soap operas, namely, *Ishq Ka Rang Safed* and *Gangaa* (both launched in 2015), discuss controversial and even provocative aspects of widowhood in contemporary Indian society, as compared to historical texts. Some of these approaches are bolder than others taken up on Indian television earlier. For example, *Ishq Ka Rang Safed* has a plot set in traditional contexts in Benares, which highlights the extreme contrasts between the textually sanctified expectations of widows and the contemporary, more open approaches to widowhood. While the traditional contexts are noticeably represented as being restrictive on individuals and hindering personal happiness, the more open approaches are promoted throughout the serial's narrative. The conflicts between traditional and contemporary views also run through the narrative of *Gangaa*, where some of the universal rights of widows, such as the right to education or to make one's own decisions, are discussed. The serial stands out for its distinctive way of employing a widow's emotional personal narrative to create public awareness for the position of widows living in traditional

Hindu contexts, even in contemporary India, and to promote the right of self-determination for widows.

The fact that this way of representing widows' struggles in Indian soap operas is openly and even officially applauded by audiences – *Gangaa* won, among other awards, the category "Best Programme with a Social Message" at the Indian Telly Awards 2015 – points to the relevance and influence of such depictions in media. Today, media are inseparable from all aspects of social life, which is shaped and reshaped by their use. Television soap opera narratives are powerful vehicles for negotiations and constructions of beliefs, opinions, and social life. Such renegotiations of historical and textually authorized gender roles in general and transformed media representations of widowhood in particular are also finding their way into debates and reflections beyond media, and actively contribute to the shaping of contemporary Indian society.

Notes

1 The word, according to some translators like Monier-Williams (1993: 967) *vi* plus *dhava*, "without husband," already appears in the Rigveda (Kane, 1974: 583).
2 See Chen (2000: 80–114) who gives details for geographical regions and communities; Bose and Sen (1966: 226–232) who for Rajasthan prove a broad acceptance; and Dubey (1965: 50–56) who presents actual remarriage numbers for central India as high as 45 percent.
3 Devi (1988: 35–45) gives a detailed overview based on Census data for 1971 and 1981. Nair (1988: 3–14) does the same for a longer period, 1951–1984, and explicitly refers to widowhood.
4 The interrelation of women, social change and soap operas has been a topic of discussion in international film studies. For a recent example, see Geraghty and Weissmann (2016).
5 The TV serials in this chapter are spelled according to their English transliteration used by the production and distribution companies. This spelling also prevails in official TV channel information and fan post on the Internet.
6 For the historical context of dying in Benares, see Justice (1997: 37–66).
7 See Saraswati (1988) and Parry (1994: 50–52) for detailed empirical material on especially the living conditions and origins of widows in Benares.

References

Altekar, A.S. (1973) [1938] *The Position of Women in Hindu Civilization: From Prehistoric Times to the Present Day.* Delhi: Motilal Banarasidass.
Anujan, Divya, Schaefer, David J. and Karan, Kavita (2004) "The Changing Face of Indian Women in the Era of Global Bollywood." In Schaefer, David J. and Karan, Kavita, (eds.), *Bollywood and Globalization: The Global Power of Popular Hindi Cinema.* New York: Routledge, pp. 110–126.
Balika Vadhu (2008–2016) TV Serial, Colors TV.
Balika Vadhu (2015) Episode 1797, January 20. Available at: www.youtube.com/watch?v=Luvz2CXfwrA (accessed December 10, 2016).
Basu, Monmayee (2004) *Hindu Women and Marriage Law: From Sacrament to Contract.* New Delhi: Oxford University Press.

Biswas, Moinak (2002) "The Couple and Their Spaces." In Vasudevan, Ravi, (ed.), *Making Meaning in India Cinema*. New Delhi and Oxford: Oxford University Press, pp. 122–144.

Bose, Brinda (2008) "Modernity, Globality, Sexuality, and the City: A Reading of Indian Cinema." *The Global South* 2(1): 35–58.

Bose, A.B. and Sen, M.L.A. (1966) "Some Characteristics of the Widows in Rural Society." *Man in India* 46(3): 226–232.

Chakrabarti, Santanu (2011) "Prime Time Soap Operas on Indian Television." *South Asian Popular Culture* 9(2): 229–231.

Chakravarti, Uma (1998) "Gender, Caste and Labour: The Ideological and Material Structure of Widowhood." In Chen, Martha Alter, (ed.), *Widows in India: Social Neglect and Public Attention*. New Delhi: SAGE, pp. 63–92.

Chen, Martha Alter (1998) "Introduction." In Chen, Martha Alter, (ed.), *Widows in India: Social Neglect and Public Attention*. New Delhi: SAGE, pp. 19–62.

Chen, Martha Alter (2000) *Perpetual Mourning: Widowhood in Rural India*. New Delhi: Oxford University Press.

Datta, S. (2000) "Globalisation and Representations of Women in Indian Cinema." *Social Scientist* 28(3/4), 71–82.

Deprez, Camille (2009) "Indian TV Serials: Between Originality and Adaptation." *Global Media and Communication* 5(3): 425–430.

Devi, D. Radha (1988) "Work Participation of Widows in India: A Census Analysis." In Nagesh, H.V., Nair, P. S., and Katti, A.P., (eds.), *Widowhood in India: A Collection of Papers Presented at the National Seminar on Widowhood in India, Dharwad March 1987*. Dharwad: Sri Dharmasthala Manjunatheshwara Educational Trust, pp. 35–45.

Dubey, Bhagwant Rao (1965) "Widow Remarriage in Madhya Pradesh." *Man in India* 45(1): 50–56.

Dor (2006) Film. Percept Picture Company. Distributor Sahara One Motion Pictures.

Douglas, Mary (1994 [1966]) *Purity and Danger: An Analysis of the Concepts of Pollution and Taboo*. London: Routledge.

Fazal, Shehina (2009) "Emancipation or anchored Individualism? Women and TV Soaps in India." In Gokulsing, Moti K. and Dissanayake, Wimal, (eds.), *Popular Culture in a Globalised India*. London and New York: Routledge, pp. 41–52.

Fisch, Jörg (1998) *Tödliche Rituale: Die indische Witwenverbrennung und andere Formen der Totenfolge*. Frankfurt and New York: Campus Verlag.

Gangaa (2015 ongoing) TV Serial, &TV of Zee TV.

Gangaa (2015) Episode 4, March 5, 2015, YouTube. Available at: www.youtube.com/watch?v=shXVknWfQTw (accessed December 10, 2016).

Geraghty, Christine and Weissmann, Elke (2016) "Women, Soap Opera and New Generations of Feminists." *Critical Studies in Television: The International Journal of Television Studies* 11(3): 365–384.

Gidumal, Dayaram (1989 [1889]) *The Status of Women in India or Handbook for Hindu Social Reformers*. New Delhi: Publications India.

Gokulsing, K. Moti (2004) *Soft-soaping India: The World of Indian Televised Soap Operas*. Stoke-on-Trent: Trendham Books.

Gokulsing, K. Moti and Dissanayake, Wimal (eds.) (2004) *Indian Popular Cinema: A Narrative of Cultural Change*. New York: Routledge.

Harper, Edward B. (1969) "Fear and the Status of Women." *Southwestern Journal of Anthropology* 25(1): 81–95.

Hepp, Andreas (2016) "Pioneer Communities: Collective Actors in Deep Mediatisation." *Media Culture Society* 38(6): 918–933.

Hiltebeitel, Alf (1981) "Draupadi's Hair." In Biardeau, Madeleine, (ed.), *Autour de la Déesse Hindoue*. Paris: Éditions de l'École des Hautes Études en Sciences Sociales, pp. 179–214.

Ishk Ka Rang Safed (2015–2016) TV Serial, Colors TV.

Jayal, Shakambari (1966) *The Status of Women in the Epics*. Delhi: Motilal Banarsidass.

Jensen, Robert and Oster, Emily (2009) "The Power of TV: Cable Television and Women's Status in India." *The Quarterly Journal of Economics* 124(3): 1057–1094.

Justice, Christopher (1997) *Dying the Good Death: The Pilgrimage to Die in India's Holy City*. Delhi: Sri Satguru Publications.

Kahāni (2012) Film. Boundscript Motion Pictures. Distributor Viacom 18 Motion Pictures, Pen India Limited.

Kane, Pandurang Vaman (1974) [1930] *History of Dharmashastra*, Vol. 2. Poona: Bhandarkar Oriental Research Institute.

Leach, E.R. (1958) "Magical Hair." *The Journal of the Royal Anthropological Institute of Great Britain and Ireland* 88(2): 147–164.

Leslie, Julia (1986) "Strisvabhava: The Inherent Nature of Women." In Allen, N.J. and Gombrich, R.F., (eds.), *Oxford University Papers on India* Vol. 1, Part I. Delhi: Oxford University Press, pp. 28–58.

Leslie, Julia (1989) *The Perfect Wife: The Orthodox Hindu Woman According to the Strīdharmapaddhati of Tryambakayajvan*. Delhi: Oxford University Press.

Mankekar P. (1999) *Screening Culture, Viewing Politics: An Ethnography of Television, Womanhood and National in Postcolonial India*. Durham, NC: Duke University Press.

Michaels, Axel (1992) "Recht auf Leben und Selbsttötung in Indien." In Bernhard Mensen, (ed.), *Recht auf Leben – Recht auf Töten: Ein Kulturvergleich*. Nettetal: Steyler Verlag, pp. 95–124.

Monier-Williams, Monier F. (ed.) (1993 [1899]) *Sanskrit-English Dictionary*. Delhi: Motilal Banarsidass.

Munshi, Shoma (2010) *Prime Time Soap Operas on Indian Television*. New Delhi and Oxford: Routledge.

Nair, P.S. (1988) "Widowhood in India: Levels and Trends." In Nagesh, H.V., Nair P.S., and Katti, A.P., eds., *Widowhood in India: A Collection of Papers Presented at the National Seminar on Widowhood in India, Dharwad March 1987*. Dharwad: Sri Dharmasthala Manjunatheshwara Educational Trust, pp. 1–14.

Nandwana, Shoba and Nandwana, Ramesh (1998) "Land Rights of Widows in Rajasthan." In Chen, Martha Alter, (ed.), *Widows in India: Social Neglect and Public Attention*. New Delhi: SAGE, pp. 228–240.

Obeyesekere, Gananath (1981) *Medusa's Hair: An Essay on Personal Symbols and Religious Experience*. Chicago and London: The University of Chicago Press.

Olivelle, Patrick (1991) "From Feast to Fast: Food and the Indian Ascetic." In Leslie, Julia, (ed.), *Rules and Remedies in Classical Indian Law*. Leiden: E.J. Brill, pp. 17–36.

Ojha, Catherine (1981) "Feminine Asceticism in Hinduism: Its Tradition and Present Condition." *Man in India* 61(3): 254–285.

Parry, Jonathan P. (1994) *Death in Banaras*. New Delhi: Cambridge University Press.

Rājnīti (2010) Film. Prakash Jha Productions, Walkwater Media Ltd. Distributer UTV Motion Pictures.

Saraswati, Baidyanath (1988) "The Kashivasi Widows: A Study in Cultural Ideology and Crisis." In Nagesh, H.V., Nair, P.S., and Katti, A.P., (eds.), *Widowhood in India: A Collection of Papers Presented at the National Seminar on Widowhood in India, Dharwad March 1987*. Dharwad: Sri Dharmasthala Manjunatheshwara Educational Trust, pp. 103–118.

Sharma, Arvind, Ray, Ajit, Hejib, Alaka and Young, Katherine K. (1988) *Sati: Historical and Phenomenological Essays*. Delhi: Motilal Banarsidass.

Somani, Indira S. and Doshi, Marissa J. (2016) "'That's Not Real India': Responses to Women's Portrayals in Indian Soap Operas." *Journal of Communication Inquiry* 40(3): 203–231.

Stafford, Roy (2014) *The Global Film Book*. New York: Routledge.

Winternitz, Moritz (1920) *Die Frau in den indischen Religionen, 1. Teil: Die Frau im Brahmanismus*. Leipzig: Verlag Curt Kabitzsch.

6 Modern technology and its impact on religious performances in rural Himachal Pradesh

Personal remembrances and observations

Brigitte Luchesi

For Christoph Auffarth

Like other parts of India, the North Indian state of Himachal Pradesh has seen a large number of technological changes during the last thirty years. Not surprisingly most of these transformations started in towns and larger settlements. But by now the rural areas, which in the 1980s lagged behind, have caught up in an amazing way. In spring 2015, a young boy who had overheard me asking about a religious ritual advised me to "go to internet!" The Internet and other modern means of communication are among the latest innovations, and they undoubtedly influence the way knowledge about religious performances are imparted – not only between actors and out-siders, but also between the actors themselves. But even earlier these tech-nological developments had a considerable impact on religious performances. The following examples are based on observations made by me over more than 30 years.[1] As a scholar of comparative religions and a trained social anthropologist, I was fascinated by the various religious rites I got to know when visiting villages in the Kangra Valley of Southern Himachal Pradesh in the early 1980s. During the following three decades I never lost my initial interest in these topics and tried to learn more about them, especially topics concerning women's religiosity, the transmission of ritual knowledge within familial groups, the organization and relevance of religious village events, and the actual importance of the major regional temples for the local population. I was also always interested in the changes and new developments taking place in the religious realm. What I observed and learned over the years is naturally only a fraction of the rich and diversified religious sphere which is characteristic of this valley, let alone of Himachal Pradesh at large or even India as a whole. It is, more-over, colored by my interests and preferences. I nevertheless hope that the following rather personal remembrances and observations may help cast some light on the impact which modern technology may have on the forms of religious performances – in Kangra as well as in other Indian regions.

Glimpses of village life in 1984 and 2016

Visits to Kangra in the 1980s

During my first visits to Himachal Pradesh I was staying with friends in Palampur, one of the larger towns of District Kangra in the southern part of the state, but used every occasion to get to know the surrounding countryside. In 1984 I was given the opportunity to stay in Andreta for a while. This village is situated in the Kangra Valley, which stretches out in a roughly west–east direction between the Shivalik mountains to the south and the Dhauladhar, the first Himalayan Mountain Range, to the north. My host introduced me to a number of people in and around Andreta with whom I became friends, among them two sisters from an established local trader family, a Brahmin couple in the nearby compound of Bahru and a Rajput English teacher and his family in the village Dattal about 3 kilometers to the west. His house and farmland are half a kilometer away from the metaled main road, at that time reached by a narrow footpath. Both villages, Andreta and Dattal, were connected by road to Panchrukhi, a market town situated near a station on the local narrow-gauge railway, which starts in the Punjabi city of Pathankot and ends in Jogindernagar further east. Bus traffic on the roads between the two mentioned villages and Panchrukhi was infrequent and irregular. People usually walked part of or the whole distance, that is, either about 2 or 5 kilometers, by foot. Private motorized transport was practically non-existent. I remember only one jeep, which belonged to a potter from Delhi who had settled in Andreta. Neither do I remember scooters, motorbikes or privately owned trucks. Some persons had bicycles. The nearest place to get a taxi was in Panchrukhi where one of the shopkeepers kept an old Ambassador. He also owned a telephone, which was quite dependable, whereas the two private telephones in Andreta rarely worked. For postal service including telegrams one had to go to Panchrukhi, too. People in this area therefore had to be good walkers. They often had to walk long distances to reach their places of employment, schools, the larger market town, medical and other services, but also relatives living in other villages. Trips to the town were only undertaken when really necessary, and then it was a matter of course to carry out errands or purchase things for others.

The accomplishment of the daily tasks in rural households was in many ways dependent on the sort of available devices and resources. Good examples are the cooking arrangements. While many urban households owned gas cookers connected to gas cylinders, cooking in the rural areas was mostly done in the traditional way. Food and water was heated in bulbous vessels on low open fireplaces (*culha*). The collection of firewood for these *culha*s, a hard and time-consuming work, was usually the task of women. Some households owned a kerosene cooker as an additional device, but it was tricky to handle and kerosene not always available. Pressure cookers had become quite popular but other modern items like fridges, washing machines, ventilators were normally lacking. This was not so much due to a lack of financial resources but to insufficient supply of electricity. Power cuts occurred regularly, and they often caused the expensive light bulbs to break. There were only few devices to light a room. People therefore went to bed soon after nightfall and got up early in the morning. They usually did not read or– in the case of children – study at night. Transistor radios, although prestige objects, were not much used, as the necessary batteries were not easily available. The few existing television sets seldom functioned properly.

Water pipes inside houses and even outside taps were rare. There were public water pumps in several places but they functioned only for a certain number of hours. Drinking water was usually fetched at a spring (*baori*), which customarily was walled in and had a small water tank attached to it where laundry could be washed. Men and boys used to take their baths at the *baori*s or the nearby stream, while women carried water for bathing to their homes. Only a few houses had toilets.

Buildings in the rural areas were still markedly different from those in the towns and larger market places where flat-roofed houses, made from baked bricks, mortar and cement, were in the majority. Although specimens of these "modern" buildings could also be found in the villages the traditional house type was still prevalent: one- or two-storeyed mud-houses with stone foundations and slate roofs. Cowsheds and huts were covered with straw or corrugated iron. Interior walls and floors were plastered with a mixture of clay, cow dung and husks. Most building materials—clay, stones, bamboo, wood, husks, cow dung etc.—were available on the spot, and slates came from the nearby slate mines in the mountains.

A revisit in 2016

When I visited Andreta and Dattal in spring 2016 the intensive building activities, which had taken place for the last twenty years, were most visible along the road between Andreta and the now very busy market town Panchrukhi. Instead of the three or four farmhouses surrounded by fields, house after house lined the road, interspersed with a gas station and workshops. All belong to the cement and baked-brick type, having flat roofs and being coated with brightly colored industrial paints. Inside both villages similar new structures had risen, either in addition to or instead of traditional houses. In Dattal a number of impressive metal gates, which separate the courtyards from the public paths, struck the eye. Several of these lanes, which used to be simple dirt paths, have been metaled. Even the old cobblestone path in Andreta, formerly part of the traditional salt route between Punjab and the high mountains, was coated with cement. Some of the courtyards were paved with flagstones, while many of the roofed-over verandas in front of main houses were covered with stone or marble slabs. Both materials are much in demand these days. Marble comes in great quantities from Rajasthan several hundred kilometers to the south and is sold in special depots near the main district roads. Interior floors may also be covered with slabs, walls – especially those in bathrooms and kitchens – with tiles. The traditional hearth is often kept in place, but is mostly used only for preparing flat breads (*capati*s) and heating the place on cold days. Cooking is primarily done on raised gas cookers (see Figure 6.1). Water pipes have become standard items, if not inside the house then very near to it; and separate toilet huts are to be found practically everywhere. A major innovation is the supply of fairly stable electricity. It not only makes for good lighting during the dark hours, but also allows the use of a lot of household implements, as for instance fridges, refrigerators, irons, fans, and electric sewing machines. Television sets and computers can be safely connected, mobiles and other modern devices charged. Landlines, which were installed on a huge scale in the 1990s, are still in use but the majority of people depend on mobiles these days. Simple mobiles are comparatively cheap and charges are moderate. Many people own mobiles with additional functions, for instance taking photos. Smart phones and tablets are still rare in the rural areas but along with the increasing Internet accessibility in all parts of the Kangra Valley they will most probably become popular soon.[2]

Another obvious development is the dramatic increase in traffic. One of its reasons is the constantly growing numbers of privately owned motorized vehicles, be it scooters, motorbikes or cars, as well as trucks and tractors used

Figure 6.1 Renovated kitchen with tiled floor and walls in a farmhouse in village Dattal, 2015. A traditional hearth is kept but the bulk of cooking is now done on a gas cooker. Photo: Brigitte Luchesi

for agricultural work. This development is accompanied by the steady extension of the road network and improved road conditions. People are now much
less dependent on public transport than before, but are able to reach distant
places more easily while, on the other hand, the path is opened for modern
commodities to come directly to their doorstep.

Impact of new technologies on religious forms of expression

A number of the new developments referred to above have had effects on
several traditional religious practices, which used to be popular in the countryside for a long time. I will sketch some of these practices in the form I
witnessed them in earlier years and then point out the changes, which came to
my attention in recent years.

Housing conditions and religious practices of rural women

Most of the religious life of the rural population in Kangra with which I
came in touch in the 1980s took place either within individual households
or together with the paternally related families living in the immediate
vicinity (see e.g. Parry, 1979: 19f.). Sometimes neighbors belonging to other
castes were included. The responsibility for a large number of religious activities lay with the female family members. They were of great importance in
the daily acts of worship (*puja*s) in the morning and evening. Even in the
cases where the actual worship was performed by men or boys the preparatory part stayed in the hands of women and girls, as for example cleaning
the places and the implements of worship and providing fresh flowers and
other items needed for worship. Places of worship were *puja* shrines inside the
house, often set up in a niche of the main room, and certain spaces in the
courtyard. Most conspicuous in high caste courtyards were pedestals made of
stone or clay with a *tulsi* plant on top. This basil plant (*Ocimum sanctum*) is
considered to be an embodiment of goddess Brinda, wife of god Vishnu.
Another widespread religious object kept outside the house was a flat stone
with engraved footprints. They represent Baba Balak Nath, one of the most
popular saints of the region whose main shrine in District Hamirpur is a
favorite pilgrimage destination.

The preparations for and organization of important yearly religious festivals
like Divali, Shivaratri, Basant Pancmi, the Spring and Fall Navaratras as well
as the first day of each solar month (*sankranti*) were exclusively done by
women. Many of them used to combine some of these religious festivals with
a fast (*vrat*) which was meant to support the requests directed to the presiding
deity of the occasion. So for instance on Haritalika Tij and Karva Cauth
requests were made for the protection of husbands, on Hoi for that of sons,
and on Raksha Bandhan and Bhaia Duj for that of brothers (see e.g. Wadley,
1976). Part of the preparatory activities were nearly always ritual designs
(*alpana*), locally known as *apan* or *rangoli*, made by the women in the

courtyard, in some cases also inside the house (see e.g. Handa, 1975: 8–18, Plates 2, 5, 6–10, 11). *Apan* are means to mark a space as the adequate place to worship deities, which is done by applying flowers, rice grains and water on top of the designs. The indispensable ritual purification of the chosen place is done by spreading a mixture of earth and cow dung on the ground, whereby the dung as a product of the revered animal is considered to be the purifying substance. For the traditional way of applying the designs lime is dissolved in water. A piece of cloth is dipped into the white liquid, put into one hand and then slightly pressed, so that the color can flow down along the two out-stretched fingers with which the lines are drawn. *Apan* for *sankranti* were comparatively simple designs on a small square, but those for major holidays were usually very intricate and skillfully done. Often they were not confined to the courtyard but also done on thresholds and inside the house. On the festival Divali it was customary to connect the large *apan* in the courtyard with the one inside the house by making a long row of footprints, which were meant to lead goddess Lakshmi, the main deity of the day, into the house.

Occasionally designs were also made on a wall inside the house, most often on the eastern wall, as the east is considered to be the abode of the gods. On Hoi, for instance, when mothers asked the goddess Hoi Mata to protect their sons, women made a drawing on the wall which, in a stylized form, depicted the goddess as well as a number of children seated around a flat object. While doing *puja* small amounts of food were pressed into this "basket."

Making drawings like the ones mentioned, especially those for Hoi, was not something that was thought to be of secondary importance or merely a decoration that made the place look festive. Making designs was understood as a ritually necessary activity and as part of the attempts to represent the divine being that one wished to worship. Characteristically many of the representations were made by devotees themselves. Handmade tangible and visible representations of deities in *pujas* on special days in the yearly round of religious festivals used to be most conspicuous on Haritalika Tij and during Rali Puja. On both occasions goddess Parvati is worshipped, Rali being one of the local names of this goddess. The Kangra region has long been known for Rali Puja, a month-long ritual performed by young girls in spring (see e.g. Luchesi, 2002). It is said that it may help them to find a good husband. For this *puja* the girls, with the help of elder women, make three cult figures from unbaked clay – for Rali, her husband Shiva and her brother Bastu – which are used in the daily worship for a month, at the end of which Rali and Shiva are married in a full marriage ceremony. Shortly after, the figures are immersed in water in a solemn ritual called *visarjan*. Similar figures were made by grown-up married women on Haritalika Tij in early fall, an occasion when Parvati's ascetic efforts to gain the attention and love of Shiva are remembered.

In the month of *Kartik* (October–November) five days are reserved for the worship of the sacred basil plant. Especially upper cast women kept a fast (*vrat*) on these days and fulfilled certain obligations, as for instance keeping oil lamps burning in front of the *puja* place with a potted basil plant in its midst for the whole period. The last day is known as *Tulsi Vivah*, the marriage of Tulsi. It is the day when the plant is married to god Vishnu. It is made to look like a bride by knotting a red ribbon around it and covering it with a red and golden veil. A red thread connects it with a stone, representing her husband. The same is done to the plant in the courtyard, which enables outsiders, too, to learn that *Saili*, as the bridal plant is locally called, is married. The event was often also indicated by new drawings on its pedestal. They typically showed two marriage palanquins surrounded by musicians and dowry items.

Women who performed a *tulsi vrat* had often taken a vow to perform this *vrat* and *puja* for a certain number of years. The final completion gave grounds for a grand celebration in which relatives and neighbors took part. Vows to perform special *puja*s over a number of years were also part of several other religious festivals, among them the already mentioned *Haritalika Tij* and *Karva Cauth*. In all cases, whether at the end of a yearly *vrat* or at the completion of a series of *vrat*s, it was common for female neighbors to gather in the home of the woman who had performed the *puja* to sing together and listen to stories one of them told. Usually the stories bore a relation to the festive occasion.[3]

Looking at women's religious performances in recent years a number of changes are noticeable. I will start with the just mentioned *vrat*s. Many women still promise to keep *vrat*s and perform them either for their own benefits or that of close kin (see e.g. Pearson, 1996). It seems that some of the occasions, as for instance *Haritalika Tij*, are less celebrated, whereas others, which formerly were not so prominent, have gained wide acceptance. One of the latter is *Karva Cauth* (literally, "Pitcher Fourth"), which is celebrated on the fourth day of the lunar month of *Kartik*. Married women will perform a *puja* and keep a full fast for the benefit of their husbands from sunrise to moonrise at night. Newspapers and television programs make everybody aware of the onset of this event, and traders in the market towns display a multitude of goods which are especially meant for this festival as for instance certain sweets, cosmetics and decorative articles. The indispensable pitchers are still available in the form of painted clay pots but tend to be replaced by fancier specimens. Special posters are available, depicting *Karva Cauth* scenes, as well as pamphlets explaining the meaning of the festival and giving advice how to perform the *puja*. Handmade designs, however, are less prominent. When I inquired about stories connected with this occasion, I was told by several women that they do not have a good storyteller in their neighborhood. But they would not mind spending the time until moonrise watching television as usually nice programs are broadcast on this day. This confirms the assumption Kirin Narayan already expressed many years ago when she wrote "village women may continue to perform the rituals, but not tell the stories" (Narayan, 1997: 221). Urmila Sood with whom she had discussed this topic had pointed out to her that the faith in the traditional stories was vanishing.

In my own discussions with Urmila Sood, her sister and other women, I had come to a similar conclusion. My general impression is that *vrats* and other religious rituals are still performed by many women, but that stories and also various activities, which formerly accompanied the festive events, are considered to be less important or even impractical under modern conditions.

In the case of *Rali Puja*, the month-long ritual performed by girls in spring, these last two aspects are prominent. Over the last twenty years there has been a definite decline in the numbers of girl groups doing *Rali Puja*. A quite reliable way to observe this development is to visit the places where the public immersion of the Rali figures is usually carried out. I did this repeatedly at three of the important immersion places of the area: the river near Camunda temple in Dadh, the fishpond in Andreta and the riverbank near the bridge in Mataur. People whom I asked confirmed that *Rali Puja* was much less in vogue than before. The reasons given to me were the following: Girls have to study a lot to acquire a good education and they have to help their mothers at home, and both activities would make it impossible to perform the two daily *pujas* and the time-consuming preparations connected with them. Another reason is said to be that often not enough girls are around to form a functioning group. I was also told that the girls themselves are not very enthusiastic about it. As a Rajput friend put it: "[g]irls don't appear to be interested in all these traditional festivities. I feel these rituals and stuff are on the way out."

Regarding the figures used in *Rali Puja* I found that in many cases they are no longer made by the girls and their female relatives themselves, but were bought from potters, and that the numbers of bought figures is rising. It is easy to discern them. Figures made by potters are produced with the help of molds and are painted with bright colors. They are still handmade but look more or less alike, and, interestingly, the figure of Rali's brother Bastu is missing. When I asked girls and women in general why they had bought the figures I was either told that they do not know how to make clay figures or that they did not have time to do it. But it was obvious that they took time to carefully dress and decorate them, and that they were proud of the results. This made me feel that they preferred them to self-made ones. In the three places where I witnessed *Rali Puja* rituals in recent years the figures were still done at home, each set in a very individual way. But I noticed another change: The special *Rali* songs which used to be connected with several of the daily rites were not sung. It turned out that the girls did not know them or only a single verse or a few lines. When they gathered to sing, they always chose well-known devotional songs and songs they had heard on tapes, usually in Hindi and not in local Pahari. They also liked to accentuate the singing with hand clapping and beating a drum, which often encouraged them to start dancing, too. Kirin Narayan who has collected traditional women's songs over many years while also paying attention to recent developments and new occasions for joint singing, as for instance during a march for single women's rights in 2006, witnessed similar trends and concluded recently:

religious singing continuous, a space to dip into and feel blessed, even as the sorts of bhajans and bhents might be changing: texts are shorter, snappier, and less likely to be in dialect, and the collective performance of religious identity can carry newly politicized dimensions. (Narayan, 2016: 222)

The various designs painted on floors and walls on the occasion of *vrat*s and various festivals which I mentioned above have become less common, especially when the women live in recently built or rebuilt houses for which baked bricks and cement were used. A reason often heard for the replacement of clay floor and clay-plastered walls is the amount of work to keep an adobe house clean and in order. Women are said to save energy and time. This is an important consideration as household help is presently hard to get and unmarried daughters may have other obligations in paid jobs or at school. A side effect of the new living spaces is, however, that women hesitate to draw designs on their walls and floors. Industrial colorfast paints leave permanent marks, and even drawings done with the traditional colored powders are difficult to erase. Another reason seems to be, although it was not directly voiced, that people consider the drawing of traditional designs on the new floors and walls old-fashioned and not in line with modern forms of life. In fact, many households do without drawings these days, especially inside the house. Occasionally drawings are done on a piece of paper which then is fixed to the wall, but most often another medium is used: colorful prints of god and goddesses available at temples and in stationary stores in great variety. They have long been in circulation (see e.g. Neumayer and Schelberger, 2003), but a certain type, namely posters for special occasions, appeared only in the late 1990s. As opposed to most of the other so-called god-posters they have a definitive function for certain chosen days only. Printed posters for Hoi Mata are a case in point; on these posters the name of the occasion is clearly given in big letters in the upper part. Head, hands and feet of the goddess are shown; her body is covered by a square, which, like the handmade designs, is filled with signs, and symbols that refer to stories about her. The strong similarity to the folk style versions may be understood as an explicit request to use them like the traditional ones, that is, applying (as described above) food on them (Luchesi, 2010: 215). Similar posters are available now for *Karva Cauth* as well. Another type are shiny prints, labeled "shubh vivah" (auspicious wedding), which are designed for marriage celebrations.

The latest invention to decorate tiled or marbled verandas without spoiling them are industrially produced stickers, which are sold in household supply shops. The round items in different sizes with designs, which vaguely resemble the folk style ones, are mainly for Divali. They go together with small stickers in form of footprints. Obviously regarded as something beautiful and desirable, these stickers have spread fast from the towns to the countryside.

Marble is now also often chosen to shelter the religious items kept in the courtyard. A variety of small roofed marble structures with three walls are offered for sale in the places selling marble. They are frequently made to house the stone footprints of Baba Balak Nath. Inside they may be covered with glazed tiles, whereby the central one often carries a picture of the Baba in full iconic form, as it is known from posters, in other words, as young boy riding a peacock. Recently these structures are often accompanied by a marble bowl on a pedestal for the tulsi plant, which is normally not decorated. This sort of development follows, I think, that which is to be observed in temples. People often equip religious spaces with the most expensive and up-to-date materials and decorative elements. It seems that they consider all items, which they appreciate and would like to have for their own profane use, the most appropriate ones for housing the representations of their revered gods.

Some impacts of stable electricity, television and electronic devices

The increasingly improved electricity supply in the rural areas has opened a number of new possibilities: first of all, good and relatively stable electric lighting and the use of a number of electrical appliances. A great demand for television sets among the rural population started in the late 1980s when the Indian public service broadcaster *Doordarshan* began to broadcast the first series of mythological dramas specially produced for television – first *Ramayana* and later on *Mahabharata*—every Sunday morning (see e.g. Lutgendorf, 1995). To watch this event people gathered in front of shops, which sold TVs and, wherever it was possible, in private houses, which already had a television set. "Come and see our gods," I was told by the head of a Rajput household in Dattal in 1987 and was given a seat between all the people who filled the room and reverently watched the events on the screen although the transmission was very poor. Here as in other places the viewers belonged to different castes and status groups. Household heads, not happy with this social mixing but unable to keep their womenfolk and children from watching the extremely popular program in other houses, often finally decided to purchase a set of their own. In the following years more and more sets were sold. At the same time the reception improved, not least because of the transmission per satellite. Nowadays a whole range of national and international TV channels may be received. Among them are channels, which cover religious ceremonies or present certain gurus. Very popular these days is the guru and yoga expert Baba Ramdev, whose televised speeches are followed by many (see e.g. Chakrabarti, 2012).

As I could observe over the years, people tend to switch on television whenever they have some free time or, mostly in case of women, tasks which may be done inside the house. This trend does affect the traditional ways of spending leisure time. Several informants confirmed that women less often gather to sing together or to tell and listen to stories. It is likely that a number of the traditional songs and stories, which were connected with local religious lore, will fall into oblivion. I was told that young girls are not much interested in them; they prefer to watch TV serials or read books they themselves choose. When I asked girls to tell me a story they had heard from their elders or sing an old local song they were rarely able to do so. The impact of television on the practice of and interest in storytelling was already discussed in the 1990s by Kirin Narayan and Urmila Devi Sood. The latter put it in a nutshell: "Whatever time is left over, you know, it's all spent before television" (Narayan and Sood, 1997: 220).

Other modern entertainment media besides television are having certain effects, too. Video recorders and audio tapes were much in demand in the 1990s and the beginning of the twenty-first century, but have lost their appeal with the introduction of CDs, DVDs and the appropriate playback devices. People interested in religious music and films find a good selection in the shops. Downloading on computers, mobiles and MP3 players is the latest possibility.

As mentioned above simple mobiles are widespread. To own a smart-phone or tablet, which especially young people like to have, is a question of money. To have one and to know how to handle it may enhance one's reputation as a modern person. Very popular is the use of all types of mobiles for taking photos. As everywhere, younger persons like to make selfies. But the interest in taking pictures encompasses many more motifs. Many auspicious life cycle ceremonies, which formerly were rarely recorded photographically, may now be photographed by a relative. Cases in point are first haircut ceremonies and sacred thread rites. One effect is that professional photographers are less often called for, and pictures taken by visitors including ethnographers are not as sought after as formerly. When visiting temples devotees like to take pictures not only outside the building, but often also inside in front of the worshipped deity. This may be understood as a way of having *darshan* (sight) of a deity with the help of an external third eye. The moment of seeing the deity with one's own eyes is seized and made permanent. In a next step a print may be made, which may then become a privately used devotional picture. Deities depicted in the form of living images (*jhankis*) are an equally popular photographic motif.

Personal computers become more and more important, especially young people deem it necessary to get acquainted with this medium. Private owned PCs seem still rather rare, but many colleges and places of higher education are equipped with PCs, and a number of private institutions offer courses. In recent years I met several young village girls who attended computer classes in towns nearby where they have also the chance to learn about the Internet and its use. The young boy who advised me to check on the Internet did obviously already know that information on religious matters could be found on the net. As I learned later, he had just visited relatives in the village but lived otherwise in a town. His parents owned a computer with Internet access, and he was allowed to use it. Either he himself or his mother or sisters had realized how easy it is to get information on religious festivals, ritual practices, mythological stories, pilgrimage sites and the like in no time. He could not be aware that there was no entry regarding the rites I was interested in, namely *Rali Puja*, and that they most probably were not the ones local people would like to know about in the first place. Up to now, it seems, women are more interested in what city women do on certain days, or, to put it differently, what they think modern women are doing. It is quite likely that in this process more of the traditional customs and performances will fall into oblivion.

Water pipes and ancestor worship

Drinking water was traditionally fetched from springs, which in the mountainous parts of Kangra district are frequent. Water for animals, bathing and various household tasks was usually taken from streams, and an elaborated channel system (*kuhls*) made the irrigation of the fields possible. The springs (*baori*) with their precious drinking water are places, which it was a time-honored custom to protect and to take care of. *Baori*s were also places thought to be suited for the construction of a small temple in their vicinity and/or a holy tree, especially a pipal tree (*Ficus religiosa*). Spring, tree and temple transform an otherwise profane space into a special one where, besides necessary daily tasks, various religious rituals may take place, among them the occasional worship of the pipal tree with water, a sacred thread and other offerings.

In Kangra the walled-in springs were also the place to keep the memorial stones for deceased family members, called *mohra* or *muhrka* (see e.g. Luchesi, 1994). The stones are hewed and usually display a figure which, according to the gender of the deceased person, is male or female. *Mohra*s used to be made for grown-up men and women and were consecrated by the funeral priest as the last act of the death rites he was performing for a deceased person. Red powder (*sindur*) was rubbed on the stones and a red cloth as well as a sacred thread was wrapped around them. These actions marked the beginning of the rites, which the descendants performed for the deceased. They consisted of applying rice grains, flower petals and *sindur* to the stones on certain days and, most importantly, offering water every day. As it was believed that *mohra*s should not be kept in the house or compound where the deceased had lived they were brought to an appropriate spot outside the house. Not surprisingly, in most cases where a household had a *baori* nearby, this place was chosen and the water offerings given by the descendants who came to fetch water and, in the case of men, bathed in the morning. After a full year the rites came to an end; the stones, however, stayed on where they had been put and began to weather.

I already pointed out that over the years more and more water pipes have been installed so that many households have now tap water inside the house or nearby. This has had some repercussions with regard to the memorial stones. By the end of the last century many springs looked neglected and memorial stones unattended. It seemed likely that the custom of erecting *mohra*s would soon become extinct. But occasionally a stone covered in remnants of red garment could be made out – a sure sign that it was newly erected and the custom still practiced. Observations and information gathered during recent years point to the following developments: In several places memorial stones are still erected but the accompanying rites have been changed. Instead of the daily offerings of water up to the first death anniversary of a person, it now may happen that all of them are given in one go right at the beginning. Daily visits to the spring are thereby rendered unnecessary. Attention to a new *mohra* can be restricted to those days when the deceased family ancestors are remembered and worshipped in their entirety, as for instance during the yearly fortnight for the dead (*pitrpaksha*). That a renewed importance is given to the whole group of stones may be inferred from the fact that *mohra*s in many places have been recently rearranged. They are now often lined up in rows on newly built steps so that all of them are shown to advantage. Although the function of *mohra*s in the death rites for individual family members has been reduced, their importance as lasting memorials is retained: they are tangible objects which represent the ancestors in their entirety and keep their memory alive for the living descendants. This was brought home to me in 2015 when I revisited a *baori* which I saw many years ago. While looking at the stones – most of them are now lying flat in neat rows on top of the new concrete structure, which covers the spring – a group of singing women appeared. In their midst was a young woman, who by her festive turn-out was clearly discernible as a newlywed bride. As is customary in the rural areas of Kangra, she was brought to all the places, which hold religious value for the kinship group, into which a young bride is incorporated by marriage. The bride took water from the spring and sprinkled it like her mother-in-law before her over the *mohra*s, thus paying reference to the deceased ancestors as a new member of the group of descendants.

Motorized vehicles and "living images"

I had already pointed to the changes in house constructions, the availability of goods and the improvement of transport, which the increase in motorized vehicles brought about. Things which formerly were carried on shoulders or heads—be it milk and agricultural products, cereals or household goods – are increasingly transported by motor scooters, cars, tractors and lorries. Not only profane things have been moved and are now moved in a different way, objects of worship, too, are often brought to other places. In the hilly areas of Himachal Pradesh, in Mandi, Kullu, Chamba, Pangi and Kinnaur, images of local gods used to be brought on festive occasions to the village gods in their vicinity or to the place of a central divinity. That was, and still is, mostly done by carrying them on palanquins. A recent trend, however, is to transport them on trucks or other vehicles at least part of the way. In Kangra Valley transportable brass images like those in the upper regions are rare and the custom of gods paying visits to each other is not widespread. But there is another popular custom, which for long required the use of palanquins, too. This is the preparation of so-called *jhanki*s, displays of Hindu gods and goddesses, of mythological themes and occasionally of historical events (see e.g. Luchesi,

Figure 6.2 Group of women with new bride at the spring in village Tatehal, 2015.
The structure around the spring is new and normally closed. On its roof
memorial stones are kept to which the mother-in-law of the bride has just
offered water and flowers. Photo: Brigitte Luchesi

2014). The deities and the other characters are represented by living persons
expected to remain motionless and silent throughout the performance. These
"living images" are made and publicly displayed on various religious holidays.
Many villages chose the holidays Holi and Janamashtami. Most often they
are taken in a procession through the village or town for everybody to see.
Over the years it became more and more common to transport them on
trucks or trailers pulled by tractors. In Andreta, the village I referred to in the
beginning, the carrying on palanquins was done until recently. But in 2015
this mode of transport was stopped here, too. Since then, the images have been
installed on tractors driven by their proud owners (see Figure 6.3). To outsiders
this change may look like a decline in religious devotion, but the organizers'
view is different. They emphasize that the transport by cars is safer for the
actors who are in most cases young boys. Indeed, when carried on a palan-
quin they had to be tied to poles and elevated seats, and quite often the whole
arrangement seemed in danger of tumbling down. I was also informed about
the difficulty to get enough strong experienced carriers these days. But behind
these explanations another reason is discernible which seems even more
important: the wish to be able to display traditional customs and religious
beliefs in a new, modern look.[4] In places like Andreta this striving after more
up-to-date performances is also inspired by the wish to align with developments in the larger places and feel less looked-down-upon by townspeople.
That the extent of technological modernization in the presentation of *jhanki*s

in Andreta and other villages is still quite moderate becomes clear when compared for instance with the yearly parade of living images which takes place in the town of Palampur during Holi. The participating *jhanki*s from Palampur and three adjacent villages compete for the approval of the public and the commission, which decides on the best one. All the tractors and trucks, which carry the images, have generators attached to them, which make all sorts of light effects possible. The electricity is also used to make props swing and turn around, while the music from huge loudspeakers adds to the spectacle. The presentations neatly blend in with the fairs – the carousels, swing boats and tremendous noise – which are going on at the same time. However, the whole event does not prevent those who want to greet and worship the presented deities in human form to do so with great devotion.

Concluding remarks

I have tried to sketch some of the impacts that the latest technological changes in parts of Himachal Pradesh have had on a number of religious performances. In order to have a certain background against which changes may be better recognized I have deemed it advisable to start out by looking at past conditions. The impacts I found are manifold. However, they were rarely so

Figure 6.3 Tractor with *jhanki* ("living image") on a metaled road in village Andreta, 2016. On the left two traditional adobe houses, on the right a modern building made from cement and baked bricks. Photo: Brigitte Luchesi

forceful that the performances in question were wiped out completely. It rather seems that in most cases the new technological means and developments have entered the field of religious practices in form of new potential offers to reshape, redesign and sometimes expand the existing religious forms of expression. The latter trend is most clearly discernible in the case of processions including the presentation of "living images" (*jhankis*). Here the new aids and appliances continuously supplement the older ones, whether in the sector of decoration or in that of transportation and sound. Memorial stones are still placed at the old springs which have lost their former function as principal source of water supply, but although the ritual treatment of the individual stones has changed, the group of stones is gaining a new importance as a representation of the collectivity of ancestors. Certain rites and religious adornments are being adapted to the new building materials and techniques. In this process handmade designs on floors and walls are slowly disappearing. As people obviously do not want to forego a certain amount of ornamental religious accessories they look for other industrially produced things which fit into the new surroundings. Some practices related to religious rites, especially those traditionally observed by women and girls as for instance storytelling and singing in groups, have noticeably been pushed into the background by the new entertainment electronics. Certain rites are said to be given up or are simplified owing to lack of time, which seems to be only indirectly connected with the new technologies. *Rali Puja* is here a case in point. A closer look, however, reveals an interesting aspect which may carry the discussion further: although self-made *Rali* figures are now mostly replaced by specimen fabricated by potters with the help of molds, the final dressing and decorating is still done by girls and women with great care as well as costs. This may be taken as a warning against prematurely speaking about a disappearance of women's creativity or a displacement of creativity due to modern developments. Instead of looking for signs of eradication of religion by technology one should, as Jeremy Stolow in his widely discussed introduction to *Deus in Machina* made clear, pay first and foremost attention to the interface between the two, to new "instruments of religious knowledge, power, imagination, and experience" and the new forms and practices which may emerge (Stolow, 2013: 10).

Notes

1 My first visit to Himachal Pradesh took place in 1982 in the course of which I made the acquaintance of a number of people in villages and towns in District Kangra. Except for two years, I revisited this district every year, staying between four weeks and six months. I usually lived with Indian friends and acquaintances in different villages, occasionally in the town of Palampur. Staying as a long-term guest in the households of these friends I not only shared their daily life but was privileged to witness festive occasions and religious activities at close quarters, not only of the household in question but also of those in the neighborhood. This opened up the opportunity for participant observation, one of the principal

research techniques of social anthropology. It was complemented by informal talks, interviews, and documentary techniques like video-recording and taking photos.

2　Literature on the distribution and use of the internet in India has become vast. A helpful short overview which addresses the history of the internet with regard to Hinduism, Hindu Web Sites, Internet Puja and online *darshan*, is by Heinz Scheifinger (2012).

3　Kirin Narayan (1997) has published stories, which she learned from Urmila Devi Sood, a gifted storyteller living in Andreta. Among them are several stories, which relate to the five days of fasting (Narayan, 1997: 39–106).

4　The same impetus was found by Tulasi Srinivas (2006) among priests of several temples in Bangalore who constantly thought of ways to use new technological items for the decoration of their temples and the elaboration of rituals. To do this "implies progress and power. Conversely to be without it implies a lack of contact with the modern world and a lack of status and power. The priests are sensitive to this difference, and accordingly incorporate technology into ritual to signify their familiarity with the modern" (Srinivas, 2006: 334).

References

Chakrabarti, Santanu (2012) "The Avatars of Baba Ramdev: The Politics, Economics, and Contradictions of an Indian Televangelist." In Pradip N. Thomas and Philip Lee, (eds.), *Global and Local Televangelism*. Basingstoke: Palgrave Macmillan, pp. 149–170.

Handa, O.C. (1975) *Pahāri Folk Art*. Bombay: D.B. Taraporevala.

Luchesi, Brigitte (1994) "Totengedenksteine in Kangra, Nordindien." *Mitteilungen der Berliner Gesellschaft für Anthropologie, Ethnologie und Urgeschichte* 15: 45–52.

Luchesi, Brigitte (2002) "'It Should Last a Hundred Thousand Years': Rali Worship and Brother Sister Bond in Kangra." *Manushi* 130: 20–25.

Luchesi, Brigitte (2010) "Darśan-Bilder: Hinduistische Verehrungspraxis und populäre Poster in Nordindien." In Bärbel Beinhauer-Köhler, Daria Pezzoli-Olgiati, and Joachim Valentin, (eds.), *Religiöse Blicke – Blicke auf das Religiöse: Visualität und Religion*. Zürich: Theologischer Verlag, pp. 201–225.

Luchesi, Brigitte (2014) "Jhankis: 'Living Images' as Objects of Worship in Himachal Pradesh." In Knut A. Jacobsen, Mikael Aktor and Kristina Myrvold (eds.), *Objects of Worship in South Asian Religions: Forms, Practices, and Meanings*. London and New York: Routledge, pp. 35–50.

Lutgendorf, Philip (1995) "All in the (Raghu) Family: A Video Epic in Context." In Lawrence A. Babb and Susan S. Wadley, (eds.), *Media and the Transformation of Religion in South Asia*. Delhi: Motilal Banarsidass, pp. 217–253.

Narayan, Kirin, in collaboration with Urmila Devi Sood (1997) *Mondays on the Dark Night of the Moon: Himalayan Foothill Folktales*. New York and Oxford: Oxford University Press.

Narayan, Kirin (2016) *Everyday Creativity: Singing Goddesses of the Himalayan Foothills*. Chicago, IL: University of Chicago Press.

Neumayer, Erwin and Christine Schelberger (2003) *Popular Indian Art: Raja Ravi Varma and the Printed Gods of India*. Oxford: Oxford University Press.

Parry, Jonathan P. (1979) *Caste and Kinship in Kangra*. London and Boston: Routledge & Kegan Paul.

Pearson, Anne Mackenzie (1996) *Because it Gives Me Peace of Mind: Ritual Fasts in the Religious Lives of Hindu Women.* Albany, NY: SUNY Press.

Scheifinger, Heinz (2012) "Internet." In Knut A. Jacobsen (Editor In Chief), *Brill's Encyclopedia of Hinduism*, Vol. 4. Leiden: Brill, pp. 700–706.

Srinivas, Tulasi (2006) "Divine Enterprise: Hindu Priests and Ritual Change in Neighbourhood Hindu Temples in Bangalore." *South Asia: Journal of South Asian Studies* 29(3): 321–343.

Stolow, Jeremy (2013) "Introduction: Religion, Technology, and the Things in Between." In Jeremy Stolow, (ed.), *Deus in Machina: Religion, Technology, and the Things in Between.* New York: Fordham University Press, pp. 1–22.

Wadley, Susan Snow (1976) "Brothers, Husbands and Sometimes Sons: Kinsmen in North Indian Ritual." *Eastern Anthropologist* 29: 149–120.

7   Pilgrimage rituals and technological change

Alterations in the *shraddha* ritual at Kapilashram in the town of Siddhpur in Gujarat

Knut A. Jacobsen

Research on Hinduism and the Internet has focused in particular on the use of the Internet by Hindu organizations to disseminate information, on temples and popular pilgrimage places that often produce their own website, and on the new ritual opportunity and business model of online *puja* (Jacobs, 2012; Scheifinger, 2010, 2012). Another influence of Internet is changes in the way visits to the pilgrimage sites are organized and, as a consequence of this the way rituals at the sites themselves are performed, as will be demonstrated in this chapter. New communication technology is being used to propagate the pilgrimage places and for attracting pilgrims and for organizing the travel and rituals of the pilgrims. Speed is a main feature of the changes in the communication technology that is currently taking place with the Internet and mobile phone, and speed characterizes also changes in the pilgrimage traditions. Pilgrims tend to spend less time at the pilgrimage places they visit as rapid communication also seems to imply rapid visits.

This chapter analyzes recent changes in the *shraddha* ritual at Kapilashram in the town of Siddhpur in Gujarat. New communication technology has impacted some of the ritual practices at this pilgrimage place. An important function for the *shraddha* ritual at Kapilashram is to give opportunity to appease the souls (*preta*s) of dead mothers or grandmothers. This is especially urgent when they are understood as the source of problems that the surviving families experience. Kapilashram is the main place in Hindu India for these *shraddha* rituals for the dead mothers and grandmothers and in fact, is unique in that it is the only Hindu pilgrimage site that is promoted as, and functions exclusively as a place for the performance of *shraddha* to the mothers. The sacredness of the place is based on the rituals aimed at giving *moksha* to the mother, which in this context, given the ambivalent status of the soul of the dead in Hinduism, means getting rid of a *preta* who for some reason cause problems because she has become stuck in this world and has become unable to move on in the death process.

The Kapila pilgrimage place at Siddhpur and the *shraddha* ritual

Siddhpur is part of a larger sacred geography associated with the ancient sage Kapila, who is the founder of the Samkhya system of philosophy, and who is also worshipped as an *avatara* of the Hindu god Vishnu. A number of sacred places in India claim to be associated with this ancient sage, and some of these places are major Hindu pilgrimage sites (Jacobsen, 2008, 2013). The Kapila pilgrimage place visited by the largest number of pilgrims annually is at the island of Ganga Sagar in the state of West Bengal, where the River Ganges meets the Bay of Bengal. Among the other Kapila pilgrimage places in India, the most important are Siddhpur in Gujarat, Kapiladhara in Uttar Pradesh, Kapiladhara in Bihar, Kolayat in Rajasthan and Kolyad in Haryana (Jacobsen, 2008). They are all associated with the mythology of the Samkhya system of religious thought, with asceticism and with the salvific goal of attainment of *moksha*. The power attributed to these places, which is the source of their pilgrimage traditions, is believed to have originated with Kapila performing asceticism at the sites. The belief is that after Kapila left the sites, his salvific power remained. The fact that Kapila was the founder of the famous Samkhya system of religious thought adds to the salvific power of the sites since Samkhya is considered the oldest of the Hindu systems of philosophy and Kapila according to Samkhya the first to have discovered, and realized the unchangeable immortal self (*purusha*) and thus attained final and eternal liberation from rebirth. Kapila was a teacher of *moksha* and therefore the focus of these places is *moksha* (which in the pilgrimage traditions often means first rebirth(s) in a rich family or in other realms of sensual pleasure, and thereafter freedom from rebirth [see Jacobsen, 2013: 168–169]). However, the concern of the teaching of the Kapila places of pilgrimage is most often the state of the soul after death, although Kolayat in Rajasthan is also promoted for its ability to heal, which is also a capacity ascribed to Kapila's power. Some features of the philosophy of Kapila are presented in the *Mahatmya* texts of the sites and each site is associated with one or several narratives about Kapila. Ganga Sagar is associated with the famous narrative of the coming to earth of the River Ganga, but many places is connected to Kapila by only a statement of his asceticism at the place which produced the presence of salvific power there, and an etymological explanation of the place name as "place of Kapila." Siddhpur claims to be the place of the conversation between Kapila and his mother Devahuti, which is the narrative of the *Kapilagita* found in the third part of the *Bhagavatapurana*. The place is in the *Kapilagita* called Siddhapada. However, as is not uncommon in the Hindu traditions of pilgrimage, several places often claim to be the site of the same mythological event. Patrons of the place Sidhabari in Himachal Pradesh claim this site to be that same Siddhapada of the *Kapilagita* (Tejomayananda, 1996: 90). The mythological foundation of the pilgrimage to Siddhpur is that Kapila gave *moksha* to his mother Devahuti, and that therefore a son in the same way can give *moksha* to his mother at this place. The story of the *Kapilagita* tells about

Kapila's birth as the son of Kardama and Devahuti, Kapila teaching to his mother the philosophy of salvific liberation of Samkhya and Yoga, Devahuti becoming a female ascetic and attaining *moksha* while her body becomes a sacred river. The most important feature of the story is that a son cares so much for his mother that he helps her to attain *moksha*, that is, the supreme goal of life. The pilgrimage place of Siddhpur is based on promoting this as the duty of the sons.

Kapila gave *moksha* by teaching his mother the salvific philosophy of Samkhya, but the method for giving *moksha* to mothers here, in other words, liberation of her from the state of *preta*, is by means of the *shraddha* ritual. This ritual is in Siddhpur called *matrigayashraddha, gayashradda* to the maternal ancestor. Regarding *gayashraddha*, L. P. Vidyarthi in his study of the ritual of *shraddha* in Gaya, which the term *gayashradda* refers to writes:

> Shraddha at Gaya is essentially observed in honour of the dead fathers and other progenitors and should be distinguished from the rites which immediately follow death (mrityu samskar or death sacrament), subsequent anniversary ancestor worship (varshik shraddha), or the annual ritual calendric ancestor worship (mahalaya or jitiya). While there are several common elements among the four forms of ancestor worship, the very fact that Gaya shraddha is observed at a public sacred ground (kshetra) rather than a domestic and local sacred centre and that its success brings final emancipation to the ancestors and happiness to the survivors gives its performance all possible elaboration, seriousness, and sacredness.
> (Vidyarthi, 1978: 33–34)

The term *matrigayashraddha* is meant to convey that the *shraddha* in Siddhpur is the same as the *shraddha* in Gaya, except that the *shraddha* in Gaya concerns the paternal ancestors and the *shraddha* in Siddhpur the maternal ancestors. In other words, what Gaya is for the dead father, Siddhpur is for the dead mother. The pilgrimage site associated with Kapila in Siddhpur and the narrative of him giving *moksha* to his mother there is the Kapilashram, or Kapila's ashram, at the outskirts of the city and the *matrigayashraddha* is performed here. At Kapilashram the main ritual is linked to the main temple, which contains statues of Kapila, his mother Devahuti, his father Kardama and Vishnu. This temple stands next to *bindusarovar* ("pond of tears"), which is one of three sacred waters here, the others being a well called *jnanavapi* ("the well of knowledge") and a tank called *alpasarovar* ("small pond"). The *shraddha* takes place in the courtyard or in one of several stone pavilions in front or in the vicinity of Kapil *mandir* and the *bindusarovar*.

While Siddhpur claims to be the place Siddhapada described in the *Bhagavatapurana*, it has also its own Sanskrit text to celebrate the site, the *Siddhapura Mahatmya* (n.d.). This is a short text of 114 verses that identifies the location at which Kapila taught the truth of Samkhya to his mother as the water tank Bindusaras or Bindusarovar in Siddhpur. The *Siddhapura*

Mahatmya is similar to the *Bhagavatapurana* structured as a conversation between Kapila and his mother Devahuti, but it is primary a pilgrimage text. It is mainly about the sacred geography of Siddhpur and of the larger area surrounding it such as Arbuda (Mount Abu). The drawing on the first page of the printed edition depicts the child Kapila in conversation with Kardama and Devahuti. The author of the *Siddhapura Mahatmya* first pays homage to the gods and his own teachers (verses 1–5 in *Siddhapura Mahatmya*, n.d.: 1–2), mentions some teachers of Samkhya (verse 6, *ibid.*: 2) and then describes Kapila as the son of Devahuti. According to the *Siddhapura Mahatmya*, Kapila was on a pilgrimage to the various sacred places, when he came to the Siddhashrama next to the water tank Bindusarovar. On arrival in Siddhpur, Kapila started to perform asceticism and reached "the highest state" (verses 8–9, *ibid.*: 3). His mother Devahuti then approached Kapila and told him that he should marry since this was considered right according to the *shastras*. Kapila then gives a remarkable answer, that the only purpose with his birth was to give moksha to the mother (verse 15, *ibid.*: 5). This statement sums up the ideological foundation of Kapilashram as pilgrimage site, that sons come here to give *moksha* to their mother. The text states that knowledge is necessary for liberation, especially the knowledge of giving up of the notion of 'mine' with respect to the body (verse 18, *ibid.*: 6). Upon hearing Kapila's instruction, Devahuti attained the highest state (19) and thereupon pure tear-drops flowed from her eyes (verse 20, *ibid.*: 6), after which she stated:

> *vande bindusarovaram ca kapilam samkhyadhipam yoginam siddham siddhapadam puram sukritinam kaivalyamokshapradam,*
> *ganga yatra sarasvati priyatama praci jagatpavini mata matrigaya sada vahati ya papapaha punyada*
>
> I offer my namaskar to the pond Bindusarovar; to the perfect yogin Kapila, the leader of Samkhya; to the city called Siddhapada which is the city of learned people and which grants moksha in the form of *kaivalya*, in which city Ganga Sarasvati, always flows, dearest Praci – which is instrumental in purifying the whole universe, the mother Matrigaya, and which is the killer of sins and granter of merit. (verse 21, *ibid.*: 6; author's translation)

It is at the site where Devahuti attained moksha, that *shraddha* or *pindadana*, the ritual of offering *pinda*s (rice balls) to dead mothers, takes place. By means of the *shraddha* ritual the soul of the dead, who is now called a ghost (*preta*) can be ensured a better rebirth or the attainment of heaven or even *moksha*. In his book on the Hindus, Julius Lipner gives a concise description of the main purposes of *shraddha*:

> it is considered very important to appease the *preta* by rites and offerings of food (*pinda*) and even clothes, for unappeased *pretas* can turn quite nasty towards human, especially their neglectful relatives, even possessing

people on occasion. In many traditional-minded and low-caste circles possession by *preta* is commonly believed to occur. The rites to satisfy the *preta* are called *shraddha* rites and are believed to effect transfer of merit to the *preta*. (Lipner, 1994: 272–273)

Most come to Siddhpur to perform *shraddha* to appease a *preta* of a mother or grandmother, who they think are causing problems for the surviving family, or in other words, a family experiences problems such as family conflicts, economic loss or psychological illness and comes to believe that these problems are caused by a dead mother or grandmother and that by pacifying the *preta* the problems will disappear.

When I first did research in Siddhpur in 1999, as part of the research for a monograph on the ancient sage Kapila, for the chapter on the sacred geography of Kapila (Jacobsen, 2008: 149–188), the *shraddha* ritual had several parts. The ritual involved the cutting of the hair of the sons, bathing in the Bindusarovar, the sacrifice of sixteen *pinda*s with its accompanying sixteen Sanskrit *shloka*s, watering the pipal tree with water from the Bindusarovar, taking *darshan* in the Kapil mandir, and giving payment to the Brahmans. With each of the sixteen *pinda*s (rice balls), which were offered to the *preta*, a different Sanskrit *shloka* in the simple *anushtubh* meter was repeated. This collection of *shloka*s, called Matrishodashi, expressed the son's sorrow and remorse for the different types of pain and suffering he may have caused his mother. The purpose was to appease the *preta* and by apologizing for the pain he may have caused the *preta* to suffer, in case the *preta* refuses to leave the family because she feels some injustice has been done to her. For each *pinda* that was offered, the son asked to alleviate a particular hardship his mother suffered as a result of performing the duty of reproduction. This included the suffering a mother feels as a result of the pain of having given birth to a son, of pregnancy, of birth when the baby is wrongly placed in the uterus, of the disgusting taste of the medicines she had to take, the mothers that die in childbirth, the pain experienced during her son's childhood, and finally the pain of fear the mother feels at the door of death. The sixteenth verse states:

> *yasmin kale mrita mata gatis tasya na vidyate*
> *tasya nishkramanarthaya matripindam dadamy aham* [1]
> For the mother who has died now, for she who did not find liberation, for the sake of her departure, I offer this pinda to my mother.
> (*Matrigayaparvanashraddham*, n.d.: 113, author's translation)

The story of Kapila provides the explanation of Siddhpur's salvific power. The power of Kapilashram in Siddhpur and the reason the *gayashraddha* takes place here is because Kapila gave salvific liberation to his mother at this place. Kapila personifies the son's wish and ability to grant *moksha* to his mother. Thus, while the verses recited in the *pindadana* ritual may express the feeling of guilt, the stated purpose of the ritual is to grant *moksha* to the mother.

When I first time visited the pilgrimage town of Siddhpur in 1999, it seemed to me like a traditional pilgrimage place, although completely focused on the *shraddha* ritual. By traditional I mean a large number of Brahman priests who performed the *shraddha* ritual for family groups individually, a main temple of Kapila with smaller surrounding temples and several shops selling various items, a temple basin for ritual bath, presence of a few *samnyasins*, a Sanskrit school to educate the Brahmans, a cow shed for feeding cows with the leftovers from the *shraddha* ritual, a large number of pilgrims, *panda*s with heaps of large books with names of families of ritual clients (see Figure 7.1) and a ritual pattern that most pilgrims performed. Pilgrims as I could observe arrived in small family groups, one or two sons and perhaps some other family members. Those I talked with had traveled to Siddhpur together with family members and they made arrangements with a priest after they had arrived in Siddhpur. Most ritual clients, who performed the *shraddha* were groups of two to five members or more belonging to one family and one priest performing the ritual with them.

Change of infrastructure

When I revisited Siddhpur, in 2013 and in 2016, around fifteen years after I had done the original research at the pilgrimage place, I was struck by how much the place had changed. In 2013, the pilgrimage site was a large construction site, which when I arrived in 2016 had been completed, and the

Figure 7.1 Priests with books with names and addresses of ritual clients. Photo: Knut A. Jacobsen

pilgrimage place had been transformed and modernized in an interesting meaning of that word, of adding heritage tourism features to the traditional pilgrimage place. New buildings had been built that looked more ancient than the older ones which had disappeared. The state of Gujarat had invested in Kapilashram as a heritage place. Most of the old buildings had been demolished new buildings had come up and the *bindusarovar, alpasarovar* and the *jnanavapi* had been rebuilt. The pilgrimage area had been expanded with a large modern park. The disorderly lively pilgrimage place had been rebuilt based on a Gujarat State rehabilitation plan. In 2012 Siddhpur had become part of a Gujarat State project of infrastructure development to promote "heritage tourism." In the Gujarat State document seeking developers for the project by the Tourism Corporation of Gujarat, the cultural heritage, as well as the connection between the economy and preservation of cultural heritage, was emphasized (see Jacobsen, 2016: 352).[2] In the document the concept of pilgrimage was replaced by the secular concepts of "tourism and cultural heritage" and preservation of the cultural heritage was seen as urgent due to economic growth and urbanization threatening this heritage (Jacobsen, 2016: 352). The goal of "heritage tourism" project seems to have been to attain economic growth, to increase the status of Siddhpur, and to transform it into a more important heritage place and thus increase the number of pilgrims. Although pilgrims arrive to Siddhpur from other states, especially from south India, Siddhpur is not as well known as the major pan-Indian pilgrimage places such as Badrinath, Puri, Varanasi, Vrindavan or Rameshvaram and so on, the annual flow of pilgrims is much smaller. The main reason for its lack of fame is that it is visited specifically for the *shraddha* ritual only and since Kapila is not a popular god worshipped by any major *sampradaya*s, no one comes to Siddhpur for the purpose merely of worshipping him. During my research in Siddhpur, in 1999, I met some pilgrims from south India, but during my visits in 2013, and in 2016 in particular, a large number was from the South Indian states. In 1999, when I asked people, unsystematically, why they had come and how they had heard about Siddhpur, some answered that a local priest or *pir* had advised them to go there in order to solve their family problems. Siddhpur was a traditional pilgrimage place but was not well known. Gujarat Tourist Department thought that it was possible to increase the number of pilgrim and tourist arrivals in Siddhpur because the city also have some tourist qualities, especially the olden wooden buildings of the Bohra traders.

One way to increase the attraction of Kapilashram for pilgrims was to make a large park next to it which was perceived as a form of beatification. Another way was to build new temples and part of temple structures in old styles as decorations, making the place look ancient and display cultural heritage. The old temple of Kapila was the same, but the rest of the pilgrimage area had been rebuilt. I have not seen any discussions of whether a place for *shraddha*, associated with death and *preta*s, could be attractive also as a tourist pilgrimage place, but it would probably not be easy to make

Kapilashram into a popular place of holiday travel. One consequence of the building of the heritage park was that Kapilashram seemed more deserted and less lively. Shops and smaller temples in the pilgrimage area had disappeared. I did not see a single *samnyasin* at the place in 2013 and 2016, which is also an indication of the number of arrivals of pilgrims and there were fewer priests. I was told that at *kartik purnima*, the main annual festival during the full moon day of the month Kartik, there would be around 10,000 pilgrims. The changes in the infrastructure did not seem to have succeeded so far to attract more tourists and pilgrims.

Changes in the *shraddha* ritual

The second change between 1999 and 2013 and 2016 I noted was dramatic changes in the *shraddha* ritual itself. When I did fieldwork in Siddhpur in 1999, there were many priests who performed *shraddha* rituals individually for each family. Small groups were seated all around the place (Figure 7.2). Each priest sat with a few persons in a circle around him or one or two persons seated just opposite to him for the *pindadana*. When I revisited Siddhpur in 2013, not only was the Kapilashram area being renovated and expanded because of the government grant in order to increase its attraction for pilgrims, but the *pindadana* ritual itself had changed. Groups of between 30 and 100 pilgrims were at this time sitting in rows like in a classroom with the *pindas* and *kusha* grass and the other ingredients in front of them (Figure 7.3). A priest led the ritual from an elevated platform using a loud speaker and had all the participants perform the details of the ritual and repeat the mantras together at the same time with an assistant going between the rows of people to assist. While the sequence of this part of the *shraddha* ritual was similar, the experience had become different. It was no longer an individual family ritual but had become an impersonal collective ritual for a group of up to more than hundred participants.

The use of new means of communication of the Web, emails, and mobile phones had led to this change in the *shraddha* ritual. When I asked the *pujari* of the Kapil mandir about how this change had come about, I was told that some priests had started to utilize the new means of communication to recruit and organize clients of their *shraddha* rituals (interview, March 2016). Other informants confirmed this explanation (interviews, October 2013, March 2016). The priests were using web pages, Internet, and mobile phones to organize a large number of people to arrive at the same time so that one priest could perform a single *shraddha* ritual for the whole group as a common ritual event. Before the new digital technologies each family group who arrived in Siddhpur would go to Siddhpur and there, at the bus station or railway station or at Kapilashram itself find a priest to have the ritual performed, or a priest would find them. The priests had collections of large books with names and addresses of the ritual clients collected over many years and they could claim ownership of clients by inheritance. Now, some of

Figure 7.2 The *shraddha* ritual in Siddhpur, 1999. Photo: Knut A. Jacobsen

Figure 7.3 Performing the *shraddha* seated in parallel rows, 2016. Photo: Knut A. Jacobsen

the priests were recruiting clients by using the new media and some had also gone into partnership with travel agents in different parts of India, who would promote and sell trips to Siddhpur with the *shraddha* ritual included in a system of profit sharing, I was informed. In the same way as the place had been given a new physical structure based on ideas of cultural heritage, the rituals had been given a new structure based on the business opportunities offered by the new media.

Among the pilgrims arriving to perform *shraddha* during my visits in 2013 and 2016 were groups from south India. According to one informant, a woman from Maharashtra who was part of the *shraddha* ritual performed in a large sitting with over 100 persons, "people who come here all have family problems. They do the *matrigayashraddha* for a grandmother and hopes it helps" (interview, March 2016). The use of the Web, Internet and mobile phones, and even Facebook according to one informant, was to recruit ritual clients, and make them come at the same time for a group *shraddha*, which had transformed the ritual into a collective with different patterns and experiences. The number of priests was greatly reduced. Before it had been ten to fifteen priests in different small groups, each with around one to five ritual clients, now it was one priest with between fifty and hundred clients in one group organized in rows. I asked several persons, after the ritual had been completed, if they would have preferred to conduct the ritual as it was done before with one priest and only one family. One of the participants said that she had been surprised when she saw how it was organized, but however the priest wanted to have it done was fine to her. Another person said that the ritual felt less personal, but she hoped that it nevertheless would help and have a good effect. All the informants I spoke with had talked with the priest on the phone, and they had been given the phone number by the travel agent who had recommended, and sold the trip to them. The old books with the names of ritual clients were still available to those who asked for them, but the new business model of cooperation with travel agents had been more successful.Another difference I noted in 2013 and 2016 was the disappearance of one ancient feature of the ritual: the cutting of the hair at Kapilashram. This might be a signal of the pilgrimage becoming more similar to tourism, but there might be other reasons as well. The priests at the Kapilashram did not seem to offer cutting of the hair as part of the ritual, maybe because it would not be practical to organize the cutting of the hair of so many people at the same time. It seems anyway to have been deemed unnecessary by the priests. Vidyarthi studying the *shraddha* in Gaya also found that the *shraddha* ritual was modified to accommodate regional practice as well as economic status, and immense variations in motivations and expectations (Vidyarthi, 1978: 34–35). Some seemed to have cut their hair at other places before they arrived. Also bathing in the pond was removed from the ritual structure by these large groups of pilgrims. I noted also that the old *pipal moksha* tree next to Bindusarovar was no longer there after the renovation, but another tree was used which was located further away from the water source. Perhaps for this reason, people would circumambulate the tree as the last part of the ritual and some tied treads to the tree, but the watering of the tree, which was an important final part of the ritual in 1999 had been terminated.

Recruiting ritual clients through the new media

An important source for the new system was several web pages which promoted the *shraddha* ritual at Siddhpur and which had been created by Brahman priests working at Kapilashram. Their email addresses and mobile phone numbers were prominent on their web pages (see www.matrugaya-siddhpur. com, www.sidhpurmatrugaya.com, and www.matrugaya.com/index.html). These web pages used the new communication technology to display the rituals the Brahman priests at Kapilashram offer and to mobilize customers. The statements "Call us" and "Send email" leave little doubt that these were commercial advertisements. Customers could send inquiry online and the priest would offer to organize the pilgrimage for them.

In the research literature on religion and the Internet, four functions of religious websites have been distinguished: presentations of institutions, groups, and doctrines; interactive communications on religious themes; offering of religious services; and finally commercial, that is, advertisement (Krueger, 2004). The web pages for the Kapilashram are commercial. They do not offer religious services so that they can be performed on the Web, but they advertise them for people to go to Siddhpur and here buy the rituals offered there. One page states:

> We are the Purohit and Pandaji of Matrugaya Tirth Kshetra, Siddhpur, for whole Maharastra Gour, Andhra Pradesh, Karnataka, Uttaranchal, Rajasthan, West Bengal, Uttar Pradesh, Madhya Pradesh, Jharkhand, Bihar, Gujarat and all Hindu who lives in India and NRI. We are providing the services of Pind Daan in Gaya, Shradh in Gaya and Dosh Nirwaran Pooja, Tarpan in Gaya. We can arrange the others facility on your behalf like stay in Hotel in Siddhpur, Tour guide and Taxi hire etc. for individual or Group. (Matrugaya, n.d.)

The web page offers all the services necessary for travel and stay in Siddhpur. By the use of the web pages ritual clients can book a *matrigayashraddha*, and hotel and travel can be organized (Matrugaya, n.d.). At the web page the priest's visiting card can be accessed (www.matrugaya.com/img/visiting-card.jpg).

At the web page is also available a ten-minute film about Kapilashram titled "Matrugaya-Bindu Sarovar – Sidhpur, North Gujarat, India." The film focuses on the priest's telephone number and the purpose of the film is to inform and promote the place, its rituals and temples and, to attract ritual clients (see "Matrugaya – Bindu Sarovar – Sidhpur, North Gujarat, India").

Another website, www.matrugaya-siddhpur.com, is run by two priests who perform *shraddha* at Kapilashram, Kirit Bhai Padhya and Darshan Bhai

Padhya, which also has printed an English version of the sixteen verses, which are recited with the offering of the *pinda*s to the *preta* (Matrugaya Shradh, n.d.).

It is notable how the *panda*s offer to organize both the ritual services, the stay in hotel, and the transport for both individuals and groups. To provide rituals along with accommodations is an old tradition. In a short study of the *matrigayashraddha* at the Kapilashram in Siddhpur from 1884, the Indian scholar S. M. Natesha Shastri described the arrangement between priest and clients and noted that in Siddhpur the ritual client "is lodged in part of the guru's house or in a separate house, as he likes. The priest himself supplies all the requisite vessels, provisions, &c., of course, expecting payment for everything in the end" (Shastri, 1884: 283). To show how the Web has partly replaced an earlier way of recruiting clients to the rituals, I quote from Shastri's description from 1884:

> When a pilgrim wishing to perform the *gaya* arrives at the station, several *purohits*, who call themselves *Tirthadhikaris* or *persons* having the (*sole*) authority over the place, receive them. Each priest brings an old moth-eaten note-book in which are written the names and designations, the village and district of all former visitors. That priest in whose note-book any trace of visitors related to the person in question is found has the sole right to officiate as head priest or *guru* to the pilgrim, who is then called his *shishya*. The mere fact that the present *shishya* belongs to the same village or district from which a former *shishya* came is caught at and given as an authority for taking up the duty of officiating priest to him. When this is once settled, the other priests finding that they have lost their game slowly return home with faces in which one may perceive an expression of dissatisfaction. (Shastri, 1884: 283)

And similarly at the end of the ritual, Shastri noted:

> Before separating, the priest takes down in his note-book the names of the pilgrim, his living relatives, &c., giving at the same time his full address to the so-called *shishya*. (Shastri, 1884: 285)

It is this tradition of fierce competition between priests for ritual clients that now is continued by using web pages, Internet and mobile phones. The new technology has given some priests a competitive edge that makes it possible for them to organize 100 clients or more to arrive at the same time and perform a common *shraddha* ritual with them while they are seated in 10 to 15 parallel rows all facing the priest and the priest using loudspeakers for all to hear.

In addition, travel agents also offer tours to Kapilashram and the *matrgayashraddha* on the Web. The travel agent *Blessing on the Net* in Ahmedabad offers one-day tours (Blessings on the Net, n.d.). It does not advertise the *shraddha* ritual, but promotes the pilgrimage place as a place of Kapila and a place at which Devahuti attained salvation:

Matru Gaya is a place of adoration where Sri Kapilaacharya also known as Sri Kapila Bhagavan a philosophic incarnation of Lord Maha Vishnu was born to the Divine parents Sage Kardhama Prajapathi and Devahuti. It is a virtuous place where Sri KapilaBhagavantha the founder and exponent of Saankhya Philosophy had preached Divine Knowledge to his Mother Devahuti. Matru Gaya is a Divine place where Devahuti attained Siddhi and Salvation and thenceforth the place came to be known as Siddhipada which in course of time referred as Siddhpur. (Blessings on the Net, n.d.)

This page exemplifies that Internet, typically, makes the myths better known, but also how simplifications of mythological narratives are promoted.

Gujarat Tourism Department has also made promotion videos for Siddhpur available on the Internet. A fifty-seconds long commercial for *matrigayashraddha* in Siddhpur was made by the Gujarat Department of Tourism playing the famous film actor Amitabh Bachchan who walks around among the ritual performers at Kapilashram and explains in Hindi that the ashram is the only place at which one can perform *shraddha* to the mother ("Mr. Amitab [sic] Bachchan Promoting Siddhpur," n.d.). Bachchan has also made a separate English version, with the same message but small difference in the wording ("Gujarat Tourism new advertisement campaign featuring Amitabh Bachchan: Sidhpur," n.d.). In the promotion videos Amitabh Bachchan tells that people come to Siddhpur from all over the world to perform *shraddha* for the departed soul of their mothers. He walks next to Kapilashram and *bindusarovar* and states that the pool is a sea of tears produced over the years by sons and daughters who have come here to perform *shraddha*. Bachchan mentions the belief that River Sarasvati once flowed to Siddhpur, and explains that Sarasvati is another name for Ma (mother). He notes that Siddhpur is a city of temples and that the visitor will feel that there are more blessings than seekers here. He concludes that Siddhpur is the only travel destination for *shraddha* to the mothers.

These are examples of how the new technology is being used to attract clients for the *shraddha* ritual. When I was in Siddhpur in 1999 I managed to make a photo copy of *Siddhpura Mahatmya* and the ritual texts that were used by the priests in the *shraddha* ritual, which had been collected in one book, a very rare text, and it took me some time to gain the trust to have a Brahman show it to me. No one would at first admit that such texts existed, no less show them to me, and I was able to make a copy only with the assistance of a helpful person who also went with me to a photocopy shop in Siddhpur. These were not texts generally available, but a collection of texts which the Brahmans used for memorization and instructions in the procedures of the rituals. In a description of the *matrigayashraddha* at Kapilashram published in 1884, the author noted "The *Tirthadhikaris*, or authorized priests of the place, keep a strict guard over the rites. They never give out a word of it to the curious *shishya* [the ritual client] if he wants to write them out" (Shastri, 1884: 283). The web pages have not replaced this secrecy around the ritual performance, but they do make more information available to people, although the information presented represents extreme simplifications and usually includes the historical narratives that legitimize the power of the place but not the ritual texts which the priests are using.

The web pages are usually in English because their purpose is to attract pilgrims from other states. It is notable that the Internet in this context is not used to develop any online rituals, but rather to encourage people to travel to the site. The site is thus not replaced by online religion, but the Web is used to encourage religious travel. It is perhaps notable that Hindu websites with online *puja*, such as www.saranam.com, offer a number of rituals, like "Pujas for Wealth," "Pujas for Health," "Pujas for Peace," "Pujas for Conceiving a Child," "Pujas for Marriage," and "Pujas for Fasting Days," but not any online performances of *shraddha*.

Concluding remarks

The example of Siddhpur has shown that new communication technologies have created new ways of organizing the ritual clients, which have changed the nature of the rituals. Mobile phones and Internet have influenced the speed of communication and the ability to reach people everywhere in an instant. For the pilgrimage and ritual tradition explored in this study, it has meant a transformation of the way in which pilgrimage and the rituals are organized and performed and the ways by which they are promoted. Web pages have been used to promote Siddhpur, and the rituals, travels, and hotels can be arranged using the web pages. The use of mobile phones and Internet to organize many pilgrims to arrive at the same time has simplified the ritual. The Internet and mobile phones make it possible to send the same message to many people simultaneously, and web pages increase the possibility for recruiting ritual clients before their arrival at the Kapilashram, just as the quick communication makes it possible to organize many people to come at the same time. One hundred people performing the same ritual activity sitting in rows like a classroom setting, simultaneously facing the same priest using a loudspeaker for all to hear, is a big change and represents a form of rationalization of religion. Many of the pilgrims also perform fewer parts of the ritual.

The state of Gujarat contributed a large amount of money to transform the pilgrimage site and India's most famous actor Amitabh Bachchan promoted it in a video available on the Web. One reason for these events is perhaps that the hometown of former Chief Minister of Gujarat and current Prime Minister of India, Narendra Modi, is the village Vadnagar, which is only 40 kilometers from Siddhpur. The place is not well known, but Modi did have local knowledge about it and perhaps wanted to promote it.

Notes

1 The Sanskrit text of the verses printed in Shastri (1884) differs: *asmin kale mrita ye ca gatir esham na vidyate, tasya nishkramanarthaya matuh pindam dadamy aham.* Shastri does not inform about his source. Shastri's translation reads: "For those that have died now, and for those that have no liberation, for the alleviation (*of their punishments*) I offer this *pinda* to my mother" (Shastri, 1884: 284, 285).
2 The document was previously available at www.gujarattourism.com/file-manager/tenders/118/siddhpur_pmc.pdf [accessed 28 December 2014].

References

Babb, Lawrence A. and Susan S. Wadley (eds.) (1995) *Media and the Transformation of Religion South Asia.* Philadelphia, PA: University of Pennsylvania Press.

Blessings on the Net (n.d.) "Tour Matru Gaya From Ahmedabad." Available at: http://blessingsonthenet.com/travel-india/tour-package/id/113/tour-matru-gaya-from-ahmedabad (accessed November 25, 2016).

"Gujarat Tourism new advertisement campaign featuring Amitabh Bachchan: Sidhpur" (n.d.) (English). Available at: www.youtube.com/watch?v=V_D3VHIPoxw (accessed November 25, 2016).

Jacobs, Stephen (2012) "Communicating Hinduism in Changing Media Context." *Religion Compass* 6(2): 136–151.

Jacobsen, Knut A. (2008) *Kapila: Founder of Samkhya and Avatara of Vishnu.* New Delhi: Munshiram Manoharlal.

Jacobsen, Knut A. (2013) *Pilgrimage in the Hindu Tradition: Salvific Space.* London: Routledge.

Jacobsen, Knut A. (2016) "Hindu Pilgrimage Sites and Travel: Infrastructure, Economy, Identity and Conflicts." In Knut A. Jacobsen, (ed.), *Routledge Handbook of Contemporary India.* Abingdon: Routledge, pp. 347–360.

Krueger, Oliver (2004) "The Internet as Distributor and Mirror of Religious and Ritual Knowledge." *Asian Journal of Social Science* 32(2): 183–197.

Lipner, Julius (1994) *Hindus: Their Religious Beliefs and Practices.* London: Routledge.

"Matrugaya" (n.d.), Available at: www.matrugaya.com (accessed December 8, 2016).

"Matrugaya – Bindu Sarovar – Sidhpur, North Gujarat, India," (n.d.). Available at www.youtube.com/watch?v=300eFhYHTCw (accessed November 25, 2016).

"Matrugaya-shradh" (n.d.) Available at www.matrugaya-siddhpur.com (accessed November 25, 2016).

"Matrugaya Shree Gaurakumar Mahendrabhai Pandya" (n.d.). Available at www.matrugaya.com/index.html (accessed November 25, 2016).

Matrigayaparvanashraddham (n.d.), Sanskrit text. No publisher.

"Mr. Amitab [sic] Bachchan Promoting Siddhpur" (in Hindi) (n.d.). Available at wwwyoutube.com/watch?v=cy55eaYZpBo (accessed November16, 2016).

"Saranam.com. World's 1st & most trusted Hindu puja service" (n.d.). Available at www.saranam.com (accessed November 25, 2016).

Scheifinger, Heinz (2010) "Om-line Hinduism: World Wide Gods on the Web." *Australian Religion Studies Review* 23(3): 325–345.

Scheifinger, Heinz (2012) "Internet." In Knut A. Jacobsen, (ed.), *Brill's Encyclopedia of Hinduism, Vol. 4.* Leiden: Brill, pp. 700–706.

Shastri, S.M. Natesha (1884), "Matrigaya at Siddhapuri." *The Indian Antiquary* 13: 282–285.

Sidddhapura [Siddhapada] Mahatmya (n.d.), Sanskrit text. No publisher.

Tejomayananda, Swami (1996) *Shri Kapila-Gita (Shri Kapilopadesha-sarah)*. Commentary by Swami Tejomayananda. Mumbai: Central Chinmaya Mission Trust.

Vidyarthi, L.P. (1978) *The Sacred Complex in Hindu Gaya*. Second Edition. Delhi: Concept Publishing.

"Welcome to Matrugaya Tirth Place – Siddhpur" (n.d.) Available at www.sidhpurma trugaya.com (accessed November 25, 2016).

8 Changing Hindutva by technology

A case study of Hindutva Abhiyan and the use of social media

Hindol Sengupta

Hindutva is a word that was first introduced in 1923 by Vinayak Damodar Savarkar (1883–1966), a leader in India's independence movement against British colonial rule. Savarkar defined Hindutva as "… not a word but a history. Not only the spiritual or religious history of our people as at times it is mistaken to be by being confounded with the other cognate term Hinduism, but a history in full" (Savarkar, 2012: 3, quoted in Gandhi 2016). He argued that any "ism" (like Hindu-ism) was inadequate for his needs because he was attempting to describe an essence that connected "all those who love the land … as their fatherland" (Deshpande, 2003: 998). As Christophe Jaffrelot has pointed out, "declaring himself an atheist, Savarkar argued that religion was only one aspect of Hindu identity, and not even the most important" (Jaffrelot, 2010: 45). Jaffrelot has noted that Savarkar considered a common geography and race as more important parameters than religion, and a common language at least as vital. He defined citizens of India as having a common *pitrubhoomi*, a "land of ancestors" (fatherland), and a *punyabhoomi*, "land of worship" (holy land), within the geography of the country, and said such people shared a common Hindu-ness or, literally, *hindutva*. It is an ongoing debate among scholars, cultural debaters and politicians whether this definition includes Muslim and Christian Indians, that is, those who belong to faiths which have "holy lands" outside the geographical boundaries of India. On caste, the Hindu system of division of society based on birth, Savarkar had more unambiguous views. Caste, he said, was not immutable, and "through their 'iron actions' individual Hindus may lose the caste status assigned to them at birth" (McKean, 1996: 81). Savarkar denounced caste-based discrimination vigorously in his lifetime. He noted "seven social chains" that kept Hindu society, and indeed India, from developing: the religious and social bar on the study of ancient theological texts including the *Veda*s, bar on changing one's caste profession (many castes had—and in some parts of India, still have—defined professions attached to them like barber, butcher and in the most exploitative form, manual scavengers), untouchability (where upper castes would not touch a lower caste or accept food or water from the lower caste), bar on crossing the seas, reconversion and inter-caste marriage (Grover, 1993: 567).

Savarkar was more concerned with so-called Muslim and Christian (British colonialism) "invasions" of India and when attacked by foreigners "argued that all castes, creeds and denominations 'suffered as Hindus and triumphed as Hindus'" (Sharma, 2003: 191). It is important to note that Savarkar was a champion of Indian independence, and spent a decade in the toughest prison of the British Raj, the island jail of Kalapani, for his revolutionary activities. His aim was to unite Hindus against the outsider, and by the time Savarkar was writing about Hindutva, caste had outlived its usefulness (Sharma, 2003: 190). To bring his much desired unity among the Hindus, Savarkar was resolutely against caste discrimination. One of the main caste barriers is people from different castes eating together, and to break this Savarkar organized many community diners where everyone ate together and asserted that the "indigenous fetter which divides Hindu society must be broken at all costs" (Bhave, 2009: 35). Savarkar wanted to create a political organization which would aggressively campaign for social reform but the movement that used his ideology most efficiently was the *Rashtriya Swayamsewak Sangh* (RSS) which was started in 1925 by Keshav Baliram Hegdewar who defined it as a national volunteer corps. It has been described as "the largest Hindu nationalist movement" (Jaffrelot, 2007: 16), or "the most potent organised Hindu cultural group of the twentieth century" (Andersen, 1972: 589). Even though Hegdewar was inspired by Savarkar and embraced the ideology of Hindutva, the RSS was founded as a cultural movement (Andersen and Damle, 1987: 40). While Hegdewar was against caste discrimination and established, for instance, the custom of RSS members of all castes eating together, he "never called for a loud campaign" and "believed in gradual social transformation" (Grover, 1993: 567).

Through its history, on the issue of caste, the RSS has consistently talked against untouchability and caste discrimination; however, politically it was also true that the location of its headquarters, in Nagpur in western India, and main areas of operation in north India, brought into it a certain upper caste conservatism that prevented it from being vigorously activist about caste issues. All its *sarsanghchalaks*, or organization heads, through history have been upper caste Hindus. In its own local units, the *shakhas*, or at any of its many offices, the RSS does not practice any caste discrimination, and, for instance, are eating together using the same utensils is one of their oldest and most steadfast rituals. But the organization's tag of being "upper caste, *bania* (petty trader)"-friendly has long stuck to, and indeed in parts strengthened, the RSS and the *Bharatiya Janata Party* (BJP), the political arm of RSS since 1951 (then called the *Jan Sangh*) and India's ruling party between 1998 and 2004 and since 2014 up to the writing of this chapter.

This chapter explores one contemporary interpretation of Savarkar's idea of a caste-free Hindu society through the work of a relatively new Hindu spiritual movement headquartered in central India called the *Hindutva Abhiyan*. The Abhiyan is led by civil engineering graduate from one of India's most elite engineering colleges Sourabh Lahiri, usually known by his ascetic name

Lahiri Guruji, who also works part-time as a risk management analyst for the American technology company IBM. The chapter analyzes the use of social media by the Abhiyan as a tool "quite like the idea of eating together using the same utensils," according to Lahiri, to push caste discrimination-free Hindu unity. The Abhiyan is not affiliated to the RSS but it has from time to time assisted RSS outreach especially in the tribal belt of central India. In this chapter it will also be noted that the Hindutva Abhiyan does not claim to be atheist, as Savarkar did, and uses two Hindu religious rituals, the chanting of the Vedic mantra *gayatri* and the performance of evening *arti*s (ceremonial image worship with fire or lamps) as part of its initiation and outreach. But in both cases the Abhiyan subverts the rituals to promote casteless-ness. Where the Abhiyan is different from the RSS is in the focus of its messaging on individuals: unlike the RSS where the focal point is always the group. Both organizations talk about empowerment but while the RSS' messaging is about empowering society, the Abhiyan always talks about individuals getting empowered. Consequently they approach the issue of empowerment from opposite sides: the RSS believes in empowering society which in turn strengthens the hand of individuals, whereas the Abhiyan pushes the idea of empowered individuals going onto strengthening society.

The chapter analyzes the work and methodology of the Hindutva Abhiyan in using social media and technology to pitch the ideology of Hindutva, that is, free from caste discrimination, combined with a major thrust towards better livelihood, which includes everything from setting up sericulture and diary projects to distributing fortified baby food in an area plagued with infant malnutrition. It analyzes the attempt by the Abhiyan and its leader to present a definition of Hindutva that puts at the heart of the message casteless-ness or a caste-free Hindu society, which is entrepreneurial in nature and uses social media as a tool to disseminate every day messages. Based on interviews,[1] the chapter specifically examines how the use of social media attempts to enhance the idea of equality among the followers of the Abhiyan, more than 80 percent of whom come from lower castes, including Dalits, or tribal communities in dense central Indian forests which are also in some of the poorest parts of the country. In India today, efforts of the lower castes to access knowledge, materials and spaces is today at an advantage because "the gaining of ritual and dogmatic knowledge is losing its dependence on direct social interaction in a spatial community, and increasingly relies on Internet based discourse" (Krueger, 2004). The contest for such access by using technology is also intrinsically related to modernity. As Anthony Giddens has claimed, "the disembedment of social interaction from temporal and spatial conditions as a distinguishing feature of modernity" (Giddens, 1990: 14). In the case of the Hindutva Abhiyan the use of technology allows for this "disembedment," and this, in turn, provides the freedom to leapfrog spatial restrictions, like entries into certain temples or certain parts of temples that are restricted by caste identity, and offer unrestricted access to spiritual guidance which otherwise would not be available for lower castes. The chapter details the extensive use of social media by the Hindutva Abhiyan to spread their message and analyze how the use of the medium of social media itself becomes a tool for empowerment and enfranchisement.

Many researchers have examined the impact of Internet-based technologies, including in bringing about a reduction in face-to-face social interaction (Nie and Hillygus, 2002), weakening or strengthening community ties (Matei and Ball-Rokeach, 2001), and whether it reinforces or subverts authoritarian political regimes (Kalathil and Boas, 2003; Meintel, 2012). The theoretical approach in this chapter assumes that when Internet-based technologies are used to promote Hindutva, then they seem to be doing two things simultaneously: on the one hand, they are breaking the traditional sources of authority, and methods of dissemination, of religious/spiritual instruction. On the other hand, they also strengthen the community, in this case the *shishya parivar* or "family of disciples" of the Hindutva Abhiyan, which includes both upper and lower castes. To convince lower castes of its seriousness about fighting caste discrimination, it has placed members from lower castes in key positions, including two recently as state unit chiefs of the BJP (Jha and Mahurkar, 2016). Not least India's Prime Minister since 2014, Narendra Modi, who is also from a lower caste, and the RSS chief Mohan Bhagwat since 2009, made it a point in 2016 to dine with sanitary workers, many of them Dalits (Indo-Asian News Service, 2016). Also long time RSS member and Member of Parliament Tarun Vijay led a large group of Dalits in 2016 to storm a temple in Uttarakhand which barred entry to Dalits (Azad, 2016).

In the history of fighting caste discrimination in India, many tools, including clauses in the Indian constitution and in the penal code of the legal justice, have been used. The most recent in the last 25 years in the free markets where the opening of the Indian economy and boom in private sector jobs have empowered lower castes by bringing unprecedented income to these communities. Among Dalits in Uttar Pradesh, economic liberalization has brought prosperity that has changed social habits (for example always sitting beneath an upper caste) and discrimination (like ending untouchability and the practice that no upper caste would accept food or drink from the hands of a lower caste) (Kapur, Prasad, Pritchett and Babu, 2010). Many Hindu groups have turned free market proponents to promote social reform in the last two decades—the RSS, shunning its early state orientation, today pitches as a champion of entrepreneurship. Caste is "a status community characterized by endogamy, hereditary membership, occupation, ritual status and a specific style of life" (Beteille, 1965, quoted in Marshall and Scott, 2009: 64), and rise in income is one of the most potent ways to change the status quo. André Beteille has argued that:

> [t]here continues to be a general association between caste and occupation to the extent that the lowest castes are largely concentrated in the menial and low-paying jobs whereas the higher castes tend to be in the best-paid and most esteemed ones. But the association between caste and

occupation is now more flexible than it was in the traditional economy of land and grain. Rapid economic growth and the expansion of the middle class are accompanied by new opportunities for individual mobility which further loosens the association between caste and occupation. (Beteille, 2012)

The loosening of caste boundaries and rituals that Beteille, and later scholars like Chandra Bhan Prasad, have observed has been fueled by free markets, and movements like the Hindutva Abhiyan seek to take this process forward by incorporating hyper use of technology in the mix. The Abhiyan itself is looking to set up diary plants[2] using foreign direct investment and promotes entrepreneurship among its followership as means to empower themselves. Faggan Singh Kulaste, the Member of Parliament of Mandla in Madhya Pradesh where the diary project is rolling out, and a disciple of the Hindutva Abhiyan, said in an interview that he joined the organization because he understood that "Lahiri Guruji proposes concrete models for change that are not based on charity only" (interview, Faggan Singh Kulaste, October 30, 2015). Kulaste is funding some of the diary project work using his MPLAD (Member of Parliament Local Area Development) funds (money that is allocated to every Member of Parliament in India for projects in their area).

Hindutva Abhiyan

Hindutva Abhiyan was started by Lahiri Guruji soon after he graduated from the Indian Institute of Technology (Varanasi) around 2016. Guruji, born in 1981, divided his time between the Abhiyan's headquarters at Dewas, a district in the central Indian state of Madhya Pradesh, and his apartment in Mumbai, the financial capital of India. Guruji used two primary tools: the messenger WhatsApp and Facebook to get his message across and argued that "social media is so easy to access, and because it is free to use, it reinforces the idea of being at par which is at the heart of fighting caste discrimination" (interview, Lahiri Guruji, November 13, 2015). Lahiri Guruji said the idea of focusing on social media and Internet-based technologies to promote the idea of ending caste discrimination occurred to him when he saw data on mobile phone purchase and use in India:

As consumer goods become cheaper more people, and even the poor at some point, will be able to afford them – this much is common sense and this had happened with all consumer goods. But in India I realized that the mobile phone was doing much more than just give the under-privileged or disenfranchised a tool. It giving them the sense of a level playing field – this is the first step towards getting justice. (interview, Lahiri Guruji, November 13, 2015)

The Abhiyan does not ask for donations from its followers and is run by using Guruji's personal earnings as a risk management consultant. The Abhiyan claims 10 million followers across the states of Madhya Pradesh, Chhattisgarh, Jharkhand, Bihar, Uttar Pradesh, Odhisha, Rajasthan, Delhi, Maharashtra, Bihar and Gujarat.

Guruji said he had been most influenced by Savarkar's idea that Hindutva "links Hindu identity to geography and that it constitutes not just religious history but the sum total of cultural history" (interview Lahiri Guruji, October 20, 2015). Lahiri Guruji used the word Hindutva in the name of his organization consciously to show an affiliation with the ideals of Savarkar. But he argued that the concept of Hindutva is "not frozen in time, and constantly adapts to particular needs of society." He said the main focus of the Hindutva Abhiyan was to fight caste discrimination which is "the part of Savarkar's work which has most influenced the Abhiyan's work" (interview Lahiri Guruji, October 20, 2015).

The Abhiyan has made a conscious choice not to create many physical centers. Lahiri Guruji says he was influenced by the "organisation skills" of the "RSS model, which used physical centers (called *shakha*s) to grow but the Abhiyan did not need physical centers. Instead our entire focus has been on using media especially social media to spread the message" (interview Lahiri Guruji, October 20, 2015). Instead it relies mainly on mobile technology and the social media to spread its message and gather followers. One common ritual the Abhiyan shares with the RSS is that at the Dewas headquarters of the Abhiyan and at any of its gatherings, meals are eaten together by followers from all castes.

Since caste discrimination manifests itself and is inherently a prejudice related to access defined from a upper caste perspective, including rituals in which utensils used by a person of a lower caste should not be used, not accepting food from the hand of a lower caste person and others, the use of technology allows for democratization and has an equalizing force to build new rituals and codes. These new rituals and codes emphasize and put in the forefront the idea that the message, in this case the key material which is being accessed online, arrives to everyone who seek it through equal and non-discriminatory routes.

The Hindutva Abhiyan is run in a pyramid structure which has Lahiri Guruji at the summit followed by 1,250 key disciples and then volunteers across 20,000 villages and towns. Disciples go through a four-to-five-hour-long one-on-one face-to-face meditation process with Guruji where they are initiated into the chanting of the *gayatri* mantra and breathing techniques during the recitation of the mantra in an otherwise silent room with no other participants. This process is integrated with the use of technology and social media. Disciples who live in remote areas and cannot easily reach Guruji, receive detailed instructions in the Hindi language on WhatsApp as a text message on how to chant the mantra, and then go through a one-on-one initiation over a telephone call which can last up to four to five hours. Once again, the disciple-to-be is told to place himself or herself in a quiet room with no one else present during the course of the phone call. The use of the *gayatri* mantra as the main methodology through which discipleship is granted is significant in a movement where nearly 90 percent of the key disciples come from lower castes. Traditionally the *gayatri* mantra "is whispered in the ear of a high caste male during his initiation ceremony ... The chant is reserved solely for upper caste Hindu males" (Bakhle, 2008: 256). Disciples in turn initiate followers by requiring them to organize weekly *arti* by adopting a neighborhood temple, including taking the responsibility to clean and repair it, if need be. Here again, the encouragement is for the followers themselves to lead the *arti* along with the temple priest, and in places where no designated priests exist, lead it by themselves irrespective of their caste and encourage people from all castes to attend. One can also become a registered follower of the Hindutva Abhiyan simply liking the Abhiyan's Facebook page and the Abhiyan's volunteer's reach out to everyone who likes the page to coordinate adding them onto a WhatsApp group and, if possible, also get them to initiate a local *arti* under the guidance of a disciple. The process of becoming part of the Hindutva Abhiyan for many followers start with liking the Facebook page, then becoming part of a WhatsApp group, followed by organizing local *artis*. Every week thousands of photos of *artis* conducted by the followers of the Abhiyan in villages across India are shared on WhatsApp groups and some of the main ones which are attended by key disciples also shared on the Facebook page of the Abhiyan. Guruji says access to worship is one of the most humiliating forms of discrimination (in the Hindu faith) and therefore Hindutva Abhiyan has made it a focal point. He also gives a weekly televised spiritual discourse on the religious national station Disha TV which is broadcast every Sunday from 9 a.m. to 10 a.m. Disha TV claims to reach 60 million households through direct-to-hold distribution and cable TV (dishatv.com, 2013). Almost all the messages, and the TV show, are in the Hindi language which is the primary language of use in the states where the Hindutva Abhiyan operates. The disciples and followers of Lahiri Guruji treat him as a guru, a "personal teacher of spirituality" (Mlecko, 1982), and he provides day-to-day guidance by addressing in his WhatsApp messages and video discourses on various aspects of life like how to become a better worker and how to fulfill familial duties with dignity. The idea of strengthening oneself by drawing inspiration from the Hindu epics and heroes of the epics is reinforced repeatedly.

The Abhiyan has more than 120,000 followers or "likes" on its Facebook page and operates 1,872 WhatsApp groups with a total membership of around 150,000 people. Facebook Insights data shows that at an average a post on the Hindutva Abhiyan's page gets around 40,000 organic (not-paid-for views). The members on the WhatsApp groups get at least four to five messages, including photos and videos, from the Abhiyan every day. These messages usually talk about empowerment, which is defined by Guruji as making life better, gaining respect, and quote stories from the Hindu epics, the *Ramayana* and the *Mahabharata*. Some of the anecdotes told in these WhatsApp messages are Guruji's interpretations of the stories of the epics, for instance, the monkey army of the god king Ram is portrayed as an army of tribal people who live in forests (quite like thousands of Guruji's own followers) empowered by Ram and the word monkey explained as only a storytelling device. Guruji urges his followers to do *"Ramtatva" sadhana* and *"Krishnatatva" sadhana*, that is, meditating upon the lives of the divinities Ram and Krishna as they are portrayed in the *Ramayana* and *Mahabharata* respectively. Popular images of Ram and Krishna in battlefield are sent along with messages and photos of Guruji every week and these often become screensavers on the mobile phones of the followers of the Abhiyan.

Guruji's live performances, *pravachans*, also emphasize, simultaneously, the image of a golden past and constant reaffirmation of positive revivalism, and a break-away, a sense of newness, talking up a "new Hindutva" for a "new age of unity." One common example is of Shabri, a tribal woman character in the *Ramayana*, who waited for years in her jungle hut for the arrival of the god Ram. Each day, she would pick berries for him and bite them to see which were the sweetest, and keep the sweetest for him. It never occurred to Shabri that Ram might not eat something bitten by her. When the god finally arrived, he lovingly ate the sweetest berries that had already been tasted by Shabri. In one *pravachan*, Lahiri Guruji said: "In the Hinduism, I know gods come to the door of the poor for food and eat food already eaten by the poor. At the most basic level, the hunger for food unites man and god; at a spiritual level, it is devotion that brings you closer to god, not everyday things like who touched what – all that is irrelevant" (interview, Lahiri Guruji, October 20, 2015).

In the Facebook messages and the WhatsApp messages, Lahiri Guruji is also photographed and video-graphed wearing the orange-colored robes of Hindu asceticism and with a thick streak of vermillion paste on his forehead. He sometimes used a makeshift chariot-like structure built on top of cars or jeeps that he is using to travel. Many of these images are shot from a low angle to give a towering sense to the photographs. When they are shared on social media, they usually also have a written message not just on the post but also sometimes on the body of the image itself. This is important because the body of the guru is sacred space for the Abhiyan's disciples and access to the physical self of the guru, albeit via technology, is an important process in the Abhiyan's outreach. The followers of the Abhiyan especially in rural areas tend to be quite financially poor and therefore devotees often behave like "participants" in the activities of the organization rather than as 'members' (Warrier, 2003). Therefore the social media output of the Abhiyan is usually, and pre-dominantly, full of activities including *pathas* and *pravachans*, work on constructing village emporiums to sell rural handicrafts and even building a local body building center is part of the activities in which the followers of the Abhiyan participate—and photos and videos of these activities are constantly sent out every day on WhatsApp and posted on Facebook to generate a sense of relentless activity. For instance, in 2016 Guruji launched a campaign promoting grassroots entrepreneurship in 100 most impoverished districts of

India and some of his main disciples have been travelling across Jabalpur, Mandla, Kanha, Amarkantak and Bilaspur straddling the tribal belt of Madhya Pradesh and Chhattisgarh organizing "skill development and tribal entrepreneurship camps" teaching villagers how to finish and package their handmade crafts products better and connecting them to local emporiums. This has been the topic of regular posts on Facebook including most recently in ten posts on Facebook between May and June 2017. Two of these posts (both on May 24, 2017) have been about meetings of Hindutva Abhiyan disciples with the ambassador of Latvia to India and the special adviser to the president of Latvia to conduct meetings of the Abhiyan and develop economic linkages with European nations like Latvia interested in organic and handmade products from India. Posts like these enthrall rural followers of the Abhiyan who can only imagine concepts like doing business with European partners and help build the aura of the Abhiyan.

It is important to note that Lahiri Guruji never uses any caste term in his messages, neither in the big *pravachan*s nor in his daily messages through social media. The euphemism used for the lower castes is always the word "poor." He argues that there is no need to use caste terms since "we are fighting for an end to caste-based discrimination; using such terms would mean reiterating these differences in the minds of the people and that is the last thing I want" (interview, Lahiri Guruji, October 20, 2015). Lahiri Guruji says his primary insight when setting up the Abhiyan was that,

> while in India it is the grouping that has been important in social relations in the past, we have been steadily moving towards a country where it is the individual not the group that holds importance. My goal was to create a model where the most important element was the individual who felt that they got individual attention. The only way to beat caste is to emphasize that Hindutva is about respecting the individual. This had never been done before. (interview, Lahiri Guruji, November 13, 2015)

Lahiri Guruji also does one or two live performances (*pravachan*s) with audience between one and four times in a year. They are usually held at a village location in Madhya Pradesh or one of the other states where the Abhiyan works, and attract between 10,000 to 100,000 people attending. All his remaining daily discourses and messages are communicated through social media. He says that the Abhiyan does not merely use social media and technology as part of its communication strategy, but the tools themselves are part of the message:

> We are attracting followers not just because of our message but also the way we are delivering it. Many of the traditional barriers of caste like upper caste people preventing lower castes from entering temples etc. are related to physical geography, the power and discrimination comes from being in that place. Social media and technology is not tied to geography.

That is why messages delivered on it give a sense of equality. (interview, Lahiri Guruji, November 13, 2015)

In a sense for the Hindutva Abhiyan, the medium is the message (McLuhan, 1964), and the use of certain medium or media adds to the power of the message.

The importance of Hindutva in social media: perspectives of disciples

According to the 55-year-old Dilip Kumar Behera, a prominent Dalit ideologue and disciple of the Hindu Abhiyan, Lahiri Guruji's choice of words, his phraseology, and the medium of delivery brings a sense of parity: "The upper caste has WhatsApp. The Dalit also has WhatsApp. They both can see the message sent by the guru at the same time—this is unprecedented power" (interview Dilip Kumar Behera, November 14, 2015). What Behera referred to was that technology seems to be subverting old barriers of access, either to religious texts or places, and therefore the idea of simultaneous access or simultaneous entry becomes a powerful code to equality. The point here is not just access to technology and the media but simultaneous access, that there is no delay in the time when the message from a guru reaches the disciples, no matter what his or her caste or tribe is.

Another disciple of Hindutva Abhiyan, Padma Charan Behera, aged 36, discovered the Hindutva Abhiyan around 2010. He was a Dalit student from the eastern state of Odhisha and the first in his family ever to go to school. He said he was impressed that "the Abhiyan used Facebook so actively and was so modern." When talking about the Abhiyan, Behera said the Abhiyan had taught him that "*jo sune aur pade voh Hindu hai*" (anyone who listens or reads is a Hindu), meaning anyone who listens to a message by Lahairi Guruji or reads a social media message on Hinduism and Hindutva from the same can be considered a Hindu. This understanding was in his view very different from the Hinduism that he grew up with in his village in the Digapahandi region of Odhisha. There, he said, a Hindu was defined by "entry," to a temple or any other place designated for upper caste Hindus. In his understanding the technology used by Hindutva Abhiyan for online practices had facilitated acts of "entry," interpreted as acts of defiance and assertion of social rights, which previously had been impossible when visiting temples because of caste discrimination in the social world. As he continued, "[w]hen we see the same thing using the same devices or gadgets, we become same to same" (interview, Padma Charan Behera, December 4, 2015). "Same to same" was a phrase he used several times to describe the experience of accessing Lahiri Guruji's words using his mobile phone.

Behera got in touch with the Abhiyan through Facebook and started to post requests for career and spiritual advice from Lahiri Guruji. He began to have conversations on Facebook with Guruji, one-on-one, to get his opinion. Behera said that on Guruji's advice he applied to study pharmacy at the Birla

Institute of Technology at Ranchi in the state of Jharkhand which is neigh-boring Odhisha. He only physically met Guruji in 2014 but for four years, he constantly took "guidance and blessings" through, first Internet cafes, and then his mobile phone. "I felt that there is a private guru only for me—this is unthinkable usually for a Dalit. On social media, through messages, I interacted directly one-on-one with Lahiri Guruji. There was no one in between and I had to follow no one else's rules" (interview, Padma Charan Behera, December 4, 2015). Behera explained that one of the most engaging things for him about the Hindutva Abhiyan was, in his words, "I am me. I am not just a Dalit. I am an individual who is interacting and being responded to as an individual." He said the Hindutva's (and even Hinduism) approach to Dalits like him was usually social and collective, "as a group," but the Hindutva Abhiyan online had opened up for an individualistic understanding of identity: "I don't want to be thought of as just one person in a group" (interview, Padma Charan Behera, December 4, 2015).

One of the most compelling phraseologies came up in the interview with the lower caste (Sutar caste) 27-years-old man Raju Carpenter from the Susner region of Madhya Pradesh. Carpenter did not only come from a lower caste background, but was also involved in petty crime for most of his early life until he got introduced to the Hindutva Abhiyan after he saw an SMS sent by the Abhiyan to one of his friends in 2009. Carpenter said that the SMS communicated that no one and no ritual had the right to come between a person and god. One of the things that appealed to Carpenter about the social media-fueled Hindutva Abhiyan was in his words that "we all have the

Figure 8.1 Raju Carpenter conducting a session in "Hindutva Abhiyan Shishya Nirman Shivir"

same profile." What he meant by this was simply that a medium such as Facebook allows social equality by its general set-up, as he explained: "Dalits and tribals and Brahmins, all the disciples needed the same thing—a Facebook profile – to be part of the Abhiyan. It was exactly the same thing—not different for different people. We never thought we could have the same profile as a Brahmin in society but because the Abhiyan is so big on using Facebook, there the profile everyone has is exactly the same" (interview, Raju Carpenter, December 1, 2015). According to Carpenter and when becoming a member of the Hindutva Abhiyan, a simple Facebook profile is attributed with new meaning and purpose. A profile becomes more than a snapshot of the user for the consumption of their "friends"; rather, as in this case, a profile is the first step that pries open closed doors. Having a profile is an acquisition of status and a sign of arrival, but not just in materialistic sense. In this case, having a profile is exactly that – an identity for those who had been for long rendered invisible by caste discrimination. Carpenter also emphasized the importance of media for fast communication of messages across borders:

> We just organized a one-day mega training programme for 500 youth from various backgrounds in Susner, one of the most backward areas of Madhya Pradesh. And the entire event was organized and managed through social media like Facebook, Whatsapp and Twitter. Messages spread like fire through social media sites. In this season of heavy rainfall, it is practically impossible to go to interior areas and invite people for the training program on a one-to-one basis. But through social networking and chat applications, we were able to reach out to even the adjoining districts for spreading awareness about this workshop. (interview, Raju Carpenter, December 1, 2015)

Another disciple of Hindutva Abhiyan, the 47-years-old Amit Rastogi, who is of upper caste (Vaishya, Bania) and a textile businessman with shops in Delhi and London, understood both the ideology and communication methods used by the organization in relation to castes in terms of a "sharing economy":

> Lahiri Guruji's work seeks to shift the equation between castes from a transaction to collaboration; when we all sit together and eat from the same utensils or access the same messages through the same medium, it is the "sharing economy" working in a new powerful way. (interview, Amit Rastogi, December 9, 2015)

As a businessman, Rastogi said that the technological interface is enabling a "seamless, simultaneous" collaborative consumption of religious discourse by all castes and tribes in new ways that were not possible before. He continued:

> [t]he focus on social media based exchange means everyone has an identity which is at par ... This is different from the almost anonymous act of just

purchasing some goods or service from a temple website. Social media allows for interaction with the guru, with everyone using the same methodology and technology. (interview, Amit Rastogi, December 9, 2015)

One of the traditional ways of breaking the caste barrier in India, apart from temple entry, is the ritual of eating together by using the same utensils and accepting food and water from each other's hands. Shravan Singh Gojawat, a lower caste disciple and the right hand man of Lahiri Guruji, emphasized the intentional practice of Hindutva Abhiyan to eat together irrespective of caste identities and how this served as model for the use of social media by Lahiri Guruji: "In the Abhiyan we all eat together and Guruji took that idea online. Being part of the same Whatsapp group is like eating together – it breaks barriers." The technology was also seen as a tool to democratize the access to religion. As Gojawat continued, "Facebook, Whatsapp, all these things were once only for rich, upper caste people. Now we can afford these things too. But what about religion, can we access that also? If religion can come on these platforms, then we are one" (interview, Shravan Singh Gojawat, October 25, 2015).

The act of forwarding messages from Guruji from a lower caste disciple to an upper caste disciple, and vice versa, became a tool for parity and contributed to collective cohesion and identity formation and the construction of a sense of "oneness." This feeling of unity was particularly felt by Bhanwar Singh Solanki, an upper caste (Kshatriya, Rajput) and former "muscle man" in the Dewas region of Madhya Pradesh. Before he joined the Hindutva Abhiyan in 2010, he said he used to "beat up Dalits every other day to teach them a lesson so that they don't act smart." After he became a disciple, Solanki said he received instructions from Lahiri Guruji daily and after this he must "SMS at least one Dalit *gurubhai* (brother follower of the guru) every day either sharing a message about the Abhiyan or asking for their well-being." This he was doing in addition to sitting and eating with Dalit followers of Lahiri Guruji. As he explained how his understanding of caste has transformed, "caste was all about touching, who to touch and who not to touch" but "now in the Abhiyan it is all about sharing" (interview Bhanwar Singh Solanki, October 25, 2015). Solanki felt that this transition from "touching" to "sharing" has been assisted primarily by technological or Internet-based "sharing" where a daily bonhomie can be established which has the added advantage of a slow initiation to breaking very old and bitter cultural prejudices because this "sharing" does not necessarily involve a face-to-face meeting and therefore can be eased into over a medium to long period time.

Hindutva Abhiyan's use of social media and technology seems to help many of its followers get a sense of equality. Their definition of this feeling of equality is close to the idea of equal rights for all the people and the abolition of all special rights and privileges (Barker, 1951). The right to access religious instruction from a guru and rituals and customs through technology is seen as equality, especially since it comes with no access barriers or special rights and privileges for upper castes. The access and equality is of course dependent on a number of factors. Hindutva Abhiyan, like the RSS, does not favor women followers as Lahiri Guruji runs an almost all men disciples-only movement. Guruji says while there is no official bar to women joining the movement and there are a few women followers, he prefers only male disciples because they have to travel to remote areas in India which are often not considered safe for women. Sampatiya Uike, a village councilor in Madhya Pradesh is one of the handful of women followers of the Hindutva Abhiyan. She said the lack of women in the Abhiyan is a deficiency of the movement. "As long as there are few women members of the Abhiyan, it is perpetuating a different kind of discrimination even though effectively fighting caste discrimination" (interview, Sampatiya Uike, October 25, 2015).

It must be highlighted that the Abhiyan's work tackles only one part of the problem of societal division due to caste by the usage of technology. It does not take into account that other forms of discrimination especially with regard to women who are a very minor part of the Abhiyan. Also in rural areas where the Abhiyan works, access to technology like mobile telephony is mostly in the hands of men – 114 million more men than women use mobile phones in India (*New York Times*, 2016) – and therefore the messaging of the Abhiyan reaches almost exclusively to men with sporadic women participation in some local functions. Considering that some of the worst atrocities of caste-related violence occur on women in India, this is a considerable gap in the work of the Abhiyan, albeit one that it is trying to fill with specific women groups which are still of negligible size and impact.

Figure 8.2 Members of the Hindutva Abhiyan.

In a population of 1.3 billion, the Abhiyan reaches a relatively small number of people. Dalits make up a little more than 16 percent of the Indian population and the impact of the Abhiyan is limited to 11 of India's 29 states and a small fraction of the population. But the Abhiyan seems to have left a deep impact in the areas where it works and among the predominantly male audience that it addresses.

It should also be mentioned here that while there are some followers in the Abhiyan who complain that Lahiri Guruji uses more and more images and more frequently videos clips that are shared to all the followers, there is a new layer of inequality being created due to the economics of high speed data access. During the interviews, three followers of the Abhiyan in Mandla complained about the cost of high speed data and that is becoming a new kind of barrier of the accessibility in the movement.

Conclusion

Hindutva, by definition, is against caste discrimination because it favors a nationalistic pitch which sees geography and place of birth, in this case India, as the primary marker of identity. But many of the founding leaders of the Hindutva ideology came from an upper caste background and this created a history of suspicion between Hindutva organizations like the RSS and its affiliates and lower caste Indians including Dalits. As protracted and vicious as caste discrimination is in India, there are clear signs that its hold is weaker in many places than ever. One of the main reasons for this weakening of caste discrimination is 25 years of Indian economic liberalization that has brought unprecedented prosperity to lower caste families.

In recent years, Hindutva organizations like the RSS and others have become proponents of free markets to help push social reform and the end of caste discrimination. The use of technology is the newest thrust in that direction, and one of the most interesting uses of technology including social media to further this cause is being done by the Hindutva Abhiyan. The Abhiyan uses technology and social media not merely as tools but as the message itself – the act of creating, say, a Facebook account and then using it to access messages from a Hindu guru, is empowering for many lower caste followers because it breaks the old barriers of access to temples.

Social media and technology create a direct interface where people from all castes access the same message, the same information and the same ritual of blessings using the same methodology. Social media, therefore, works a bit like the old ritual of people from all castes eating together to break the barriers of untouchability. The use of social media and technology to fight caste discrimination gives new meanings to ideas like what a Facebook profile means—status inducing, something that brings parity of access between castes—and new ways of looking at identity – on the Facebook wall reading and liking the same messages from the guru at the same time brings a rare sense of temporary equality which is prized.

Figure 8.3 Education and awareness through Facebook

Hindutva Abhiyan has created methods of initiation into the movement through mobile telephony and social media where the followers absorb guidance from the guru mainly through daily WhatsApp messages and Facebook posts. The act of direct feedback which is in-built in social media, whether it is commenting on posts on Facebook, or replying to group messages on WhatsApp gives many lower caste followers a platform where they feel not discriminated against or placed lower in any way compared to upper castes. The use of social media and technology, then, in this case, works to fight caste discrimination, even though with the relative higher price of high speed data access, it creates new disparities, by leapfrogging the issues of access that religious sites often have.

Notes

1 All interviews were done in Mumbai, Delhi and Mandla in Madhya Pradesh. In total, Lahiri Guruji and 15 prominent members of the Abhiyan were interviewed. Lahiri Guruji was interviewed thrice, while the others were interviewed once.
2 The diary plants are being set up in association with Holland Milk of the Netherlands. See http://milk-milk.ch/index.html.

References

Andersen, Walter (1972) "The Rashtriya Swayamsevak Sangh: Early Concerns." *Economic and Political Weekly* 7(11): 589, 591–597.

Andersen, Walter and Shridhar Damle (1987) *Brotherhood in Saffron: Rashtriya Swayamsevak Sangh and Hindu Revivalism.* New Delhi: Vistaar Publications.

Azad, Shivani (2016) "Tarun Vijay, Dalits Pelted with Stone for Defying Temple Ban." *The Times of India*, May 20. Available at: http://timesofindia.indiatimes.com/india/ Tarun-Vijay-Dalits-pelted-with-stone-for-defying-temple-ban/articleshow/52367193. cms (accessed July 1, 2016).

Bakhle, Janaki (2008) "Music as the Sound of the Secular." *Economic and Political Weekly* 50(1): 256–284.

Barker, Ernest (1951) *Principles of Social and Political Theory.* Oxford: Clarendon Press.

Beteille, Andre (2012) "India's Destiny Not Cast in Stone." *The Hindu*, February 21. Available at: www.thehindu.com/opinion/lead/indias-destiny-not-caste-in-stone/a rticle2913662.ece (accessed November 30, 2016).

Bhave, Y.G. (2009) *Vinayak Damodar Savarkar.* New Delhi: Northern Book Centre.

Deshpande, S.H. (2003) "Savarkar's Portrait." *Economic and Political Weekly* 38(11): 998, 1084.

dishatv.com (2013) "Distribution of Disha TV." Available at: http://www.dishatv.com/ index.php?option=com_content&view=article&id=64&Itemid=88 (accessed December 6, 2016).

Gandhi, A.K. (2016) *The Life and Times of Veer Savarkar.* Delhi: Prabhat Prakashan.

Giddens, Anthony (1990) *The Consequences of Modernity.* Stanford, California: Stanford University Press.

Grover, Verinder (1993) *Political Thinkers of Modern India.* Delhi: Deep & Deep Publications.

Indo-Asian News Service (2016) "Mohan Bhagwat Breaks Bread with Sanitary Workers at Kumbh Mela." NDTV.com, June 17. Available at: www.ndtv.com/india -news/mohan-bhagwat-breaks-bread-with-sanitary-workers-at-kumbh-mela- 1405967 (accessed June 25, 2016).

Jaffrelot, Christophe (2007) *Hindu Nationalism: A Reader.* Princeton, NJ: Princeton University Press.

Jaffrelot, Christophe (2010) *Religion, Caste and Politics in India.* Delhi: Primus Books.

Jha, Ajit Kumar and Uday Mahurkar (2016) "United Colours of RSS." *India Today*, April 14. Available at: http://indiatoday.intoday.in/story/rashtriya-swayamsevak-sa ngh-rss-sangh-parivar-mohan-bhagwat/1/642499.html (accessed May 4, 2016).

Kalathil, Shanthi and Taylor C. Boas (2003) "Open Networks, Closed Regimes: The Impact of the Internet on Authoritarian Rule." *First Monday* 8(1): 150–153.

Kapur, Devesh, Chandra Bhan Prasad, Lant Pritchett and D. Shyam Babu (2010) "Rethinking Inequality: Dalits in Uttar Pradesh in Market Reform Era." *Economic and Political Weekly* 45(35): 39–49.

Krueger, Oliver (2004) "The Internet as Distributor and Mirror of Religious and Ritual Knowledge." *Asian Journal of Social Science* 32(2): 183–197.

Marshall, Gordon and John Scott (eds.) (2009) *A Dictionary of Sociology.* London: Oxford University Press.

Matei, Sorin and Sandra J. Ball-Rokeach (2001) "Real and Virtual Social Ties: Connections in the Everyday Lives of Seven Ethnic Neighbourhoods." *American Behavioral Scientist* 45(3): 550–563.

McKean, Lise (1996) *Divine Enterprise: Gurus and the Hindu Nationalist Movement.* London: University of Chicago Press.

McLuhan, Marshall (1964) *Understanding Media: The Extensions of Man.* New York: Mentor.

Meintel, Diedre (2012) "Seeking the Sacred Online: Internet and the Individualization of Religious Life in Quebec." *Canadian Anthropology Society* 54(1): 19–32.

Mlecko, Joel D. (1982), "The Guru in Hindu Tradition." *Numen* 29: 33–61.

New York Times (2016) "Women and Girls in India Denied Smartphones because Men Consider it 'Indecent' and Shameful," October 14, 2016.

Nie, Norman H. and D. Sunshine Hillygus (2002) "The Impact of Internet Use on Sociability: Time Diary Findings." *IT & Society* 1(1): 1–20.

Savarkar, Veer (2012) *Hindutva: Who is a Hindu?* Mumbai: Hindi Sahitya Sadan.

Sharma, Jyotirmaya (2003) *Hindutva: Exploring the Idea of Hindu Nationalism.* New Delhi: Penguin Books India.

Warrier, Maya (2003) "Guru Choice and Spiritual Seeking in Contemporary India."*International Journal of Hindu Studies* 7: 31.

9 Promoting Punjabi Deras' ideologies online

A case of Dera Sacha Sauda

Anna Bochkovskaya

Recent decades have witnessed an unprecedented growth of various religious and pseudo-religious communities (*dera*s[1]) in the Indian state of Punjab and in adjacent areas. Multiple reasons for the flourishing of *dera*s have been thoroughly analyzed by Surinder Jodhka (2008), Ashutosh Kumar (2014), Meeta and Rajivlochan (2007), Harish Puri (2003), Ronki Ram (2016a, 2012, 2008, 2007), Neeru Sharma (2012), Surinder Singh (2009) and other scholars. According to rough estimates (Ram, 2016b), there might be over 10,000 *dera*s of different types in present-day Punjab, and almost 80 percent of the state's population are affiliated with them (Dogra, 2007).

A majority of such communities generally function around a single guru and/or the place where he currently lives or used to reside in the past: a number of older *dera*s boast long histories, which in some cases (as with saints—Hindu *nath*s or Muslim *pir*s) are expected to be traced to pre-Sikh times. Jodhka (2008) notes that "as institutions of popular or folk religion outside the more organized structures such as mosques and temples, [deras] represented the enchanted universe of pre-modern religiosity" and possibly contributed to passing the message of the Sikh Gurus to inhabitants of the region (Jodhka, 2008). Given the multiplicity and diversity of such communities in Punjab, it is feasible to differentiate between Sikh and non-Sikh *dera*s: in the former, *dera* followers strictly adhere to the Sikh code of conduct, while in the latter, they can follow various religious practices (Ram, 2007: 4067). Another important divide is whether a *dera* follows the "living god/guru" principle: within the Sikh fold, most important is the physical presence of the *Guru Granth Sahib* that features an ultimate source of spirituality and is regarded as eternal Guru, whereas some of non-Sikhs *dera*s praise own leaders as godmen and worship them. Six such communities – namely, Namdhari, Sant Nirankari, Radha Soami Satsang Beas, Sacha Sauda, Divya Jyoti Jagrati Sansthan, and Bhaniarawala – have been listed as most "dangerous" anti-Sikh *dera*s by the Shiromani Gurdwara Prabandhak Committee (SGPC), the highest religious authority of the Sikhs.[2]

The bulk of the *dera*s' devotees comprise rural Dalits of different lower caste groups, and marginalized peasants. In comparison to other states, Punjab has the highest proportion of Scheduled Castes who constitute 8.86

million or almost 30 percent of the state's population of 27.7 million.[3] In various proportions they represent all religions of Punjab. Having become relatively wealthy owing to the earlier shift in occupation patterns and also to remittances from Punjabi migrants (Singh, 2012: 55; Puri, 2003: 2695–2696) the lower castes are trying to get their share in the resources and assert themselves in Punjab's politics. To this end, they resort to religion simultaneously looking toward distancing from Sikhs due to the overwhelming dominance of upper Sikh castes (mostly, Jats) in the ritual sphere and in the SGPC.

As of today, there are two main symbols that have been setting off the increasing caste confrontation within the Sikh community of Punjab: *gurdwara*s (places of worship) and the scripture. Since in many cases lower caste Sikhs received humiliating treatment in Jat-run *gurdwara*s or were not allowed to enter common places of worship at all, they started building their own shrines (Ram, 2009: 6, 12; Judge and Bal 2008: 51–53; Jodhka and Louis, 2003: 2924–2925). To emphasize the autonomy, Dalits deliberately avoid the term "gurdwara" and call them *gurderas*, *gurghars* or *bhawans*. As a result, in a majority of Punjab's villages there currently are at least two shrines—one used by higher castes and the other one serving for the needs of lower castes (Puri, 2003: 2700).

Equally important for both sides is the *Guru Granth Sahib* that occupies the central place in *gurdwara*s as an object for worship and on certain occasions can be carried home to perform some rites. There have been numerous evidences that higher caste Sikhs forbid lower castes to use the scripture or restrict their access to it (Ram, 2007: 4070–4072; Puri, 2003: 2700). Thus, the *Guru Granth Sahib* is nowadays regarded by a major part of Punjabi Dalits as another manifestation of higher caste power. Consequently, within the past decades there have been several attempts of *dera* leaders in Punjab to adopt own holy books as "alternative" scriptures. The most controversial cases included the *Bhavsagar Granth* compiled by/for Bhaniarawala Baba of Ropar in 2001 (Meeta and Rajivlochan, 2007),[4] and the *Amritbani Guru Ravidass* proclaimed in 2010 a separate scripture for Ravidassias, that is, contemporary followers of medieval Sant (Saint) Ravidass whose largest *dera*, Sachkhand Ballan, is located near Jalandhar (Ram, 2016a, 2009, 2008; Singh, 2012; Jodhka, 2009).

In this context, the lower castes' struggle for identity has become a perfect framework for the activities of such *dera*s as the above Radha Soami Satsang Beas, Divya Jyoti Jagrati Sansthan, and Sacha Sauda, which advertise themselves as universal spiritual or socio-spiritual organizations "based on the spiritual teachings of all religions" (Radha Soami Satsang Beas, 2016), or representing "a confluence of all religions" (Dera Sacha Sauda, 2016a-h). Having become part of social and religious landscapes not only in Punjab, but also in some other Indian states, these three popular *dera*s aim at expanding their activities both in and outside India and widely use advanced media technologies, specifically the Internet, for this purpose.

Based on the concepts of "religion online" and "online religion" proposed and developed by Christopher Helland (2000, 2004, 2005) and further elaborated by Jeffrey Hadden and Douglas Cowan (2000), Lorne Dawson and Douglas Cowan (2004) as well as by Glenn Young (2004), this chapter focuses on the Internet performance of *dera* Sacha Sauda (colloquially DSS), which is one of the largest, most powerful, and most controversial *dera*s in India.

Ideology of the "True Deal"

Founded in Punjab in 1948 by Shah Mastana Ji Maharaj, Dera Sacha Sauda[5] (literally meaning the *dera* of "True Deal") remained a rather unremarkable community for decades, but things began to change since 1990 when its third guru and current leader Sant Gurmeet Ram Rahim Singh Ji Insaan came to power. With the headquarters currently based in Sirsa[6] (Haryana), the *dera* nowadays operates over 40 branches (*ashram*s) in several Indian states[7] and is most popular in southern Punjab and Haryana. It boasts *lakhs* of followers (figures in various sources vary from 10 to 60 million[8]), while the proportion of Dalits within Sacha Sauda is estimated at up to 70 percent (Swami and Sethi, 2007).[9]

Dera Sacha Sauda claims to be not a religious entity but "a social welfare and spiritual organization that preaches and practices humanitarianism and selfless services to others" (Dera Sacha Sauda, 2016a, b). The role of the living guru is central in its ideology as he is the one who guides all followers in worshiping god and in daily life. Dera Sacha Sauda's principles feature an eclectic combination of pieces of philosophy taken basically from Sikhism, but also from Hinduism, Islam and Christianity, that is, all major religions that in various proportions[10] can be found in contemporary Punjab. This is why the Dera Sacha Sauda emblem (Figure 9.1) carries symbols of these four religions—*ik onkar, om/aum*, crescent and star, and cross. Names of Dera Sacha Sauda's second and third gurus (Param Pita Shah Satnam Singh Ji and Gurmeet Ram Rahim Singh Ji Insaan) are a combination of Sikh, Hindu and Muslim components, which also serves to the purpose of recognizing the unity of all faiths in Punjab.

At the same time, the present guru's name also suggests that unity should be embodied in the word "insaan" (*insan*, meaning human being): every adherent is supposed to use it after his surname or, preferably, instead of it (Dera Sacha Sauda, 2016d). This idea has a strong connotation with the tradition of adopting the name Singh for Sikh males and Kaur for Sikh females, especially if taken in combination with a ceremony of "the pledge for humanitarism" (*jam-e-insan* or "nectar of humanity") introduced by Ram Rahim Singh in 2007. The pledge includes partaking of a pink-colored sweet "holy drink" that resembles *amrit*, or holy water used during the baptism ceremony in Sikhism. When photos of the Dera Sacha Sauda's guru drinking and distributing the holy substance to his followers were published in Punjab's newspapers in May 2007 the entire state went aflame (Deep, 2007), since mainstream Sikhs considered this "blasphemous act of impersonating Guru Gobind Singh" (Singh, 2015) and as a deliberate insult to the Sikh

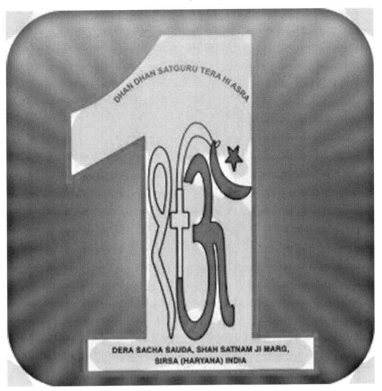

Figure 9.1 Dera Sacha Sauda's emblem

community (see e.g. Khalsa Press, 2007). What aggravated the situation was Ram Rahim Singh's dress clearly visible in the photos that "imitated" the attire of Guru Gobind Singh, the tenth Sikh guru (for details, see Baixas, 2007; Baixas and Simon, 2008; Copeman, 2012).

Violent clashes between mainstream Sikhs and followers of Dera Sacha Sauda in 2007 took place not only in Punjab and Haryana, but also in Delhi, Himachal Pradesh, Jammu & Kashmir, Uttar Pradesh and even in Kolkata and Mumbai, in other words, in all states or cities with large Sikh communities. The SGPC demanded imposing government ban on all branches of the *dera*, and the situation in the state in many ways reminded that of the late 1970s and early 1980s when a stand-off between Nirankaris and mainstream Sikhs took place followed by a decade of militancy in Punjab (Meeta and Rajivlochan, 2007: 1909). As a result, the Akal Takht issued an edict (*hukamnama*) urging all Sikhs to boycott Dera Sacha Sauda and its followers. At the same time, the 2007 row stirred up interest toward Dera Sacha Sauda and its leader and, as I will show in the following, allowed the *dera* to gain additional popularity among lower castes in Punjab and beyond.

Unsurprisingly, Dera Sacha Sauda's ideology implicitly emphasizes the tenets resembling those of Sikhism – a religion open to everyone at least at the early stages of its history. The *dera*'s first principle declares: "In Dera Sacha Sauda all religions are equally honored and welcomed" (Dera Sacha Sauda, 2016h). Putting forward the idea of universalism it obviously connotes the statement "There is no Hindu, there is no Muslim" associated with Baba Nanak, the first Sikh Guru, which "pointed the way to towards the common humanity underlying the external divisions" (Singh, 2014: 21).

Nanak's concept of *dan* ("giving") in relation to the society is supported by Dera Sacha Sauda's second principle: "Dera Sacha Sauda believes in humanity as the greatest religion and is involved in the true service of humanity. The poor, helpless and sick are helped here in every possible manner" (Dera Sacha Sauda, 2016h). Every person is supposed to earn his living "through hard work and rightful means," and within this context, the *dera*'s major domains include voluntary work (*seva*) within its premises, and versatile social and relief activities outside them.

As far as the first domain is concerned, celibate volunteers of the *dera* work for 15 to 18 hours a day and practice meditation (Principle 12, Dera Sacha Sauda, 2016h). About 450 resident *sevak*s (300 men and 150 women) permanently stay in the central *ashram*, and many others come to work in Sirsa-based central *ashram* and in other branches for weeks or months. Their labor is very important as the *dera* claims "not to accept any offerings, donations or fees for the meditation" that is taught within its premises (Principle 4, Dera Sacha Sauda, 2016h).

It has been reported that Dera Sacha Sauda owns more than 700 acres of land, and the main bulk of it is located in Haryana followed by southern Punjab.[11] Agriculture is the main source of the *dera*'s income: Dera Sacha Sauda owns several processing companies including the "Sach Foods," "Sach Herbotech Products" and the recently established "MSG All Trading International" that deal with food grains, vegetables, aloe vera leaf and juice, candies, spices, biscuits, fruit juices, tea, and so on. These companies have been set up with the mission "to serve society by offering products which are helpful for attaining a perfect health & hence achieving a perfect state of mind"(Sach Herbotech Products, n.d.), for which purpose they focus on products of organic farming that meet international standards (Press Trust of India, 2016).

The income coming from agriculture is supposed to be used for funding Dera Sacha Sauda's second domain, that is, large-scale social and relief work carried out at local and national levels. This work is performed by the *dera*'s dedicated wing, Shah Satnam Ji Green "S" Welfare Force Wing founded in 2001 (Shah Satnam Ji Green "S" Welfare Force Wing, 2016). According to the wing's website, it is an agency uniting over 70,000 trained volunteers including doctors, paramedics, engineers, rescuers and other experts required in humanitarian aid missions. They took part in helping victims of the 2001 earthquake in Gujarat, the 2004 tsunami in Tamilnadu and the Andamans, in eliminating the aftermath of several snow avalanches in Jammu and Kashmir, and provided help at different times to drought-stricken districts in Rajasthan, flood affected areas in Punjab, Haryana, Orissa, Uttarkhand and other states. Not downplaying the importance of all these activities it should be noted that the Green "S" Force (introduced at its website as "World's only #1 humanitarian force working for humanity without any salary") is extensively used for advertising the comprehensive performance of Dera Sacha Sauda and its guru.

Thus, within the past two decades Dera Sacha Sauda has turned into a big business enterprise and is largely dubbed "commercial" *dera* (Chaudhry, 2012; Manav, 2016). One substantial component of *dera*'s success is its vast propaganda activity carried out mainly through its Sirsa-based media center. Dera Sacha Sauda addresses all strata of society and applies a variety of means for self-advertising, which primarily include broadcasting, print media, and the Internet.

Holy sayings and doings on the Web

Since 2000s, large and influential *deras* have successfully been using online marketing options for promoting their ideologies and attracting new followers. In most cases such activities represent both *online religion*, which is generally perceived as provision of information about religious groups, rituals and traditions, and simultaneously, *religion online*, which offers Internet users various types of interaction or practices that may include online prayers, meditation, observance of rituals, spiritual counseling, astrological charts etc. (Dawson and Cowan, 2004: 7–8). A majority of *dera* websites amalgamate both options confirming Glenn Young's suggestion that religion online and online religion do not feature a strict opposition, but "are two types of religious expression and activity that exist in continuity with one another" (Young, 2004: 93).

In this respect, Dera Sacha Sauda is no exception. The *dera* boasts a very informative and constantly updated English-language website (www.derasachasauda.org) that provides detailed information on its history, ashrams, and spiritual masters, lists the principles, and brings forward *seva* news lavishly supplemented with visuals. Importantly, every page has a link to Dera Sacha Sauda's official sources of information that include *dera*'s Twitter, Facebook and Google+ accounts; a website personally dedicated to Ram Rahim Singh; DSS mobile applications and SMS service websites; YouTube channels; sites of educational institutions run by DSS; newspaper and magazine websites, and some others.

In the past six years that I have been tracing Dera Sacha Sauda's performance, the *dera*'s media resources intensively expanded. The *Sach Kahoon* ("Speaking True" or "Saying the Truth") daily newspaper (www.sachkahoon.com) currently publishes Haryana, Rajasthan, Punjab, Delhi, and Uttar Pradesh printed and e-paper versions (http://epaper.sachkahoon.com) available in Hindi, and also Punjab and Delhi editions available in Punjabi; there also is an online version of *Sach Kahoon* in Hindi (http://sachkahoon.in/). With the total circulation estimated at over a *lakh* (100,000), the newspaper's printed version is distributed by Dera Sacha Sauda's followers in all its branches. Focusing on Ram Rahim Singh's sermons and *seva* activities, the *Sach Kahoon* also gives a good coverage of local, national as well as international news. Supplement to the *Sach Kahoon* is another digital-and-print edition, the monthly *Sachi Shiksha* ("True Education") magazine (www.sachishiksha.in), which is intended for women and published in Hindi, Punjabi, and English.

Broadcasting efforts focus on speeches of Ram Rahim Singh, called *ruhani satsang*s / *majlis* (spiritual gatherings), which are in most cases delivered in Hindi. Four daily TV programs intended mostly for Punjab and Haryana and showing live sermons of the guru are on the list, but in the past two-three years the DSS has shifted to the maximum use of computers and mobile phones for this purpose. One recent novelty is the Dera Sacha Sauda Mobile Application for Android and IOS users that allows watching and/or listening the live telecast of *satsang*s from Sirsa.

Other self-advertising means include books (*granth*s), CDs and DVDs with *satsang*s and *bhajan*s (spiritual singing), in other words, "regular" or "conventional" resources used by other *dera*s as well. A majority of these products is available in Hindi and Punjabi while some books are in English; all of them can be purchased online.

Spirituality and the contribution of Dera Sacha Sauda in the spiritual awakening of the mankind is the keynote of the entire website. The *dera*'s home page opens with pictures of the three gurus / spiritual masters and the "holy slogan" *Dhan Dhan Satguru Tera Hi Aasra* (*dhan dhan satguru tera hi asra*, meaning "praise the true guru, your sole reliance"), that comes up together with a photo of the present Dera Sacha Sauda's head. Actually, it is Ram Rahim Singh whose visual presence, either in photos or videos, accompanies visitors through all pages of the website. Pursuing the idea "to lead humanitarian endeavors" (Dera Sacha Sauda, 2016b) he discusses such issues as true meditation "to attain inner self confidence and see God"; promotion of love and tolerance among people of all religions, castes, color and regions; healthy living; humanitarian work and so on.

Addressing the widest possible audience, Dera Sacha Sauda uses targeted channels for different social groups to achieve the desired effect. The Internet and the English language are meant for educated public at local and national levels and also outside India.[12] TV broadcasting along with publication of books and CD-DVD matter is also aimed at a vast audience, but with an emphasis on the locals. Print media is largely limited to the Punjabi- and Hindi-speaking area and is primarily intended for the rural grassroots level—the strata of Dera Sacha Sauda's utmost success in Punjab and Haryana.

The content of Dera Sacha Sauda's public-awareness campaigns serves the same purpose of suiting various tastes so in focus is the comprehensive character of *seva* activities. As I have mentioned, the Shah Satnam Ji Green "S" Welfare Force Wing – the Dera Sacha Sauda's champion in the *seva* field – contributed to disaster management in various states thus showing the flag during major relief operations broadcast all over India. Its website lists 127 humanitarian activities that have involved the active participation of *sevak*s. Among them are environment protection and cleanliness campaigns, improvement of medical service and schooling, motivating de-addiction campaigns, blood donation (*rakt-dan*) and many others.

A majority of these activities are not Dera Sacha Sauda's invention. For example, blood donation has been a very important sphere of other *deras'* work for decades.[13] Sant Nirankaris successfully ran large-scale *rakt-dan* campaigns in the early 1980s; websites of Radha Soami Satsang Beas (Radha Soami Satsang Beas, 2016) and Divya Jyoti Jagrati Sansthan (Divya Jyoti Jagrati Sansthan, 2017) also mention the many-year engagement of these *deras* in blood donation activities. Even the mainstream Sikhs also resort to such actions (for example, Copeman, 2012: 170–174) as they give a perfect opportunity to combine *seva* and propaganda efforts.

Unlike Dera Sacha Sauda, other *deras'* public-awareness campaigns are less publicized on the Internet. Dera Sacha Sauda's aggressive and flexible style marks it out against the background of other communities. To this end, setting records turns out to be an impressive subject of self-advertising, and the *dera* has been using the *Guinness Book of World Records* as a perfect medium for the purpose. Dera Sacha Sauda's website informs that these actions started with setting two sequential records for blood donation in 2003 and 2004, and with listing the smallest mobile hospital "Farishta" in the *Limca Book of World Records*. In 2009, Dera Sacha Sauda shifted to another option, that is, environment protection through planting trees: over 938,000 trees were planted in just one hour and recorded in the *Guinness Book*. The action took place on August 15, 2009, on India's Independence Day that also happened to be the birthday of the *dera*'s guru, seemingly no mere coincidence. The date has been used not only to celebrate, but to mark the *dera*'s efforts in preservation of environment, which is another issue given a wide coverage at the website.

Though much popularized and invariably "consecrated" by the presence of the *dera*'s head, the record-setting actions are insignificant for the *aam admi* (common man) of Punjab and neighboring states. For a majority of people most important are those of the above programs that are aimed at practical improvement of their living conditions. These include employment generation projects, community marriages, tribal reintegration schemes, crusades against drug addiction and alcoholism, medical aid including organization of regular eye camps that provide free eye checkups and operations, etc. These targeted actions substantially contribute to the *dera*'s success in rural Punjab, Haryana and beyond.

It is in addressing the grassroots audience that Dera Sacha Sauda's Sikh bias becomes more evident regardless of all statements of Ram Rahim Singh and other officials about the "universal character" of the *dera*. Dera Sacha Sauda has effectively used Sikh symbols as an instrument for attracting lower caste Sikhs and, simultaneously, for self-advertising through the effective use of media resources. For example, the *dera*'s 2007 confrontation with mainstream Sikhs started in May 2007 when at least three leading newspapers of Punjab published photos that they had received from the Dera Sacha Sauda showing Ram Rahim Singh dressed like Guru Gobind Singh stirring some *amrit*-like liquid intended for the *jam-e-insan* ceremony. Importantly, the ceremony had taken place in Sirsa before that without any advertising and media coverage and had gone unnoticed (Baixas and Simon, 2008: 13). After the row calmed down, the ceremony has been taking take place on a regular basis—outside Punjab and without using Guru Gobind Singh's attire—as routine work on local level.

But the unrest stage-managed by Dera Sacha Sauda through media in 2007 actually served three purposes: first, it was supposed to divert attention from a number of other scandals that involved Ram Rahim Singh: sexual harassment of *sadhvi*s (women followers) and two alleged murders including one of a journalist who investigated the sexual offense cases (Rajalakshmi, 2003). Secondly, it attracted attention to introduction of the *jam-e-insan* ceremony as a perfect psychological means for establishing a sense of belonging to a new community that is so important for lower castes. Last but not the least, it was a general propaganda masterpiece that in the long run helped the *dera* to attract other followers.

Spiritual Q&A Book: holy text on the Web

Web publications of holy books partially bridge the gap between religion online and online religion, as they provide information and/or advertise a religion or ideology, and to an extent allow using scriptures for actual practices. A specific version of own holy text was produced by Dera Sacha Sauda in 2011: the need for an official explanation of *dera*'s ideology and its guru's performance had become obvious in the confrontation of the *dera* and mainstream Sikhs boosted by the 2007 controversy. Consequently, the volume titled *Kuch bhi saval kaho uska ruhani javab* (*Spiritual Answer to Any Question*) was published in Hindi and Punjabi, and from 2011 to 2014 was available online at Dera Sacha Sauda's website tagged in the menu bar as *Spiritual Q&A Book*. Both Hindi and Punjabi versions were uploaded in form of printed copies where one could "turn over" the virtual pages.

Formally, the *Spiritual Q&A Book* is not a scripture like the Sikh *Guru Granth Sahib* or the Ravidassia *Amritbani* or any other text, which is either venerated like a guru or used during worship. But it might be considered as a version of counter-scripture, well disguised considering its form and content. To this end, one important argument is that the book represents the *bani*—words of the *satguru*, the spiritual leader of the *dera*—that are considered sacred for the followers. In compliance with its title, the book features a dialogue: it contains 725 questions and answers to them given by the Dera Sacha Sauda head Ram Rahim Singh.

Both the questions and answers are very short, in most cases not exceeding three or four lines. There is no system in the arrangement of questions, and some of them are rephrased and come up more than once. The range of topics erratically discussed in the "dialogue" is very wide, but if summed up the following concepts and ideas are in focus:

- Divine omnipotence. Every aspect of everyday life is explained by the guru a result of God's will (*prabhu ke hukm*). Importantly, Ram Rahim Singh uses a variety of epithets from different religions when referring to God (*malik, satguru, Ram, bhagvan, paramatma, parbrahma* etc.).
- The holy name (*nam*) and the necessity of repeating it (*nam simaran / nam japna*) in meditation. In a number of answers the intertwining of Sikh and Hindu elements comes up: *Ram nam kahna* ("Say the name of Ram") is often used instead of or in parallel with *nam simaran / nam japna*.
- Significance of the guru. Ram Rahim Singh's answers emphasize that God conveys part of his own self in *sants/gurus* (questions 34, 39), which implicitly means that considering the full title, that is, Sant Ram Rahim Singh Maharaj Ji Insaan, Dera Sacha Sauda's guru is of divine origin.
- Explanation of the categories of "good" and "bad" (*acchai* and *burai*) and, subsequently, the importance of *ruhani satsangs* (spiritual gatherings) in Dera Sacha Sauda's ashrams as the embodiment of *acchai*. Such gatherings attended by thousands of people in the Sirsa-based ashram are the main place where the guru regularly delivers his speeches and explains the above concepts.
- Universal character of Dera Sacha Sauda's ideology. This most important provision is reiterated through the idea of unity of the mankind: the slogan "We all are one" (*ham sab ek hain*) is frequently used in the text. To this effect, the term *insan* (human being) is also repeatedly explained by the guru. The derivative *insaniyat* (question 689), or the "mankind," is the religion of Ram Rahim Singh, as he puts it, and also the synonym of the universal religion (*sarvadharam*) preached in the *dera*.
- Global/international issues and ways to solve them. Such questions as reasons for global warming (questions 50, 510), terrorism and its roots (question 589), complicated relations between India and Pakistan (question 596), possible end of the world (question 479) etc. are briefly discussed by the guru who constantly stresses the role of *sants* in coping with such problems.

The *Spiritual Q&A Book* also contains several comments of Ram Rahim Singh concerning sacred books (*dharmik/pavitra granth*), which is another argument for considering the "dialogue" as a specific alternative scripture. Nonrandom questions together with the answers aim at stressing the secondary role of "regular" scriptures versus the primary role of the guru and his words (*bani*) in giving followers the name of God. In question 82 Ram Rahim Singh

Figure 9.2 Questions and Guru's answers

says that guru's words are most simple for memorizing, understanding, and finally obtaining *moksha* (liberation).

Another question – whether live (*dehdhari*) gurus excel sacred books – is probably a clue to understanding the message of the "dialogue." The Dera Sacha Sauda guru's answer is that "all the sacred books – no matter of their number – were all written by live *sant*s, gurus, or prophets," which allows Ram Rahim Singh to further develop his idea of remaining "above" all the religions and relevant scriptures.

Thus, the book intends to contribute to the general image of the Dera Sacha Sauda as a spiritual entity boasting its own "spiritual" book essential for any organization of such a type, and also to "officially" clarify some controversial stories and reproaches concerning the *dera*'s performance. It is necessary to mention here that a majority of Dera Sacha Sauda's Punjab- and Haryana-based low caste followers do not know English and do not use the Internet, so the online version of the holy book uploaded at the English-language website was of no use to them. At the same time, the English-language website was also meant for attracting foreign followers so the Hindi or Punjabi versions of the *Spiritual Q&A Book* were less important for the potential overseas audience. Consequently, the book further evolved into two English-language volumes *Holy Discourses* and *Spirituality: A Plethora of Answers* (Dera Sacha Sauda, 2016f) and a number of Punjabi- and Hindi-language books with the same contents.

In 2014, the book was removed from the website, which was radically changed. In the updated version, all theses proposed by the guru in the *Spiritual Q&A Book* were transformed into new informative and easy-to-read web pages. For example, the page listing 15 main principles of Dera Sacha Sauda (Dera Sacha Sauda, 2016h) briefly covers a large number of repeating portions in the *Q&A Book* about the universal religion, *acchai* and *burai*, the role of *satsang*s and the guru, and so on. The same refers to the pages explaining the ideas of *jam-e-insan* (Dera Sacha Sauda, 2016d), humanitarian works (Dera Sacha Sauda, 2016e) and other important issues. Thus, the manner of presentation of the *Spiritual Q&A Book* by Sacha Sauda can be perceived as a well-calculated strategy, especially considering the irreconcilable attitude of mainstream Sikhs to the *dera* and its guru. Objectively, it was quite difficult to accuse the guru of creating an "alternative" scripture: explicitly, the Hindi and Punjabi versions of the book online were just a compilation of questions and answers, and none of them seemed to insult the tenets of Sikhism or Hinduism since the guru's answers sounded very diplomatic. But the general message was and still is quite clear. Placed together in the book called "spiritual" the guru's words or *bani* implicitly acquired a traditional form of a "holy" text, which is essential for any religious or quasi-religious ideology.

Messages of the "Messenger"

Since 2014, the focus of Dera Sacha Sauda's self-advertising efforts shifted to the film industry domain with the aim of widening the coverage and gaining more profit. The Dera Sacha Sauda head revealed himself in multiple capacities of film director, producer, script writer, composer, singer and actor, and subsequently released three films, *MSG: The Messenger* (February 2015), *MSG-2: The Messenger* (September 2015) and the most recent *MSG: The Warrior Lion Heart* (November 2016).

All of them have been aggressively promoted in India (Figure 9.3): Dera Sacha Sauda engaged all its online resources including the *dera*'s main website and social networking services to advertise these products. Noteworthy, the first film was initially titled *MSG: The Messenger of God* and was marketed as "a Bollywood movie which aims to spread social awareness in the society" and "a blend of entertainment and social message" (Dera Sacha Sauda, 2016g) since its main character—the Guruji with *lakhs* of followers – fought with such evils (*burai*) as drug addiction and sexual abuse. As early as at the promotion stage the *MSG* proved to be in the center of controversies: in January 2015 it was denied certification by the Central Board of Film Certification on the grounds that the film was likely to provoke conflict and hurt religious sentiments (Rajalakshmi, 2015) and was sent to the Appellate Tribunal. An argument of the officials was that the *MSG* trailer had already aggravated the situation in Punjab and some other states due to the growing stand-off of Dera Sacha Sauda's followers and mainstream Sikhs who considered the title of the film most insulting (Bajwa, 2014; Kamal, 2015). The tribunal's positive decision in relation to the film predictably outraged Sacha Sauda opponents, primarily the Sikh authorities, and the movie was banned for release in Punjab until the final clearance of the Punjab and Haryana High Court came up (Sriram, 2015). Ram Rahim Singh's compromise with the authorities

Figure 9.3 The MSG Poster

boiled down to muting some phrases in the movie and shortening its title to *MSG: The Messenger.*

In a way, the *MSG* controversy followed the 2007 pattern when promotion of a "product" started with a provocative action for marketing reasons. After some minor adjustments a compromise was achieved, and the *MSG* brand became operational. The film started to set records at the trailer stage (Kapoor, 2015) and despite the utmost primitiveness of the plot[14] managed to get a wide audience all over India as it was dubbed not only in Hindi, but also in Tamil, Telugu, Malayalam, and English.

Its sequel, *MSG-2*, was released in several months and took the same path of aggressive advertising at the trailer stage followed by banning in some states,[15] which nevertheless allowed Dera Sacha Sauda to further promote own activities by taking advantage of the effective and profitable *MSG* brand. For example, it has been applied in the name of the *dera*'s new wholesale firm "MSG All Trading International Pvt Ltd" that deals with over 150 products including high-demand organic food items and widely uses online trading through teleshopping and mobile apps (Press Trust of India, 2016).

Leaving aside the details of Dera Sacha Sauda's commercial success on the path of "encouraging spiritual awakening" as well as "preaching and practicing humanitarianism" (Dera Sacha Sauda, 2016b), I would point out the effective use of terminology in *dera*'s self-advertising: those were both religious and hi-tech connotations of the term "messenger" that have made the films and the MSG brand so attractive for younger followers of Dera Sacha Sauda. Besides, there is a small but indicative detail on the *dera*'s website: the only email contact given there is msg@derasachasauda.in, which conveys the message of personal interaction with the "Messenger of God," or the *satguru* Ram Rahim Singh.

Thus, the performance of Dera Sacha Sauda on the Web is a combination of basically religion online supplemented with minor elements of online religion. The Dera Sacha Sauda is mostly a business project, which tells on the way of online representation of the guru's words or *bani*: the *Spiritual Q&A Book* initially uploaded on the *dera*'s website finally evolved into a more profitable collection of online information that has absorbed major ideas from the book and simultaneously offered up-to-date options for online communication with the living guru.

Though Dera Sacha Sauda's ideology is not meant to be a religion, the anatomy of its online efforts shows that the *dera*'s advertising of reform activities represents a fusion of religious and social components. Dera Sacha Sauda's self-representation is situational: religion – or spirituality, as the *dera*'s authorities put it – comes to the surface whenever and wherever it becomes necessary to offset the (sometimes) excessively pragmatic approach shown by the "True Deal" enterprise in tackling a variety of topical issues. Dera Sacha Sauda's success is largely a result of well-calculated social strategy, flexible propaganda policy, and pragmatism involving the use of cutting-edge media technologies.

***

In August 2017, the special Central Bureau of Investigation court in Haryana found the DSS leader Ram Rahim Singh guilty of having sexually assaulted two female followers of the dera *(as far back as the early 2000s) and sentenced him to 20 years of jail. This new phase of DSS history has not been covered in the chapter.*

Notes

1 In Hindi and Punjabi *ḍera* means "camp," or "settlement."
2 Orders and messages of SGPC in connection with these *deras* are available in (Hukamnāme, 2003) and also at the old and current websites of SGPC (http://old.sgpc.net and http://sgpc.net/).
3 Figures available in Census of India, 2011. Patterns of Scheduled Castes distribution in Punjab as well as issues pertaining to Punjabi Dalits' social mobility are discussed in Gosal, 2004: 21–42; Judge and Bal, 2009; Judge, 2014: 108–128.
4 The SGPC strongly condemned the publication, and the book was immediately banned by the Punjab Government. The decision was followed by a long investigation that resulted in quashing the ban by the High Court of Punjab and Haryana in 2008, but still the "alternative" scripture has not been available anywhere.
5 The *dera*'s name comes from Guru Nanak's hagiography and recalls an episode when Nanak gave away to the poor all the money he was supposed to invest in some business and told his father that he had done a True Deal, *saca sauda* (see Baixas and Simon, 2008).
6 After bifurcation of the Indian Punjab in 1966 its eastern part was named Haryana, and Sirsa district became part of the newly emerged state. Sirsa city is located in the vicinity of the Haryana-Punjab border.

7   The *dera*'s website lists 40 ashrams that are located in Punjab, Haryana, Rajasthan, Uttar Pradesh, Madhya Pradesh, Chattisgarh, and Maharashtra (Dera Sacha Sauda, 2016c). There also are branches in Delhi, Himachal Pradesh, Gujarat, Karnataka and Orissa (Bhatia, 2014).

8   Kumar (2014: 342) estimates the number of DSS followers at 10 million. According to Dera Sacha Sauda's website, over 60 million people worldwide are followers of the organization (Dera Sacha Sauda, 2016b), which seems to be an exaggeration.

9   Lal (2009: 226) notes that a majority (70 percent) of all *dera* followers in Punjab are lower caste or Dalit.

10   Sikhs account for 57.7 percent of Punjab's population followed by Hindus (38.5 percent). Muslims (1.9 percent) and Christians (1.2 percent) are hardly visible in the state (*Census of India*, 2011).

11   This information seems to have first appeared in media after the 2007 controversy, which additionally boosted the interest towards Dera Sacha Sauda and its head, Ram Rahim Singh. Since then this figure has been cited in different publications, for example (Tiwari, 2007; Panwar, 2015).

12   Dera Sacha Sauda aims at its widest possible representation worldwide. Currently, two overseas branches of the *dera* operate in Australia and Italy.

13   A comprehensive research of voluntary blood donation as part of spiritual service in India is given in (Copeman, 2009).

14   According to a co-director of the film, the *MSG* featured "basically no storyline or plot" (Banerjee, 2015).

15   *MSG-2* was banned in Jharkhand, Chattisgarh and Madhya Pradesh for some scenes hurting the sentiments of adivasis (tribals) (Express News Service, 2015). A number of theaters in Punjab refused to show the film fearing possible resentment of Dera Sacha Sauda's opponents (Sharma, 2015).

References

Baixas, Lionel (2007) "The Dera Sacha Sauda Controversy and Beyond." *Economic and Political Weekly* 42(40): 4059–4065.

Baixas, Lionel and Charlène Simon (2008) "From Protesters to Martyrs: How to Become a 'True' Sikh." *South Asia Multidisciplinary Academic Journal* 2. Available at: http://samaj.revues.org/document1532.html (accessed October 25, 2016).

Bajwa, Harpreet (2014) "Furious Sikh Groups Demand Ban on the Dera Chief's Messenger of God Film Stunt." *The New Indian Express*, December 28. Available at: www.newindianexpress.com/thesundaystandard/2014/dec/28/Furious-Sikh-Group s-Demand-Ban-on-the-Dera-Chief%E2%80%99s-Messenger-of-God-Film -Stunt-698869.html (accessed December 12, 2016).

Banerjee, Debesh (2015) "They Came for Their Hero's Movie, Didn't Matter it Wasn't Shown." *The Indian Express*, January 17. Available at: http://indianexpress.com/a rticle/india/india-others/sikh-organisations-hold-protests-in-punjab-against-con troversial-film-messenger-of-god/ (accessed December 12, 2016).

Bhatia, Varinder (2014) "All Parties Come to Me, All Get the Same Blessings. There is no Special Blessing", *The Indian Express*, October 26 (online edition). Available at: http://indianexpress.com/about/dera-sacha-sauda/page/2/ (accessed December 9, 2016).

Census of India (2011) "Population by Religious Community (Punjab)," "Scheduled Caste Population by Religious Community (States/UTs)". Available at: www.cen susindia.gov.in/ (accessed September,17, 2016).

Chaudhry, Amrita (2012) "Over 9,000 Deras in Punjab, Some as Old as Sikh Religion Itself." *The Indian Express*, January 28. Available at: http://indianexpress.com/article/cities/chandigarh/over-9-000-deras-in-punjab-some-as-old-as-sikh-religion-itself/ (accessed December 12, 2016).

Copeman, Jackob (2009) *Veins of Devotion: Blood Donation and Religious Experience in North India*. New Brunswick, NJ: Rutgers University Press.

Copeman, Jacob (2012) "The Mimetic Guru: Tracing the Real in Sikh – Dera Sacha Sauda relations." In Jacob Copeman and Aya Ikegame, (eds.), *The Guru in South Asia: New Interdisciplinary Perspectives*. London and New York: Routledge, pp. 156–180.

Dawson, Lorne L. and Douglas E. Cowan (2004) "Introduction." In Lorne L. Dawson and Douglas E. Cowan, (eds.), *Online Religion: Finding Faith on the Internet*. New York: Routledge, pp. 1–16.

Deep, Kiran (2007) "Dera Chief Seeks Centre's Intervention." *The Tribune*, May 17 (online edition). Available at: www.tribuneindia.com/2007/20070518/punjab1.htm#8 (accessed December 9, 2016).

Dera Sacha Sauda (2016a) official website. Available at: www.derasachasauda.org (accessed October 26).

Dera Sacha Sauda (2016b) "About Dera Sacha Sauda." Available at: www.derasachasauda.org/about-dera-sacha-sauda/ (accessed October 26).

Dera Sacha Sauda (2016c) "Ashrams." Available at: www.derasachasauda.org/ashrams/ (accessed October 26, 2016).

Dera Sacha Sauda (2016d) "About Jaam-E-Insan." Available at: www.derasachasauda.org/jaam-e-insan/ (accessed October 26).

Dera Sacha Sauda (2016e) "127 Humanitarian Works." Available at: www.derasachasauda.org/humanitarian-works/ (accessed October 26).

Dera Sacha Sauda (2016f) "Literature/Publications." Available at: www.derasachasauda.org/literatures-publications/ (accessed October 26).

Dera Sacha Sauda (2016g) "MSG – The Rapturous Movie Full of Excitement and Thrill." Available at: www.derasachasauda.org/msg-the-rapturous-movie-full-of-excitement-and-thrill/ (accessed October 26).

Dera Sacha Sauda (2016h) "Principles of Dera Sacha Sauda." Available at: www.derasachasauda.org/principles/ (accessed October 26).

Divya Jyoti Jagrati Sansthan (2017) official website. Available at: www.djjs.org/ (accessed August 27, 2017).

Dogra, Chander Suta (2007) "The Morphed Gene." *Outlook*, May 27. Available at: www.outlookindia.com/article.aspx?234750 (accessed October 15).

Express News Service (2015) "Jharkhand Bans 'MSG 2 – The Messenger'". *The Indian Express*, September 19. Available at: http://indianexpress.com/article/entertainment/bollywood/jharkhand-bans-msg-2-the-messenger/ (accessed December 12, 2016).

Gosal, R.P.S. (2004) "Distribution and Relative Concentration of Scheduled Caste Population in Punjab." In Harish K. Puri, (ed.), *Dalits in Regional Context*. Jaipur: Rawat Publications, pp. 21–42.

Hadden, Jeffrey K. and Douglas E. Cowan (2000) "The Promised Land or Electronic Chaos? Toward Understanding Religion on the Internet." In Jeffrey K. Hadden and Douglas E. Cowan, (eds.), *Religion on the Internet: Research Prospects and Promises*. London: JAI Press / Elsevier Science, pp. 3–24.

Helland, C. (2000) "Online Religion/Religion Online and Virtual Communitas." In J.K. Hadden and D.E. Cowan, (eds.), *Religion on the Internet: Research Prospects and Promises.* New York: JAI Press, pp. 205–224.

Helland, C. (2004) "Popular Religion and the World Wide Web: A Match Made in (Cyber) Heaven." In Lorne L. Dawson and Douglas E. Cowan, (eds.), *Online Religion: Finding Faith on the Internet.* New York: Routledge, pp. 23–36.

Helland, C. (2005) "Online Religion as Lived Religion: Methodological Issues in the Study of Religious Participation on the Internet." *Online-Heidelberg Journal of Religions on the Internet* 1(1). Available at: http://archiv.ub.uni-heidelberg.de/voll textserver/5823/1/Helland3a.pdf (accessed October 20, 2016).

Hukamnāme (2003) *Hukamnāme Ādeś Sandeś, Srī Akāl Takhat Sāhib* (A Collection of Edicts, Orders and Messages from Sri Akal Takht Sahib), Rup Singh (ed.), Amritsar: Singh Brothers. Available at: http://old.sgpc.net/CDN/hukamname_Aadesh_Sandesh.pdf (accessed November 2, 2016).

Jodhka, Surinder S. (2008) "Of Babas and Deras." *Seminar.* Available at: www.india-seminar.com/semframe.html (accessed September 25, 2016).

Jodhka, Surinder S. (2009) "Ravi Dasis of Punjab: Contours of Caste and Religious Strife." *Economic & Political Weekly* 44(24): 79–85.

Jodhka, Surinder S. and Prakash Louis (2003) "Caste Tensions in Punjab: Talhan and Beyond." *Economic and Political Weekly* 38(28): 2923–2926.

Judge, Paramjit S. (2014) "Egalitarian Religion and Caste-Based Exclusion in Rural Punjab." In Paramjit S. Judge, (ed.), *Mapping Social Exclusion in India: Caste, Religion and Borderlands.* Cambridge: Cambridge University Press, pp. 108–128.

Judge, Paramjit S. and Gurpreet Bal (2008) "Understanding the Paradox of Changes among Dalits in Punjab." *Economic and Political Weekly* 43(41): 49–55.

Judge, Paramjit S. and Gurpreet Bal (2009) *Mapping Dalits: Contemporary Reality and Future Prospects in Punjab.* Jaipur: Rawat Publications.

Kamal, Neel (2015) "Now, Baljit Singh Daduwal too Demands Ban on 'Messenger of God'". *The Times of India,* January 12. Available at: http://timesofindia.indiatimes.com/entertainment/hindi/bollywood/news/Now-Baljit-Singh-Daduwal-too-demands-ban-on-Messenger-of-God/articleshow/45847385.cms (accessed December 12, 2016).

Kapoor, Shruti (2015) "Five Reasons Why Censor Board Should Clear MSG: The Messenger of God." *India Today,* January 15. Available at: http://indiatoday.intoda y.in/story/five-reasons-why-censor-board-should-clear-msg-the-messenger-of-god/1/413388.html (accessed December 12, 2016).

Khalsa Press (2007) "Sirsa Cult Leader Makes Mockery of Guru Sahib!" *Panthic,* May 16. Available at: www.panthic.org/articles/3288 (accessed October 20, 2016).

Kuch bhī savāl kaho uskā ruhānī javāb (2011). Publisher Rakesh Kumar.

Kumar, Ashutosh (2014) "Deras as Sites of Electoral Mobilisation in Indian Punjab: Examining the Reasons that Political Parties Flock to the Deras." *Asian Ethnicity* 15(3), 335–350.

Lal, Madan (2009) "Gurudom: The Political Dimension of Religious Sects in the Punjab." *South Asia Research* 29(3): 223–234.

Manav, Sushil (2016) "Dera Sacha Sauda Launches 'MSG' Products." *The Tribune,* January 31. Available at: www.tribuneindia.com/news/haryana/community/dera-sa cha-sauda-launches-msg-products/190148.html (accessed December 12, 2016).

Meeta and Rajivlochan (2007) "Caste and Religion in Punjab: Case of the Bhaniarawala Phenomenon." *Economic & Political Weekly* 42(21): 1909–1913.

Panwar, Preeti (2015) "Pics: Indian Spiritual Gurus and Their Empire of Wealth." *Oneindia*, November 20. Available at: www.oneindia.com/feature/pics-indian-spiritua l-gurus-and-their-empire-of-wealth-1319476.html (accessed December 12, 2016).

Press Trust of India (2016) "Dera Sacha Sauda firm MSG All Trading Launches 151 Products." *Business Standard*, March 27. Available at: www.business-standard. com/article/pti-stories/dera-sacha-sauda-firm-msg-all-trading-launches-151-products -116032700483_1.html (accessed December 12, 2016).

Puri, Harish K. (2003) "Scheduled Castes in the Sikh Community: A Historical Perspective." *Economic & Political Weekly* 38(26): 2693–2701.

Radha Soami Satsang Beas (2016) official website. Available at: www.rssb.org (accessed October 26, 2016).

Rajalakshmi, T.K. (2003) "Godman under a Cloud." *Frontline* 19(26) (online edition). Available at: www.hinduonnet.com/fline/fl1926/stories/20030103003404000.htm (accessed October 20, 2016).

Rajalakshmi, T.K. (2015) "Problem Message."*Frontline*, February 20 (online edition). Available   at: www.frontline.in/the-nation/problem-message/article6847869.ece (accessed October 16, 2016).

Ram, Ronki (2007) "Social Exclusion, Resistance and Deras: Exploring the Myth of Casteless Sikh Society in Punjab." *Economic and Political Weekly* 42(40): 4066–4074.

Ram, Ronki (2008) "Ravidass Deras and Social Protest: Making Sense of Dalit Consciousness in Punjab (India)." *Journal of Asian Studies* 67(4): 1341–1364.

Ram, Ronki (2009) "Ravidass, Dera Sachkhand Ballan and the Question of Dalit Identity in Punjab." *Journal of Punjab Studies* 16(1): 1–34.

Ram, Ronki (2012) "Beyond Conversion and Sanskritisation: Articulating an Alternative Dalit Agenda in East Punjab." *Modern Asian Studies* 46(3): 639–702.

Ram, Ronki (2016a) "Sacralising Dalit Peripheries: Ravidass Deras and Dalit Assertion in Punjab." *Economic & Political Weekly* 51(1): 32–39.

Ram, Ronki (2016b) "Why Politicians are Making a Beeline for Punjab's Ever-proliferating Deras." Interview to Scroll.in. Available at: http://scroll.in/article/ 809298/deras-cant-be-ignored-as-they-have-a-significant-socio-political-role (accessed October 25, 2016).

Sach Herbotech Products (n.d.). Available at: www.indiamart.com/company/1708040/ (accessed June 25, 2014).

Shah Satnam Ji Green "S" Welfare Force Wing (2016). Available at: www.shahsatnam jigreenswelfareforcewing.org (accessed October 5, 2016).

Sharma, Neeru (2012) "Caste in Punjab: Political Marginalization and Cultural Assertion of Scheduled Castes in Punjab." *Journal of Punjab Studies* 19(19): 27–47.

Sharma, Sachin (2015) "'MSG-2' Set for Low-key Release on Friday in Punjab." *Hindustan Times*, September 17. Available at: www.hindustantimes.com/chandigarh/m sg-2-set-for-low-key-release-on-friday-in-punjab/story-aQ7jke9SGcaU4xcyNfb9LN. html (accessed December 12, 2016).

Singh, Gurharpal (2012) "Religious Transnationalism and Development Initiatives: The Dera Sachkhand Ballan." *Economic and Political Weekly* 47(1): 53–60.

Singh, Pashaura (2014) "An Overview of Sikh History." In Pashaura Singh and Louis E. Fenech, (eds.), *The Oxford Handbook of Sikh Studies*. Oxford: Oxford University Press, pp. 19–34.

Singh, Perneet (2015) "SGPC Okay with Takht Decision: Sikh Clergy under Fire." *The Tribune*, September 26 (online edition). Available at: www.tribuneindia.com/

news/punjab/sgpc-okay-with-takht-decision-sikh-clergy-under-fire/138062.html (accessed December 9, 2016).

Singh, Surinder (2009) "Deras, Caste Conflicts and Recent Violence in Punjab." *Mainstream Weekly*, XLVII (26).

Sriram, Jayant (2015) "Film Passed with Cuts, Disclaimers." *The Hindu*, January 17. Available at: www.thehindu.com/news/national/film-passed-with-cuts-disclaimers/article6797208.ece (accessed December 12, 2016).

Swami, Praveen and Aman Sethi (2007) "Politics, Religion, and Resistance." *The Hindu*, June 4 (online edition). Available at: www.thehindu.com/todays-paper/tp-opinion/Politics-religion-and-resistance/article14772779.ece (accessed December 9, 2016).

Tiwari, Tribhuvan (2007) "Is Sacha Sauda the Real deal?" *Outlook*, May 28. Available at: www.outlookindia.com/magazine/story/is-sacha-sauda-the-real-deal/234751 (accessed December 12, 2016).

Young, Glenn (2004) "Reading and Praying Online: The Continuity of Religion Online and Online Religion in Internet Christianity." In Lorne L. Dawson and Douglas E. Cowan, (eds.), *Online Religion: Finding Faith on the Internet*. New York: Routledge, pp. 93–106.

10 Digital derasars in diaspora

A critical examination of Jain ritual online

Tine Vekemans and Iris Vandevelde

> Look at how things are changing with the technology. My guru-ji, he's a Jain monk. He's not gonna travel outside India, but he's real into technology. He is high-tech. He does livestream, and we can talk back. He's on WhatsApp. Every day I get his message on WhatsApp. (interview, Pradeep, retired, Florida, December 2015)[1]

Rapid media developments and their impact on everyday existence constitute one aspect of modernity that has received growing scholarly attention in the last three decades. Since the mid-nineties, researchers with a background in sociology, media sciences, and religious studies have consequently examined the relation of new media to religion and religious change (e.g. Dawson and Cowan, 2004; Campbell, 2012; Grieve and Veidlinger, 2014). Indeed, an analysis of the mediatized, mediated, and "virtual" manifestations of religion, including their transformative potential and use, has become an essential aspect of any attempt to come to grips with the contemporary dynamics of different religions (Stout and Buddenbaum, 2008). However, the relation between Jainism and new media, although partly addressed in Tine Vekemans' publications (Vekemans, 2014; 2015) and mentioned in the work of John E. Cort and Peter Flügel on Jain modernism (Cort, 1995; Flügel, 2012), has as yet not been fully delved into.

Within the entanglements between Jainism and new media, we can distinguish different degrees of religious "virtuality": on one end of the virtuality scope, technology is used as a tool in organizing and enhancing *offline* place-bound events and practices. Large religious ceremonies, such as initiations of new monks and nuns (*diksha*), have turned into media events, attended and watched by increasing numbers of people, both in India and abroad. Such events clearly show how aspects of modern technology are being used to facilitate communication and enable the participation of larger audiences. This is of course not a new phenomenon: the microphones, cameras, screens, and television broadcasts have been around for quite a while, and the printed flyers and posters have been used for even longer. Yet, we find that these technologies have been increasingly replaced or encompassed by newer, computer-mediated versions. This has not only broadened the scope of traditional media and increased their efficiency and quality, but has also added livestreaming, WhatsApp communications, Skype connections and text messages to the list of available supportive technologies. But the new media are not just a handy logistical tool. Over the past decades Jainism has developed an increasing online presence, consisting mainly of informational websites, discussion groups, mobile applications and social media accounts, but also containing ritual tools and resources, which this chapter will focus on.

Scholars have argued that diasporas are often areas of religious change, because of their need to rethink common narratives, practices, and customs in order to adapt to new geographical, social, cultural, and climatological environments (see e.g. Scheifinger, 2008: 241; Vertovec, 2009). Interestingly, in the story of the entanglements between Jainism and new media, the diaspora plays an important role indeed that is dual in character.[2] On the one hand, Jains living outside India are considered an important target audience amongst India-based webhosts and producers of Jainism-related online content. On the other hand, the Jain diaspora seems to be exponentially more active online with regard to religion, with about half of all findable Jain websites[3] hosted outside India. This is part of a broader commitment of diaspora Jains to sponsor religious projects in the shape of (online) publications, educational videos and CD-ROMs, as well as academic collaborations. Indeed, when a community is geographically spread out, or still in the process of being established, an increase in the immediate relevance of new media can be seen on a social, organizational, informational, and communicative level (e.g. Alonso and Oiarzabal, 2010). During one of our focus group interviews in Ohio, one young female respondent illustrated this relevance very aptly when she described her family's move to the USA:

> When we moved to Ohio, my mom googled 'Cleveland Indians' – which is a baseball team [everyone laughs]. Then she refined her search to 'Cleveland Jains' or something, and she found this one Jain family who she called. They introduced us at the temple and all ... I look online for the activities of JAINA [Federation of Jain Associations in North America] and YJA [Young Jains of America] and the like ... It is pretty remarkable what these organizations have accomplished here ... being able to connect people from all over the world and have them come together at one convention, it is only possible because of the Internet. (focus group, Meena, student, Michigan, October 2015)

But does this relevance of new media to the diaspora population extend beyond the social, organizational, informational, and communicative levels into the realm of ritual praxis? This chapter critically examines the role and transformative potential of new media in contemporary diasporic Jainism, especially focusing on the case of online rituals. Our insights are developed through a multi-method approach, which subscribes to a relatively new development that has been theorized, implemented and advocated in the last few years (Kozinets, 2010; Diminescu, 2012; Hiller and Franz, 2004; Nedelcu, 2012; Fazal and Tsagarousianou, 2002; Kissau and Hunger, 2010). This approach combines a topological and representational analysis of Jain websites (i.e. structural analyses, where ritual is analyzed as a type of content) with interviews with the (potential) users of such online features (i.e. reception analysis, where ritual is analyzed as a mode of action).[4] Given the pre-eminence of the diaspora in the Jainism-new media nexus, fieldwork was conducted in different locations in the USA and Belgium. All these data were gathered by Tine Vekemans in the course of 2014 and 2015.

The chapter first gives an outline of our methodology, followed by a brief exploration of existing literature related to new media, religious change, and ritual. Then it presents a tentative typology of Jain "ritual" tools and resources online. Lastly, the chapter provides an analysis of our field data with some insight into the reception and use of these features in the everyday life of diaspora Jains. As a conclusion, we assess the importance of these developments for Jainism as a lived religion today, and reiterate how the results of our research can add to ongoing discussions on computer-mediated ritual, and on religion and technology in general.

The impact of technological innovations on religious praxis

In addressing issues of media development, migration, and religious change, this chapter fits into a body of research addressing the impact of modernity on religion. Scholars in the field of religion have been intrigued by the potential of the Internet for religious change. New media technologies have been praised where they provide possibilities of diversification, connection to a wider audience and new avenues for religious practice (Brosius and Polit, 2011: 271). On the other hand, many studies have indicated that new media bring about changes in wrappings rather than essential and radically new changes (e.g. Jacobs, 2007). As the focus of this chapter is on computer-mediated ritual (CMR), it especially strikes a chord with a subcategory of religious studies, commonly termed "ritual dynamics" or "ritual transfer." This relatively new line of research breaks with the long held idea that rituals are by definition static and unchanging, but rather conceptualizes them as living and dynamic elements of traditions that are prone to change (subtly or radically) when elements in their context change (Brosius and Polit, 2011; Miczek, 2007: 199; Langer et al., 2006: 2). Taking into account the field sites used for the interviews and focus groups that are part of the backbone of this chapter, our case study involves two such context shifts: from offline to online and from India to the diaspora, which involves movements that not only entail changes in geographic context, but also possibly in climate, community size, available infrastructure and legal framework. Through the new possibilities, restrictions and necessities they occasion, both these shifts arguably open up "new arenas of sacredness" (Zavos, 2013).

But what impact can we expect the Internet to have on Jain religious practice? What will these new areas of sacredness look like? Existing research on online rituals has so far not specifically addressed Jainism. Research into CMR in other religions can be useful for comparisons with our findings. However, this should be done with great care and circumspection because of differences in cosmology, accepted modes of religiosity, and religious institutionalization, and so on. Theories of religion and ritual based on Christianity or other Abrahamic religions cannot easily be extended to South Asian traditions (King, 1999). Studies on ritual in other South Asian traditions seem more suited for comparison, although a deeper similarity on the basis of apparent parallels between Jain, Hindu, Buddhist, and Sufi forms of worship cannot be safely assumed either (Hirst and Zavos, 2011: 112). Studies of CMR in Hinduism describe some of the potential changes the online context may engender. For instance, Nicole Karapanagiotis has found that "novel ritual adjustments" have occurred amongst Vaishnava Hindus to ensure that the computer provides a pure environment for *puja*. Similar to Heinz Scheifinger, she noticed that online religious ritual is approved of among Hindus in theory, but is hardly done in practice (Karapanagiotis, 2010; Scheifinger, 2008). This is in contrast with Phyllis Herman's findings on the frequent use of online *darshan* as offered by the website of a Hindu temple in LA (Herman, 2010). The switch to an online setting may also generate broader societal dynamics, such as a "democratizing potential" in matters of access (Mallapragada, 2010: 115): certain groups who were previously excluded from participation in rituals on the basis of caste and gender, now gain access online. At the same time, the changes brought about by digitalization should not be overestimated. From studies about Hindu rituals on the web, it turns out that online versions are kept as close to offline reality as possible. This view is also shared by web designers of both Hindu and Christian ritual sites studied by Stephen Jacobs, who admittedly changed offline characteristics of ritual as little as possible when recreating them online (Jacobs, 2007: 1117). Indeed, as Madhavi Mallapragada argues, "Hindu temple sites ... are repurposing 'older' media forms such as photographs of deities, Hindu calendar art" and so on (Mallapragada, 2010: 111). Although parallels of many of these dynamics can be seen in the case of Jainism, the way in which they are articulated is often typically Jain.

Of virtual venues and digital *derasar*s

Jainism online comes in different shapes, and serves different purposes. The vast majority of the content on websites, but also on a growing number of apps and social media accounts is dedicated to *informing* Jains and non-Jains on Jainism. When it comes to the information they present, these sources display a varying intricacy: some of them present basic information about the religion, while others provide more elaborate explanations or indeed scholarly explorations of Jain doctrine. Some focus on one specific part of Jain tradition, whereas others aim to provide an exhaustive picture. They propagate a variety of views, ranging from global humanitarian to strongly sectarian interpretations (Flügel, 2012). Among the most popular topics are the ethical implications of the Jain way of life, such as diet rules and non-violence. Additionally, many local Jain centers and temples, especially in the diaspora, have their own websites and/or Facebook pages, offering practical data about the daily working of the temple or center, and thus are serving both *organizational* and informational purposes. In this way, the Internet represents a billboard for various Jainism-related organizations and a new arena for spreading information, used by organizations that may previously have used other, offline media for conveying the same information, but also eagerly appropriated by a growing group of new voices, often present exclusively online (like the Atlanta-based website www.jainworld.com or activist websites like www.ja invegans.org). A small number of websites and mobile applications also provide content that moves beyond the purely informational. This content comes in the shape of downloadable tools and materials for *ritual* uses offline, at the home shrine, and/or possibilities for ritual action online. Sometimes, their intended ritual use of these website and apps is explicit. On other occasions, the suggestion of a possible ritual use is more implicit, subtly presented in the way materials are portrayed or phrased. However, before analyzing and interpreting these digital *derasars*, a brief introduction into the workings of the real-world Jain *derasars* (temples) they are based on is in order.

Real-world shrines, public and private

Jain ritual praxis in a real-world temple is an experience that engages all senses, includes performative actions, and (often) generates social interactions. It is important to note that some groups within Jainism do not engage in image-worship. The place reserved for them in a temple takes the shape of a meditation hall and/or reading room.[5] However, the majority of Jains in the diaspora belong to a *murtipujak*, or image-worshipping sect. In Jain temples, the statues (*murti*) do not represent a god in the Abrahamic sense of the word, but rather an exemplary human figure that has reached enlightenment (a Jina).[6] The most straightforward form of devotional praxis in such temples is the act of looking upon the statue, henceforth called *darshan* (Cort, 2012). More elaborate forms of worship include bathing the *murti* (*abhishek*) and offering food, flowers and other substances in front of it, and are called *puja*.[7] These practices can be done individually, but larger ceremonies are often performed collectively. Apart from *darshan* and *puja*, a temple visit may include the chanting of mantras, the singing of hymns, the playing of music, study, and meditation. Although the correct performance of the prescribed ritual acts is important, most Jains agree that what matters most is the inner disposition or mind-set of the devotee (*bhava*).

Sometimes instead of, and often in addition to, their religious life organized around the Jain temple or center, most Jain families have some form of house shrine. These shrines range from very elaborate miniature temples, to a simple arrangement of a small statue or picture adorned with attributes such as oil lamps or incense. It is rare to find elaborate *pujas* being performed at home shrines, but they do serve an important purpose as locations of everyday religious practice: for daily *darshan*, meditation, and study. For Jains living in an area without an established temple, home shrines tend to become the focal point of religious and ritual practice. In what follows, we will look at different types of online ritual tools and resources that have been developed, and describe how they aim to fit into Jain ritual practice. Subsequently, we will address the (im)possibilities of computer-mediated ritual (CMR) as perceived by Jains living in the USA and Belgium.

The Jina in the cloud: typology of CMR in Jainism

The transfer of the offline multi-layered performative actions that make up a ritual to a holistic online experience seems less straightforward. However, Jain materials aimed at ritual use find an increasing presence online (Vekemans, 2014). In what follows, we will describe three different types of such resources: religious downloads, live *darshan*, and online *puja*. Through an analysis of the aesthetics of these resources and the discourse employed to present them, we will conceptualize their purported use. We argue that the choice of imagery and words displayed within and surrounding these online resources and tools clearly suggests their intended ritual use. Moreover, we observe how they aspire to contribute to an inclusive religious experience by bringing in different sensory stimuli, introducing performative aspects, and establishing concrete ties to real-world sacred spaces.

Downloading the home shrine

A first type of online resources for application in a Jain ritual context, are auditory and visual materials available for download, such as devotional songs (*bhajan*) and devotional images. The main aim of these downloads, as some of the websites explicitly state, is to supply materials for home rituals and meditation. As such, their function is essentially the same as that of the ubiquitous religious music tapes, printed pictures and DVDs, which have since long been part and parcel of Jain homes and home-shrines, but new media have exponentially expanded the range of materials available and the ease with which they can be acquired.

Pictures and images found online, of the 24 Jinas, but also of monks, nuns, and pilgrimage places, are downloaded and printed, and may supplement or even replace the *murti* that is usually the center of a home shrine. Hymns and devotional music are available for listening online (from different websites, but also through a number of online radio stations), and may be used as a background music for meditation, or to help the devotee enhance his or her *arti* ceremonies at home. All these materials are immediately recognizable to Jain practitioners as subject or part of ritual praxis because of both the content and the iconography, even where the content provider does not make explicit claims about their suggested use.

However, apart from the websites and sources we conceptualize as "offering materials for ritual use," we find a broader online supply of downloadable religious materials, similar in content, but produced with a more mundane use in view. In this way, downloadable materials have become a new way of infusing religious content into different spheres of life, in the guise of ring-tones and screensavers for example, as they came along with the increasingly common presence of PCs, laptops and smartphones in Jains' daily lives. Although such websites have an arguably religious aim, their intent is perhaps rather to provide tools for religious identity formation than to contribute to any real ritual practice. As one website offering desktop wallpapers proclaims:

> Desktop Wallpaper[s] of Gods, Gurus and Holy Places on our working desktops are a way to reassert their subtle presence in our day to day life ... To effuse your working atmosphere with a divine presence grace your desktop with the Desktop Wallpaper of Shree Dharmachakra Prabhav Tirth. (http://dharmachakra.in/Downloads/Jain-Desktop-Wallpapers.aspx. Last accessed August 15th, 2016. This website has since been taken offline)

Darshan through the looking glass

A second way in which the Internet offers material for ritual use among Jains, is through video footage of the inner sanctum and/or icons in temples, and the activities going on in this area of the temple. Although most "temple-cameras" were initially installed for security reasons, the images they record are increasingly made available online to a wider public, in some cases, such as the temple in Columbus, Ohio, only to members of the local temple community through a system of logins – in other cases, such as the Jain Center of Southern California, to anyone who accesses the website. The way this footage is pre-sented ranges from the posting of asynchronous recorded material on YouTube, over occasional streaming of special events, to synchronous 24/7 livestreams on the temple website. In general, this video footage can be seen as the next step in the category of "downloadable visual materials" discussed above.

However, synchronous livestreaming constitutes a distinct and ritually meaningful category. Some temples, such as the Jain Center of Southern California (http://jcsc.homeip.net/), have started labelling the synchronous footage they make available online as "live *darshan*." This choice of words is telling, in the sense that it indicates that the content providers conceive of it as a way of participating or engaging in ongoing ritual action; as a legitimate means of gaining *darshan*. Taking our cue from one respondent who com-pared the practice of "live *darshan*" with looking at the *murti* through glasses, we want to conceptualize live *darshan* as a proposed online ritual action that relies on a transportation of the user to a real-world sacred space. This is achieved through an immediate connection, often providing the viewer with a unique, uninterrupted view of the *murti*. As most livestreams include visuals as well as audio, at least two senses of the user are engaged in what is going on in the temple. Given the fact that people who are present in the temple (whether meditating, performing *puja*, chanting, or just visiting) also come into view of the user, we may even add a social function to our analysis of such websites. The performativity that will turn out to be the main focus in online *puja*, as described below, is not established in any direct sense here.

Puja in the digital derasar

The most obvious cases, where ritual action appears in its fully virtualized form, is online *arti*, or in its more elaborate form, online *puja*. Here the practitioner can actually perform the ritual, by clicking and thus setting in motion consecutive animations which constitute either a simple *arti* ceremony, or a more elaborate *puja* ritual.

Apart from giving the user the possibility of being the performative agent in the *puja*, most online temples reveal a strong preoccupation with providing a close approximation of the sensory experience of real-world temple worship. Not only does the user see the image, the offerings, and often some temple-like background, he or she can also ring the temple bell, and hear the appropriate music and/or mantras of the type commonly used in temple worship. As the starting of different animations requires a mouse-click on the right part of the screen (i.e. the right offering, the right part of the Jina image, etc.), we can argue that there is at least some indirect engagement of the sense of touch as well.

Although the *puja* itself is in this case "virtual," often, these digital *derasars* are tied to the real world by the use of a picture of a recognizable *murti* of a famous temple or pilgrimage destination (e.g. www.jainuniversity.org uses the *murti* from the temple at Palitana; www.shreenakoda.com uses a picture of the temple at Nakoda[8]); other, mostly older sites use a simpler, computer generated image not directly based on any specific real-world *murti* (e.g. www. jain.8m.com).

Finding the Jina in the cloud: reception and use

Other researchers inform about the presence, availability, and prevalence of online ritual features in other traditions, often building upon the intention of the content providers (see e.g. Jacobs, 2007; Scheifinger, 2008; Mallapragada, 2010). Our fieldwork, however, was aimed specifically at assessing the reception and use by (potential) users of computer-mediated ritual features in the Jain diaspora (for a similar analysis, see also Karapanagiotis, 2010; Herman, 2010). True to the Jain creed of "live and let live," the general opinion is that everyone should decide for themselves whether these mediated forms of ritual praxis work for them or not. And yet, when invited to reflect further and formulate an opinion, either in individual conversations or in a group, a number of recurring objections to and contestations of computer-mediated ritual praxis came to light.

When it comes to downloading visual and audio materials for use at a home shrine, or indeed to watching recorded sermons or ceremonies online, there is very little contestation among the informants we interviewed. When confronted with websites offering live *darshan* and online *puja*, more objections were raised, and although both were often problematized, most interviewees preferred live *darshan* to online *puja*. Even though they could not participate in a performative way, they felt that a mediated relocalization to a real sanctified place made more sense than the complete virtual of a computer generated (or at least computer compiled) imagery that is the basis of online *puja* websites. As one respondent phrased it:

> If you want to do the darshan in the morning, in the large cities such as in California, the live darshan is always available. You can just do that, and that's important. But not the puja part you know click click click, nobody is gonna do that. (focus group, Manoj, businessman, Ohio, November 2015)

Clearly, in the eyes of most of our respondents, such practice is not (yet) an organic extension of the offline religious life.

Ritual use of CMR: emergency back-up

Our informants in India indicated that they saw live *darshan* and online *puja* mostly for Jains living abroad, meaning far removed from (or too busy to go to) actual temples and gurus. This is sometimes confirmed by statements on the websites themselves (Mallapragada, 2010: 118). Nevertheless, as mentioned above, our fieldwork in different diaspora communities did not reveal an elaborate use of online *puja* as a form of ritual praxis. However, our respondents in the diaspora did agree on the point that these online devices are meant for people with limited access to real-world temples and communities. One respondent opened the discussion, stating that: "The intention of these [ritual] websites is obvious. They are made for people who for some reason don't have access to a Jain community" (focus group, Rohit, student, Michigan, October 2015). A number of categories were then established: the old, the sick, those living very far from a temple or community, those living in places where public worshipping is inadvisable or forbidden, those that are traveling. One respondent gave the example of his mother-in-law:

> In fact, my mother in law, she does it. She can't come to the temple every day. She opens up the computer, and does Palitana darshan [on jainuniversity.org], and she has links to YouTube, and then she does arti ... but

it is not the same and she knows it is not the right thing. When she does go to India, she makes a point of visiting the real thing. (interview, Bhindesh, businessman, Florida, December 2015)

In sum, in theory online ritual resources can meet the needs of those with limited access to offline Jain communities, rituals or temples. At the same time, this respondent stresses that "the real thing" remains preferable. Indeed, in practice, most respondents indicated that, if put in a situation where temple worship is unlikely, they would rather turn to home shrines than to online alternatives.

Objections to ritual use of CMR

If computer-mediated ritual is accepted in theory, why is it so little used in practice? We found that most of our respondents' reluctance centered, on the one hand, on the absence of sensory and social elements in computer-mediated practices, and on questions related to *bhava* and commodification, on the other hand. Research on online devotional practice in other South Asian religious traditions has brought to light similar limitations and objections (e.g. Hawkins, 1999; Karapanagiotis, 2010).

Talking to Jains in different places and from different sectarian backgrounds, we learned that online practices are seldom denounced out right, but neither are they generally accepted as an equal alternative to offline devotional practice. When asked why this was the case, respondents said that they missed "something"; there was a general feeling of things being out of context. One respondent described it as a feeling: "No, online puja is not the same. The feeling isn't there," (Prakash, Georgia), and another spoke of ambience: "what I would look for are the people and the ambience ... so that whatever I'm doing, I can connect," (Abhishek, Michigan). Yet another talked of vibrations: "there's a lot of emphasis on the vibrations that are in the parikrama ... that's why it is not the same" (Neha, Ohio).

What these answers point to is the absence of the sensory and social experiences that together make up and are therefore crucial for the act of temple worship. Although content providers are clearly trying to include as many sensory elements as possible, sensory impressions such as the smell of incense and flowers, the ringing of the temple bell, the sound of the voices of other devotees singing, the view of the temple as one approaches for morning worship or the feeling of the cool marble floor are difficult to transfer into the online realm and therefore often are lacking in computer-mediated *darshan* and *puja*.

Another recurring theme of contestation centers on the idea of *bhava*. Our respondents share this preoccupation with mind-set as the benchmark for authenticity in religious praxis with scholars studying rituals (Helland, 2005: 6). The emphasis on the appropriate spiritual mind-set leads some respondents to minimize the importance of how or where an individual chooses to perform ritual. However, many other respondents expressed doubts about the possibility of establishing the right mind-set for worship when surfing the Internet. While both interpretations agree that the inner, spiritual disposition of the devotee is the key parameter in devotional practice, this latter position asserts that the environment in which devotional practice takes place has a vital impact on this disposition. Inappropriate elements might be invasive commercial ads on the website or work stored on the computer that might grab the devotees' attention or compel them to rush through rituals. One young female respondent concurred, saying:

> I feel that going to an actual temple makes me feel a lot more at peace and stuff, as opposed to sitting down in front of my computer. I would feel that online, I would just you know, play around, and click random things, as opposed to doing the full thing. (focus group, Priya, student, Michigan, October 2015)

Apart from echoing to a certain extent the ritual purity argument that became apparent in Karapanagiotis's analyses of Vaishnava Hindu views on online *puja* (Karapanagiotis, 2010), these objections also relate to discussions about the commodification of religion. Although religious content is now widely available in all sorts of formats, on all sorts of platforms, this is not uniformly considered positive. Indeed, the few objections to the downloading or streaming of audio-visual material occur in the case of perceived disrespectful use. One of our informants in Delhi illustrated this dual attitude very well. This middle-aged man had a devotional hymn as a ringtone on his mobile phone, but, when asked about this, he indicated that ... "our hymns really shouldn't be used as such" (interview, Akhilesh, Delhi, July 2014). An older male respondent in the US voiced the same concern, saying: "It may be okay, but it is not for me. You lose reverence for these things when you are in front of your pc on a comfy chair ... putting it on your laptop ... that's not how you do it" (interview, Manish, retired, Georgia, November 2015).

Some websites address these concerns implicitly, by adding a barrier between the ritual and the rest of the website (e.g. a hyperlink or a "do puja" button, such as on www.jain.8m.com). Some content providers make things more explicit, with disclaimers informing the users how to use the provided material. For example, one informative CD-rom on Jaina worship (Jina Worship) starts with a banner reading that "the Cd should be handled with care in the same way we handle a religious book," and "kept in a place where there will be no disrespect." It then proceeds to say one should not be eating, chewing, wearing footwear or menstruating when watching the CD.

Non-ritual use of CMR

The subtle and less subtle objections to computer-mediated religious practice raised by respondents, may lead some to consider online ritual resources as mere gimmicks. Yet, respondents who problematized computer-mediated ritual practice, even as an "emergency back-up," often considered these proposedly ritual features potentially useful in different non-ritual contexts. One of our respondents hinted at the most prevalent of these alternative uses when he shared his opinion on online *puja*: "No, online puja is not the same. The feeling isn't there. Virtual reality does not work. Maybe its use is acceptable for meditation purpose, or for youngsters who do not come to the temple, or for older people" (Prakash, Georgia; interview November 2015). When we unpack and analyze this statement, we find that the initial denouncing of "virtual reality" is followed by a recognition of its possible use as an emergency back-up, as discussed above. Additionally, this respondent proposes two possible alternative functions for computer-mediated ritual features, namely contemplation aid and educational tool. A number of respondents saw a possible third alternative function: a way to (re-)connect to a particular place or community.

First, the proposed use of CMR as contemplation aid rests on the fact that Jain religious practice does not only consist of rituals (not even for the sects practicing temple worship). In addition to performative actions, contemplative practices and study are also considered necessary (or at least beneficial) components. Although there is no requirement of visual aids or music in this type of meditation, such material can help some practitioners concentrate. In this respect, online *puja* software may be used as any other online or offline image, as something to contemplate on. The music that is part of most software can function as any other online, or offline *bhajan*: to help the devotee get into the right mood.

Secondly, the educational value of CMR in Jainism lies in the complexity of the temple-going process. Although the act of *darshan* is pretty straightforward, different *puja* ceremonies are quite complex, consisting not only of series of offerings to be made in the correct order, but also entailing a set of standardized movements and mantras, and possibly songs and music. These are traditionally learnt by joining one's family at a young age, and/or in regular *pathshala* (Sunday school) classes. The degree to which Jains are familiar with all aspects of such ceremonies varies. Especially respondents of the second and third generation indicated that they were not entirely proficient in this respect: "A lot of people here, like myself, have a hard time remembering and pronouncing the *sutra*s to go with *puja*" (interview, Girish, businessman, Ohio, November 2015). Online resources can meet this deficit, by playing a role in the transfer of religious knowledge and ritual proficiency. Another respondent agreed, saying:

> I think this [online puja software] has incredible merit. We already use online *bhajan*s, this is just the next step. Now you have Video. With the right *sutra*s playing … it's just like having a pandit next to you explaining … people can learn from it, and then take it to the temple. (focus group, Nareshbhai, IT professional, Ohio, November 2015)

Thirdly, during a focus group discussion on live *darshan*, one graduate student told the group how his family in India would occasionally set up a webcam so that he could be present and follow the proceedings at their house shrine. He did not feel like he was performing any ritual action in this way, but he did feel included and connected. Similarly, (former) members of the community whose temple is the subject of live *darshan*, can use the video-feed to (re-)connect to the community, rather than just to "do *darshan*." One student respondent said: "I would agree that, if I were to use this, I would use it more in a reminiscent sort of way, rather than a purely religious act." The same potential for connection through online *darshan* is available for families and friends of community members, as one respondent noted: "For large events it is nice, then our family in India can join in and watch" (focus group, Anish, student, Michigan, October 2015).

Conclusion

The introduction of new media possibilities may not have radically changed Jain religious praxis, but the increasing prevalence of Jainism-related content on new media platforms does lead us to the conclusion that there is a process of appropriation at work. As with previous technological innovations that changed the transmission of religious information (printing press, radio) or that altered the organization of religious gatherings (amplification, micro-phones, etc.), it makes sense that new media will have to be negotiated and tested against habitual practices and ritual prescriptions before their use in a religious context is entirely accepted and adopted (even if people have no problem using these technologies in other fields of life). This negotiation is often an uneven process: some functions of these new technologies are more easily adopted than others, and some people will make more active use of them than others.

The easy availability of information and the possibility to connect immedi-ately to individuals and organizations (however geographically distant) are con-sidered to be the main assets of ongoing developments in new media. The sharing of information through conference calls, streaming events, but also regular text messaging by religious figures (ascetics, gurus) are new, mediated ways of interacting with the Jain tradition that are accepted as such by the lay community both inside and outside India. In the case of computer-mediated ritual (CMR), it is acknowledged that these websites and apps are useful to open up religious actions for those with limited access. However, as we have seen, this acknowledgement does not readily translate into their ritual use. Indeed, the more things get virtualized, the more discussion arises about the validity of computer-mediated praxes. What is clear when we start look-ing at the reception of CMR, is that the motivations of the (potential) users are not identical with the intentions with which the content is put online. In most peoples' opinion, online *puja*, if it is to be used in a ritual way, is clearly meant as a last resort alternative for practitioners living in far-flung places, with very little or no access to an established Jain community. But even in those cases, many respondents still thought that performing the rituals at home at a house shrine (however simple), would be more beneficial.

Although an all-out denouncing of computer-mediated ritual praxis is rare, with many respondents saying it is up to the individual devotee to decide, websites and apps providing *puja* and *darshan* services are not very well-received as new avenues of ritual praxis. But, as our research has shown: this does not mean these features are considered useless. Our choice of reception analysis including both individual interviews and open discussion in focus groups allowed us to move beyond the objections to ritual use of CMR, and see how Jains creatively engage with these materials and repurpose them. Apart from their ritual function, CMR are seen as advanced forms of audio and visuals for meditative praxis, as educational material, or as forms of social connection, and, at least it that sense, they are becoming more and more known about and accepted.

As noted by Scheifinger (2008) and Mallapragada (2010) in the Hindu context, matters of access play a crucial role in the appreciation of new media developments in general, but they have a special relevance for Jains living outside their region of origin. As one third-generation Jain student explained:

> These days, a lot of people ... tape things: lectures, speeches by sadhus and pandits, and share it via WhatsApp and such. My mom is always playing that sort of recordings. She says that the main thing we miss here in the US is the teachings of the sadhus and sadhvis. And it's only through recent technologies that we can access these more easily here. (focus group, Rohit, student, Michigan, October 2015)

Of course, the diaspora community cannot be seen as monolithic, nor are the communities in diaspora disconnected from each other or from the communities of Jains in India. Although the number of field sites for this research was limited, it already revealed that the degree to which communities and individuals in the Jain diaspora are actively involved with new media varies. In general, the Jains in North America seem to be the most actively involved on both the user and the producer side of new media. The Jain community in Belgium has very little visibility online, but that doesn't mean its members do not use new media in different ways. As more research on the Jain diaspora is being conducted, we hope that this discrepancy and other findings in our study can be substantiated and expounded further.

As things stand, the development of CMR has not revolutionized the daily religious practice of Jains in the diaspora. But, as technological innovation and its various concomitant processes of negotiations are ongoing, it is difficult to predict what developments in online Jain religious and ritual praxis will be elaborated. Some of the objections voiced to the ritual use of CMR today might be overcome as new technologies become available, which may lead to a broader acceptance and use of them. However, meanwhile, other developments in modern Jainism in India and in the diaspora are at work, which may counter such a growth of CMR, such as a shift towards an emphasis on ethics and contemplation, away from ritual. Only time will tell whether these digital *derasars* will soon be a thing of the past, or they will continue to develop and in time turn into accepted avenues of ritual praxis.

Notes

1 For reasons of privacy, we have chosen to anonymize our respondents. The names given in the text are pseudonyms.
2 In addition to the 4,450,000 Jains in India, Jainism has developed a relatively extensive diaspora over the past century. The contemporary Jain diaspora numbers about 300,000 lay people. Monks and nuns are not allowed to travel by mechanical means, and are thus traditionally not found outside South Asia. Although this means that more than 6 percent of the total number of Jains now lives abroad, standard works on Jainism only briefly address the specificities of the diaspora (Carrithers and Humphrey, 1991; Cort, 1998; Dundas, 2002; Laidlaw, 1995). The few works which address the Jain diaspora itself generally consist of case studies describing one particular community of Jains from a sociological or religious point of view (North America: Jaini, 1998; Radford 2004. Antwerp (BE): Vandevelde et al., 2015; Helmer, 2009. Leicester (UK): Banks, 1992).
3 The corpus of websites, apps and pages that is the basis for our broader research project, was compiled by conducting google-searches on "Jain," "Jainism," and key concepts such as "ahimsa." These searches were done in Hindi, Gujarati, English and Dutch. For the purpose of our research, a website, app or page is considered Jain if the majority of its content is related to Jainism. That means that not every website produced by a Jain counts as a Jain website, and that some of the sources labeled "Jain" may be produced by non-Jains.
4 For the structural analysis, data are derived from a topological and representational study of more than 300 interconnected "Jain" and Jainism-related websites hosted worldwide. The reception analysis is based on data assembled through 40 in-depth interviews and a number of focus groups with Jains in Europe (Antwerp) and the USA (Michigan, Ohio, Georgia, and Florida), supplemented with a series of exploratory, informal interviews with Jains in India.
5 The practice of having a separate room for non-image worshipping sects within the parameter of a temple is rare in India, but quite prevalent in the diaspora.
6 Most of the main *murti*s in large temples in India and the diaspora have gone through the *prana pratistha* (life-instilling) or *anjana shalaka* (eye-opening) cere-mony, which means that they are considered—literally or symbolically—to possess a form of consciousness, soul, or life. In that sense, the function of these images goes beyond mere depiction.
7 For an elaboration on *puja*, see Babb (1988) and Humphrey and Laidlaw (1994: 16–63).
8 Both Palitana and Nakoda are Jain pilgrimage places located in the state of Gujarat in India.

References

Alonso, Andoni and Pedro Oiarzabal (eds.) (2010) *Diasporas in the New Media Age: Identity, Politics, and Community*. Reno, NV: University of Nevada Press.
Babb, L.A. (1988) "Giving and Giving up: The Eightfold Worship among Śvetāmbar Mūrtipūjak Jains." *Journal of Anthropological Research* 44(1): 67–86.

Banks, M. (1992) *Organizing Jainism in India and England*. London: Oxford University Press.

Brosius, Christiane and Karin Polit (2011) "Introducing Media Rituals and Ritual Media." In A. Michaels, (ed.), *Reflexivity, Media, and Virtuality (Ritual Dynamics and the Science of Ritual IV)*. Harrassowitz: Wiesbaden, pp. 267–275.

Campbell, Heidi (ed.) (2012) *Digital Religion: Understanding Religious Practice in New Media Worlds*. Abingdon and New York: Routledge.

Carrithers, M. and C. Humphrey (eds.) (1991) *The Assembly of Listeners: Jains in Society*. Cambridge: Cambridge University Press.

Cort, J.E. (1995) *Defining Jainism: Reform in the Jain tradition*. Toronto: University of Toronto, Centre for South Asian Studies.

Cort, J.E. (ed.) (1998) *Open Boundaries: Jain Communities and Cultures in Indian History*. Albany, NY: State University of New York Press.

Cort, J.E. (2012) "Situating Darsan: Seeing the Digambar Jina Icon in Eighteenth- and Nineteenth-Century North India." *International Journal of Hindu Studies* 16(1): 1–56.

Dawson, Lorne L. and Douglas E. Cowan (eds.) (2004) *Religion Online: Finding Faith on the Internet*. New York: Routledge.

Diminescu, D. (2012) "Digital Methods for the Exploration, Analysis and Mapping of e-Diasporas." *Social Science Information* 51(4): 451–458.

Dundas, Paul (2002) *The Jains*. London: Routledge.

Fazal, S. and R. Tsagarousianou (2002) "Diasporic Communication: Transnational Cultural Practices and Communicative Spaces." *Javnost/ The Public* 9(1): 5–18.

Flügel, Peter (2012) "Jainism." In Helmut K. Anheier and Mark Juergensmeyer, (eds.), *Encyclopedia of Global Studies* 3. Thousand Oakes: SAGE, pp. 975–979.

Grieve, Gregory P. and Daniel Veidlinger (eds.) (2014) *Buddhism, the Internet and Digital Media: The Pixel in the Lotus*. New York and London: Routledge.

Hawkins, Sophie (1999) "Bordering Realism: The Aesthetics of Sai Baba's Mediated Universe." In C. Brosius and M. Butcher, (eds.), *Image Journeys: Audio-Visual Media and Cultural Change in India*. New Delhi: SAGE Publications, pp. 139–162.

Helland, C. (2005) "Online Religion as Lived Religion: Methodological Issues in the Study of Religious Participation on the Internet." *Online – Heidelberg Journal of Religions on the Internet* 1(1): 1–16.

Helmer, G.R. (2009) *Jaina in Antwerpen: Eine Religionsgeschichtliche Studie*. Munich: AVM.

Herman, Phyllis K. (2010) "Seeing the Divine through Windows: Online Puja and Virtual Religious Experience." *Online – Heidelberg Journal of Religions on the Internet* 4(1): 151–178.

Hiller, H.H. and T.M. Franz (2004) "New Ties, Old Ties and Lost Ties: The Use of Internet in Diaspora." *New Media Society* 6(6): 731–752.

Hirst, Jacqueline S. and John Zavos (2011) *Religious Traditions in Modern South Asia*. London: Routledge. http://dharmachakra.in/Downloads/Jain-Desktop-Wallpapers.aspx (last accessed August 15, 2016. This site has since been taken offline).

Humphrey, C. and J. Laidlaw (1994) *The Archetypal Actions of Ritual: A Theory of Ritual Illustrated by Jain Rite of Worship*. Oxford: Clarendon Press.

Jacobs, Stephen (2007) "Virtually Sacred: The Performance of Asynchronous Cyber-Rituals in Online Spaces." *Journal of Computer-Mediated Communication* 12(3): 1103–1121.

Jain Center of Southern California (n.d.) *YouTube*. Available at: http://jcsc.homeip.net/ (accessed August 15, 2016).

Jain University (2016). Available at: www.jainuniversity.org (accessed on August 15, 2016).

Jain Vegans (n.d.). Available at: www.jainvegans.org (accessed on October 5, 2016).

Jain World (2011). Available at: www.jainworld.com (accessed on October 5, 2016).

Jaini, S. (1998) "Evolution of Jainism in North America." In S. Jain and S. Pandey, (eds.), *Jainism in a Global Perspective*. Benaras: Pārśvanātha Vidyāpī tha, pp. 293–300.

Jina Worship (2 DVDs) Rushabh Creation.

Karapanagiotis, Nicole (2010) "Vaishnava Cyber-Pūjā: Problems of Purity & Novel Ritual Solutions." *Online – Heidelberg Journal of Religions on the Internet* 4(1): 179–195.

King, Richard (1999) *Orientalism and Religion: Postcolonial Theory, India and the Mystic East*. London: Routledge.

Kissau, K. and U. Hunger (2010) "The Internet as a Means of Studying Transnationalism and Diaspora." In R. Baubröck and T. Faist, (eds.), *Diaspora and Transnationalism: Concepts, Theories and Methods*. Amsterdam: Amsterdam University Press, pp. 245–266.

Kozinets, R.V. (2010) *Netnography, Doing Ethnographic Research Online*. New Delhi: SAGE Publications.

Laidlaw, J. (1995) *Riches and Renunciation: Religion, Economy and Society Among the Jains*. Oxford: Clarendon Press.

Langer, R., D. Lüddeckens, K. Radde and J. Snoek (2006) "Transfer of Ritual." *Journal of Ritual Studies* 20(1): 1–10.

Mallapragada, Madhavi (2010) "Desktop Deities: Hindu Temples, Online Cultures and the Politics of Remediation." *South Asian Popular Culture* 8(2): 109–121.

Miczek, N. (2007) "Rituals Online: Dynamic Processes Reflecting Individual Perspectives." *Masaryk University Journal of Law and Technology* 2: 197–204.

Nedelcu, M. (2012) "Migrants' New Transnational Habitus: Rethinking Migration through a Cosmopolitan Lens in the Digital Age." *Journal of Ethnic and Migration Studies* 38(9): 1339–1356.

Radford, M.A. (2004) "(Re) Creating Transnational Religious Identity within the Jaina Community of Toronto." In Knut A. Jacobsen and P. Pratap Kumar, (eds.), *South Asians in Diaspora: Histories and Religious Traditions*. Leiden: Brill Publishing, 23–51.

Scheifinger, Heinz (2008) "Hinduism and Cyberspace." *Religion* 38(3): 233–249.

Shree Nakoda (n.d.). Available at: www.shreenakoda.com (accessed on August 15, 2016).

Stout, Daniel A. and Judith M. Buddenbaum (2008) "Approaches to the Study of Media and Religion: Notes from the Editors of the Journal of Media and Religion with Recommendations for Future Research." *Religion* 38(3): 226–232.

Vandevelde, Iris, Philippe Meers, Sofie Van Bauwel and Roel Vande Winkel (2015) "Sharing the Silver Screen: The Social Experience of Cinemagoing in the Indian Diaspora." *Bioscope-South Asian Screen Studies* 6(1): 88–106.

Vekemans, Tine (2014) "Double-clicking the Temple Bell: Devotional Aspects of Jainism Online." *Heidelberg Journal of Religions on the Internet* 6: 126–143.

Vekemans, Tine (2015) "Transnational Connections and Religious Development in the Jain Diaspora through an Exploration of the e-Diaspora." In Tine Vekemans and

Natasha Miletic, (eds.) *Discovering Diaspora: A Multidisciplinary Approach.* Oxford: Inter-Disciplinary Press, pp. 109–120.

Vertovec, S. (2009) *Transnationalism.* Abingdon: Routledge.

www.jain.8m.com (n.d.). Available at: www.Jain.8m.com (accessed on August 15, 2016).

Zavos, John (2013) "Hinduism in the Diaspora." In Joya Chatterji and D.A. Washbrook, (eds.), *Routledge Handbook of the South Asian Diaspora.* London: Routledge, pp. 306–317.

Index